Praise for
The Grace of Troublesome Questions

"In this autobiographical theology, Richard Hughes offers readers a transformative collection of writing that reflects decades of scholarly and spiritual labor. No one has loved, studied, or wrestled more with the American Stone-Campbell religious tradition than Richard. And no one has expressed with more clarity its massive gifts and flaws, always with an eye to pressing it to become the 'beloved community.' Thank you, Richard, for your example of faith so evident in this volume."

—**Douglas A. Foster,** Scholar in Residence, Graduate School of Theology, Abilene Christian University

"The words and deeds of Alexander Campbell and Barton W. Stone have never been so well explained and their long shadows over the paradox of Christian approaches to racial justice never as well grounded. Richard Hughes's struggle to reach his own fully informed commitment to racial justice and reconcile it with both his deep faith and a scholar's knowledge of the flawed histories of the United States and Christianity provides a model of earnest introspection that evolves into his commitment to a new vocation. All Americans who care about social justice, both people of faith and those who are secular, can learn a great deal from Richard Hughes."

—**Richard Ekman,** President Emeritus, Council of Independent Colleges

"Characterized by honest reflections and compassionate observations, American religious historian Richard Hughes has written a compelling memoir that speaks words of wisdom and hope into our current national context. By embracing the 'grace of troublesome questions,' his story offers a guiding path for the work of reconciliation and a path that is particularly timely for this cultural moment."

—**Dr. Kim S. Phipps,** President, Messiah University

"*The Grace of Troublesome Questions* is a serious reflection on *the meaning* of Richard Hughes's scholarship and life. Hughes's compelling and technically rooted memoir provides a guide for those unwilling to turn their back on their religious tradition while awakening to the lament of the oppressed. In short, Richard Hughes is one who embodies the noble principle that he and his tradition advocate—'the importance of an unbiased and open search for truth.'"

—**David Fleer,** Director, Christian Scholars Conference

"This book is a genuine treasure! It collects a career's worth of scintillating insights and profound spiritual wisdom from one of the finest scholars associated with the Churches of Christ. Hughes is always the master of his subject and invariably manages to think outside the box. To top it off, Hughes is a superb communicator who delivers his insights in beautiful, clear prose."

—**Grant Underwood,** Richard L. Evans Chair of Religious Understanding, Brigham Young University

"In *The Grace of Troublesome Questions*, Richard Hughes invites you to join him on the sacred journey that shaped his work and changed his life. Pay attention and it will change your life as well."

—**Robert M. Randolph,** former Chaplain to Massachusetts Institute of Technology

"A careful reading of this collection yields rich rewards. Readers see the historian's mind at work as he reflects upon 'the restoration vision' and offers astute observations about our current vexed moment in history. Interspersed with retrospective personal essays about his unfolding vocational journey, readers are offered a glimpse into the heart of this loving husband, grateful student, devoted teacher, and humble scholar. There is a prophetic element, too, as we are invited to resist White supremacy and confront Christian nationalism in its more subtle forms. For those familiar with Richard's work, this collection will be a joyful reminder of what you already know to be true of his great mind and capacious heart. For those who are not, prepare to be elevated—inspired *and* challenged—in your understanding of American Christianity."

—**Hannah Schell,** Editor of *Vocation Matters*, blog of the Network for Vocation in Undergraduate Education (NetVUE), coauthor of *Christian Thought in America: A Brief History*

"Few historians have deepened our understanding of American religion more than Richard Hughes, who developed the interpretive paradigms of restorationism and of founding mythologies to understand, among other things, the complex tensions within his own Churches of Christ tradition and the way White supremacy undergirds American religion and culture. This volume collects in one place Hughes's far-ranging essays and works of memoir that together convey a restless mind seeking to understand what drives religious belief, action, and reaction in his own life and in history writ large. Hughes's determination to understand violent opposition to nonviolent prophetic figures ranging from Menno Simons to Colin Kaepernick, along with his elegant and probing prose, speak volumes to the present political, religious, and racial landscape. A must read."

—**Joe Creech,** Director, Lilly Fellows Program

THE
GRACE OF
TROUBLESOME
QUESTIONS

This book is a genuine treasure. It collects a career's worth of scholarly moments and profound spiritual wisdom from one of the finest scholars associated with the Churches of Christ. Hughes is always the master of his subject and invariably chooses to think outside the box. To top it off, Hughes is a superb communicator able to deliver his insights in historical, clear prose."

—Grant Underwood, PhD, adj. Leonard Arrington Chair of Religious Understanding,
Brigham Young University

In *The Grace of Troublesome Questions*, Richard Hughes invites us to join him on the inward journey that shaped his work and changed his life. Pay attention, and it will change your life as well."

—Robert M. Randolph, Chaplain to the Institute, Massachusetts Institute of Technology

A gratifying sum of this collection yields a glimpse into Hughes's life, his labors, his mindful work as historian and writer. Those of us familiar with his work and others scarcely observe his passion in our current engagement, in today's context especially. In retrospective personal essays about his unfolding vocational journey, too, here are offered a glimpse into the heart of milk loving husband, grateful teacher, devoted teacher, and humble scholar. There is a prophetic element, too, as we are invited to resist. While vigorously and confident Christian nationalism in part the subtle forms. For those familiar with Hughes's work, this collection will be a joyful reminder of what you already know: the interest of his exacting mind and a passionate heart. For those who are not, prepare to be moved—inspired and challenged in your understanding of American Christianity."

—Danny Hughes, Editor of *Situating Martyrdom: The Rhetoric of Our Recent Controversies*
—Brian Steaven Burgos, PhD, coauthor of *Church's Theme in American Religious Journey*

Few historians have shaped the understanding of American religion more than Richard Hughes, who developed the interpretive paradigms of Restorationism and of primitive mythologies to understand, among other things, the complex forces within his own Churches of Christ tradition and beyond. Whose supreme scholar persists, from disciplined and others, this volume collects in one place Hughes's ranging inquiries and works of significance that together convey a restless spirit seeking to understand the drive to human action, and religion in justice while looking into his own tribe. Hughes's latest important work underlies us to examine our deepest presuppositions through an engine from Martin Luther King to Howard Thurman and Bob Dylan and primitive prophets speaks immeasurably to our moment as he points us toward liberation. A must-read."

—Richard T. Hughes, Pepperdine University

THE
GRACE OF
TROUBLESOME
QUESTIONS

Vocation, Restoration, and Race

RICHARD T. HUGHES

Abilene Christian University Press

THE GRACE OF TROUBLESOME QUESTIONS
Vocation, Restoration, and Race

ACU
PRESS

Copyright © 2022 by Richard T. Hughes

978-1-68426-022-5

Printed in the United States of America

Library of Congress Cataloguing in Publication Data is on file at the Library of Congress, Washington, DC.

Cover design by Bruce Gore
Interior text design by Sandy Armstrong, Strong Design

For information contact:
Abilene Christian University Press
ACU Box 29138
Abilene, Texas 79699

1-877-816-4455
www.acupressbooks.com

22 23 24 25 26 27 28 / 7 6 5 4 3 2 1

This Book Is Dedicated to Truth-Seekers

From Every Nation, Every Religion,

And Every Ethnicity,

With the Hope That by Seeking Truth,

We Might Hasten the Day When Peace Will Prevail on Earth.

And to Jan and AJ,

Whose Passion for Truth Inspires Me Every Single Day

THE GRACE OF TROUBLESOME QUESTIONS

Vocation, Restlessness, and Faith

ACU
PRESS

CONTENTS

FOREWORD

While reading through this collection of remarkable essays, I was struck by the parallels with my own life—and I suspect that other readers will have glimmers of recognition as well. Like Richard Hughes, I grew up with a rather constricted notion of what it meant to be *Christian*, a definition so uncapacious that it did not include Presbyterians or Methodists, much less Episcopalians or (heaven forbid) Roman Catholics. (I suspect that even Richard's Church of Christ might have fallen beyond the pale in my evangelical world.)

Similar to the author's experience, my first attempt at "witnessing" (proselytizing) did not go well. Stanley, my next-door neighbor and a Roman Catholic, took the wind out of my sails when he responded in the affirmative to my opening gambit, "Stanley, are you a Christian?" Clearly, he was lying, but I had been warned that the "unsaved" were duplicitous, so I shouldn't have been surprised. The conversation spiraled downward from there, and I was unable to score a conversion. I told no one of my chastening encounter for years thereafter, so I did not have the benefit of the challenge posed by Richard's mother following his own misbegotten evangelistic sortie: ". . . if you discover that they are right and you are wrong, then you must be the one who is willing to make the change."

This is a book about changes—changes in tradition, changing historical circumstances, but also, most arrestingly, changes in the author. Like many adolescents, and driven by his restless intellect, Richard began to question some of the shibboleths of his childhood understanding of the faith. The challenge of living in two worlds, like Danny Saunders in Chaim Potok's novel *The Chosen*, can be excruciating and disorienting, but it can also be an occasion for growth. And what I admire most about Richard's story is that, unlike many adolescents from similar backgrounds, he chose the middle course between two extremes that characterize most crises of faith. Rather than elect either to embrace the faith of his parents without question or to reject it completely, he chose to make it his own, an often messy process—one that requires patience and determination, a willingness to explore new ideas and challenge long-standing assumptions.

Wise and patient mentors are essential to this process, and Richard's introduction to the Anabaptist tradition at the suggestion of a professor proved crucial to a richer understanding of his own restorationist tradition; it also led to an enhanced appreciation for the New Testament mandate to care for "the least of these." Richard acknowledges that familiarity with the Anabaptists very likely figured into his late-career decision to decamp from Pepperdine to Messiah University.

Anabaptist thinking also very likely contributed to another shift in emphasis. The first edition of Richard's book *Myths America Lives By* was good and important, but the response to that book prompted the author to take a deeper look at the persistence of White supremacy in American life—and he did so at a time when racism was festering anew everywhere from neighborhoods and street corners to the southern border and the Oval Office. Undaunted by the challenge of revisiting his earlier thinking, Richard embarked on a major revision, and the second edition, subtitled *White Supremacy and the Stories That Give Us Meaning*, provided (as I said in my endorsement) "both a searing critique and a summons to embrace our common humanity."

From a larger perspective, because Richard's church was clearly a restorationist enterprise, he began to see over the course of time that the restorationist vision that defined his church also defined the United States. As a result, his scholarship evolved from casting a critical eye on his church to doing the same for the nation, recognizing it for the restorationist project it is. Richard's focus on restorationist thinking, therefore, has been constant throughout his career, but the shift from scholarship on church to scholarship on nation is yet another of the changes that define his vocation.

Changes. Aside from the intrinsic merit of each essay, this book demonstrates what might be characterized as (bordering on oxymoron) the continuity of change on the part of the author. One of the great contributions of Richard's life and scholarship has been his willingness to entertain new ideas and challenge old assumptions—and then the courage to alter his thinking, if necessary, all the while remaining faithful to his faith.

In a world wracked by dogma, that's an example worthy of emulation.

Randall Balmer
John Phillips Chair in Religion at Dartmouth College

PREFACE

"For there is always light, if only we're brave enough to see it.
—Amanda Gorman, "The Hill We Climb," Inaugural Poem 2021

Richard Hughes, my friend and fellow pilgrim on this long journey of seeking the best way to see the light and walk in it, is a joy to hold in my heart. It is not a simple matter for a man who grew up in a religiously conservative, segregated world to join hearts and build deep and abiding connections with an African American woman who grew up in that same type of world, though lightyears apart. But Richard's vigilant search for the truth opened his head and heart in ways that enable him to build bridges.

It is a gift from the Spirit that enables a journey like his—a journey to make sense of a world made by others and handed to us as the only possible way to see. The typical response is to accept that world without too much questioning because it is too frightening to interrogate it. One never knows where the search for deeper understanding will lead, and the fear about that journey is generally enough to extinguish the search for many people. But this is not the case for Richard Hughes. He engaged that search to the point of making it a major part of his vocation.

That search has enabled him to produce an amazing body of scholarship grounded in both Christian history and issues of justice and equity.

In addition, the search led him to question the conviction of his youth that he was "separate and more virtuous than the unwashed masses, and better even than my friends who belonged to what they claimed were other Christian traditions." The ways in which the idea of superiority regarding his belonging to the alleged "one true church" and the idea of White supremacy as a White person intersected were powerful enough to have completely erased any possibility of his liberation. But God had plans for him to be free.

Richard's description of the troubling questions that haunted him as he moved through his high school and college years as questions "filled with grace" helps the reader catch a glimpse of the soul that was not going to be satisfied with the easy answers that might have supported his living in the unconsciousness of personal darkness. When the invitation to live in the dark has been handed to you by your family, your immediate community, and your religion, it is much easier to seek affirmation for remaining in the dark than to heed the challenge from those who are offering invitations to step into the light.

While it is never easy to discern all the factors that lead people from darkness to light, Amanda Gorman is correct in asserting "that there is always light" and the light will shine "whether or not anyone acknowledges it." Thus, at age twenty, when Richard discovered that the idea of "the one true church founded in the first century" was not the whole story for his denomination, he began to ask questions about the story that was told. He wondered, What was its history? What were its roots? What were the cultural and religious forces that had produced this particular tradition that had shaped him so deeply?

He writes, "These questions were hardly academic. These were questions that assaulted my very sense of self since my sense of self was so completely bound up with my church's claim to be true and right while others were false and wrong." The discomfort caused by these questions led to his decision to study history to seek the answers. One can only wonder if he would have had the courage to choose such a path had he known how much this decision was going to totally transform his life. But the amazing grace about the journey with God is that the path to consciousness reveals itself slowly if one will only live one day at a time. God's slow work led him

forward to complete his undergraduate education and move on to graduate education and beyond.

The truth-seeking continued to grow, and as he worked to understand his religious root system, he began to see the undeniable intersection
between membership in his church and the larger issue of citizenship in
this country—a country that used God and religion to justify marginalizing
and oppressing Indigenous People, African Americans, and any persons of
color, as well as the poor and others who were not deemed worthy of full
access to freedom and all the resources necessary to live an empowered
life. His interrogation of this indefensible system of oppression—a system
built on a foundation of White skin and religious supremacy—led him
to the conclusion that one could not hold to such ideas and follow Jesus.

One cannot become human alone. A community is needed to help in
the continual process of creating dissonance between tightly held points of
view that support unconsciousness, on the one hand, and the challenge to
awaken, on the other. Richard found these voices first in his grandmother,
then in his mother, and then in caring professors and others. But he must
be given credit for his willingness to listen and to be impacted by what he
both heard and saw since one always has the personal freedom to live an
entire lifetime as an unconscious person who imagines that there is no
other way to see reality.

The way of seeing that characterizes Richard Hughes today—the scholar,
the person of faith and prophetic witness, the justice seeker, teacher, and
overall wise person—was carved into reality through challenge and great
disturbance to his spirit, as described in this book. But this discussion
would be quite incomplete without acknowledging the generosity Richard
demonstrates when it comes to supporting all who cross his path. He has
worked to see all people as beloved children of the Creator. He demonstrates the grandest level of collegiality that I have ever experienced in the
academy, exhibited in the way he seeks to include his colleagues whenever
possible in scholarly projects and to make sure he collaborates as much
as he can. He does this both by extending to others as many invitations as
possible and graciously accepting the ones that come to him.

Such generosity grows from having honestly interrogated one's inner community, which leads, in turn, to a clear-headed understanding of the need to be in community with those in the external world in a way that verifies the light that calls everyone. As the young poet, Amanda Gorman, says about the light, "There is always light, if . . . only we are brave enough to be it." The capacity to be brave enough to be the light comes from encountering the inner darkness and the outer darkness with a determination to stay open to the light and to the healing work the light will bring.

Perhaps the most challenging space anyone can embody when doing this work is the space that exists in the family of origin and the religious orientation that accompanies that foundation. This is the place Richard has inhabited for many decades with both his head and heart. Thankfully, he is not a person who is trying to clean up the truth so that it will fit into a nice container of his choosing. No, he is a person who has turned in many directions in the search for the truth and who, when he was young, took the wise advice of his mother to acknowledge the truth when he finds it.

This is the type of integrity that makes it possible to keep digging for the truth no matter what one uncovers. Richard's work regarding his religious journey in the Church of Christ has been fraught with much turmoil and is certainly to be appreciated and respected. The scholarly work he has produced in regard to systemic racism and the personal vulnerability he shares by doing this work is heartening to me and many others. As an African American, I am thankful to find a White man who is willing to follow the truth regarding this country and the myths it has created to justify the indefensible systems that have caused so much suffering to Indigenous People, African Americans, and other people of color.

Richard is a truth-teller when it comes to race and injustice in this land. He does not try to make it better or worse than it happens to be. He investigates and reports his findings. But he does more than the typical historian does, since he places the results of his findings in the container of his vocation of serving as a truth-seeking and truth-telling person of faith. Thus his message becomes more than good scholarship, for it is transformed into material that can help facilitate a new way of seeing that can help to heal.

Richard's remarkable vocational journey of seeking truth reflects the layering that is necessary for that search to bear the best fruit. Thus the search for truth became a part of his vocational quest as he sought to discern both the deep call of the heart and the needs of the world.

The world needed the truth that Richard brought, and his heart needed answers to the many questions that challenged his very existence. But his was a dual search. He had to find answers to his questions about his religion, and he had to interrogate his Whiteness and the world that it represents. He could not have done one without the other because of their intricate intersection, though he could have spent a lifetime trying to choose between the two. His journey models for seekers of vocation a path that can be followed. It makes it clear that the search for vocation is a journey rather than an arrival. While there are certainly points along the path that allow for rest and rejuvenation, the road is continuously offering an invitation to the pilgrim to keep going. Richard says yes with such enthusiastic energy. He is curious. He has such an active life of the mind. He seeks to occupy brave spaces where truth-telling is valued.

Richard Hughes has been a good friend for the past two decades as we have shared this pilgrim's path. His truth-telling encourages me and helps me. He is not simply someone who is attempting to be an ally in the quest for justice and freedom for African Americans and others. He is willing to be in a relationship built on the foundation of vulnerability and truth-telling. He is not a fragile White man who cannot allow himself to hear or see the truth because of the perceived threat involved in such revelations. He takes the truth about race and the history of America as he has found it and has the courage to allow that truth to inform his way of being in the world. He is grounded in enough truth about himself to do the work he is called to do. He is not afraid to ask questions because he does not have the need to appear to know everything. He listens. He is willing to learn and unlearn. He is an amazing storyteller. *Humble servant of God* and *truth seeker* describe him best. He and his way of being in the world are gifts for which I am deeply grateful.

Catherine Meeks
Founding Executive Director of the Absalom Jones Center for Racial Healing,
Atlanta, Georgia

ABBREVIATIONS

CH   *Church History*

CM   *Christian Messenger*

D&C   *Doctrine and Covenants*

GA   *Gospel Advocate*

MH   *Millennial Harbinger*

RQ   *Restoration Quarterly*

INTRODUCTION

This is a book about vocation, about who I am, deep down inside, and who I have been called to become. It is a memoir, but an unconventional memoir, as the reader will quickly discern—for in addition to a handful of autobiographical narratives, I have allowed my work to speak for itself, as my work is the product of my life.

I learned from Frederick Buechner that when we grow old—and I am now seventy-eight years of age—we often seek to discern the plot that may have defined our lives. If my life has a plot, it is surely bound up with the Christian tradition in which I was raised—the Churches of Christ.

It is no small thing to grow up in a religious tradition that claims for itself the title "the one true church" and proclaims that it alone is right while everyone else is wrong. How does one make sense of such a tradition and such a bold and audacious claim when one grows up in the religiously pluralistic world of the United States of America?

Granted, religious pluralism in my West Texas world of the 1950s was, for the most part, limited to a handful of Christian denominations—a far cry from the broader religious pluralism in the United States that embraces virtually all the religions of the world. Still, to be taught that I alone was right while all my friends were wrong and on the road to eternal perdition was for me a troubling proposition and one that would define the plot line of my life.

The centerpiece of that bold and audacious claim was what my church described as "the restoration vision"—the attempt to restore in the United States of America the primitive church that existed in the first-century world of Jesus and his Apostles. When my church began in the early nineteenth century on the American frontier, most envisioned the restoration vision as an ideal they strived to achieve. With that tentative understanding, the search for truth was central to their work. But it didn't take long—only thirty years at most—for many in Churches of Christ to transform that ideal into a realized achievement. From that point on, Churches of Christ, for the most part, began to proclaim themselves as the one true church, outside of which there could be no salvation.

I have spent much of my life trying to make sense of the restoration ideal and its often-audacious claims; and along the way, I have found that it has driven many Christian traditions besides my own, most notably the Church of Jesus Christ of Latter-day Saints.

But I was stunned when I discovered that the restoration ideal also defined my nation, the United States of America, which claimed to have been built on "self-evident truths" embedded in nature from the time of creation. Like my church, the nation has vacillated between inclusion and exclusion—between living out the meaning of its Creed that proclaims the equality of all human beings, on the one hand, and affirming, on the other, that nature's "self-evident truths" apply only to people we have labeled as "White."

As I saw how the restoration vision played itself out in the life of the nation, I found myself drawn inescapably into the study of race. And by 2012, thanks to an African American professor—Dr. James Noel—I began to explore in earnest the role White supremacy has played in American culture.

I must confess that I have not been an unbiased scholar. Indeed, one of my colleagues at Messiah College—Professor John Fea—used to say I was more a preacher than an objective historian. Perhaps that is so. At any rate, I discovered many years ago another Christian tradition that also embraced the restoration ideal—the Anabaptists of the sixteenth century. Their story introduced me to one of the driving narratives in the biblical text—the upside-down kingdom of God. And it is that vision that, for good or for ill, has underpinned virtually all my historical work and has formed in many ways the plot that defines my life.

The final section of this book pays tribute to a variety of people who have shaped my sense of vocation: my wife, Jan; my teachers, from Mrs. Derryberry at Stonewall Jackson Elementary School in Dallas to Professor James Spalding at the University of Iowa; and a Black pastor who taught me lessons I could only learn from someone who is Black, Reverend Wayne Baxter, pastor emeritus of Faith Chapel Church of God in Christ in Harrisburg, Pennsylvania. But along with Reverend Baxter, two other Black people have profoundly shaped my sense of vocation: the late Professor James Noel, who taught for many years at San Francisco Theological Seminary, and Dr. Catherine Meeks, Founding Executive Director of the Absalom Jones Center for Racial Healing in Atlanta, who has been my friend and mentor for almost twenty years.

Finally, I am grateful to Dr. David Fleer, my dear friend and colleague at Lipscomb University, without whose suggestion, encouragement, and prodding, this book would never have materialized.

Richard T. Hughes
Franklin, Tennessee
August 15, 2021

CALLED BY TROUBLESOME QUESTIONS

THE GRACE OF
TROUBLESOME QUESTIONS

F inding good work to do—work that can bless the world and enrich the soul, not just for a moment but for a lifetime—is an incredible gift of grace. In my case, that gift first appeared in the form of deeply troubling questions about the church in which I was raised, the Church of Christ.

Over the years, I have often thought that my birth relation to that church was a little like being born Amish. Separate and all-consuming, my church defined the boundaries of my life, and I understood from an early age that I was separate, different, and other.

We were separate for one simple reason: ours was the one true church since we alone had restored the primitive church described in the biblical text.

Not only was I separate, but throughout my teenage years, I also knew that I was better, more virtuous than the unwashed masses, and better even than my friends who belonged to what they claimed were other Christian traditions. But we knew better. We believed those churches weren't really Christian at all. They were cheap imitations, phonies, and frauds, though we used much nicer language to describe them. We called them "the denominations"—a label that could never describe the one true church.

I grew up a lot like Danny Saunders in Chaim Potok's novel *The Chosen*. The son of a Hasidic rabbi, a first-generation immigrant to the United States, Danny thrived on mainstream American culture in his newly adopted land, but each afternoon when school was out, he returned to his deeply separatist Hasidic world, and the tension he felt between the two was palpable.

Like Danny, my life as a teen was a sheer paradox. I thrived in the public schools in San Angelo, Texas, but my church was a world apart. My parents forbade me to attend the school-sponsored dances or even to learn to dance, for that matter. But they required that our entire family attend Sunday school every Sunday and church three times every week—Sunday morning, Sunday evening, and Wednesday evening. And when the week-long gospel meetings rolled around, as they did twice a year, we were there for every service.

One story illustrates well the tension I felt between my church and my school—a story that played itself in the context of Texas high school football. If you saw the movie *Friday Night Lights*, then you will understand at least part of the world in which I grew up, a world in which high school football was king. For every home game, the San Angelo Central High School Bobcats packed the stadium—a magnificent partial bowl built especially for our team—with 11,000 screaming fans, 20 percent of San Angelo's population.

As student body vice-president during my senior year, it fell to me to lead the invocation on one of those nights before the game began. Just before I climbed the stairs to the press box, the student body president caught my arm and offered some advice. "There are many Jews at this game tonight," she said—though looking back, I'm sure she was wrong about that since the Jewish population there was small—"and out of respect to them," she continued, "why don't you just end your prayer with a strong 'Amen' and leave off the words, 'In Jesus's name'?"

I had been taught always to pray "in Jesus's name" since we believed that our prayers reached the Father only through him. But on this particular night and at this particular place, a healthy dose of compromise made good sense to me. So I prayed for the players, and I prayed for the fans, and I prayed for our country. And when I was finished, I simply said, "Amen."

Two days later, on Sunday morning, several men in our church accosted me. They didn't accost me one by one. They accosted me as a group. They clearly had talked things over among themselves and selected one to speak for the rest. That man got in my face and said, "Boy, that prayer you prayed at that game the other night didn't get no higher than them light poles!"

I felt my face grow hot and red. These men had embarrassed me deeply. I had done what I thought was right in the context of my school, but it turned out to be wrong—profoundly wrong—in the context of my church.

The tension I felt between the world of my school and the world of my church was unrelenting. In spite of the fact that I had found acceptance among my peers, I knew I was "other" and would never be like them.

Mine was—and still is—a profoundly regional church. It has always enjoyed considerable strength in a belt that runs from Tennessee to Texas, but its numbers plummet when one leaves its four-state geographical heartland. But until I was twenty years old, as far as I was concerned, it embodied the whole of Christendom.

And that is why, in the late 1950s, I seriously wondered why the major television networks devoted so much coverage to what the Pope said about this or that global crisis, but never covered the perspectives of the leading preachers in my church.

Never mind the fact that the Catholic Church was a global church while mine was largely confined to four states in the American mid-South. And never mind the fact that the Catholic Church had over a billion adherents while mine had perhaps a million. If ours was the one true church and therefore the whole of Christendom, I firmly believed that our preachers deserved fully as much coverage as the networks gave the Pope, and probably even more. Why didn't they interview Batsell Barrett Baxter, the most famous preacher in what we called "the brotherhood" and therefore, as we computed reality, the leading preacher in the whole of the Christian world?

My growing up in Texas helped sustain my provincial view of the world, which in turn reinforced my true-church mentality. As far as I was concerned, Texas was the only world there was. Michigan and Tennessee? India and Mozambique? Those were mythical places that might exist somewhere out in the great beyond, but they clearly held no relevance for my world and me, for my world was the all-encompassing universe known as Texas.

All that changed, however, during my senior year in high school. In the spring of 1961, my parents and I visited St. Louis, where we stayed in a large downtown hotel. The first morning there, my dad invited me to accompany him on a prebreakfast walk, just to see the sights in downtown St. Louis.

I was shocked, utterly shocked, when I saw people, and not just people, but large crowds of people—hundreds, perhaps thousands of them— making their way down the streets and sidewalks of downtown St. Louis.

I suppose I knew that there were people in St. Louis. But on a deep, emotional level, I had never really considered the fact that there were people outside of Texas. Nor had any adult I knew encouraged me to consider that possibility. Instead, most Texans—at that time, at least—believed at a basic, primal level that our state was the center of the universe, a conviction I absorbed by osmosis. That fact that I lived at the *axis mundi*—at the center of the world—never challenged my true-church mentality but only sustained it.

Then, when I was sixteen, my mother said something that began to open my mind to a larger world. A preacher in our tradition had produced a series of filmstrips designed to aid in the task of converting one's friends and neighbors to the one true church. The idea was to invite them in for coffee and dessert and, in that nonthreatening environment, to help them see the error of their ways.

When I discovered those filmstrips, I made up my mind to show them to my high school buddies. All my friends belonged to one Christian denomination or another. They were mainly Baptists, Methodists, and Presbyterians. But I didn't consider them genuinely Christian, and I firmly believed they would burn in the fires of hell if they remained outside the one true church. So one day after school, they came to my house to see and hear the great and marvelous truths I hoped they might embrace.

When I reached the end of my filmstrip presentation, my friends ridiculed me. They thought my perspectives were astoundingly narrow, and that's saying something, considering how narrow all our perspectives were when we were sixteen years old in Texas in the 1950s.

But the most important truth anyone taught that day was imparted neither by the filmstrips nor by me nor by my friends, but by my mother, for once my friends had left our house, my mother spoke words that have shaped my thinking—and, indeed, my life—in far-reaching ways.

"Son," she said, "if you want to convert your friends to our church, that is entirely up to you. But if you discover that they are right and you are wrong, then you must be the one who is willing to make the change."

As I reflect on those words my mother spoke over half a century ago, I realize she gave me that day one of the greatest gifts a mother can give a child, short of life itself and a mother's love. The gift was the charge to see the world through someone else's eyes.

My mother's words placed a dent in my true-church armor, but that armor began to crack in serious ways during my college years. One day a friend told me something I had never grasped before—that our church was essentially confined to four Southern states—Tennessee, Arkansas, Oklahoma, and Texas. As insular as I was, it somehow made no sense to me that all God's children—all the saved from throughout the earth—were essentially confined to four states in the American South.

While still in college, I encountered religions other than the Christian religion in a world literature textbook that contained selections from the Koran and the Bhagavad Gita. Before reading those selections, I had never given the slightest thought to the fact that millions of people in the world embrace religions other than the Christian faith.

Making that discovery shook me to the core, for it forced me to ask if the fact that I was a Christian—indeed, if the fact that I belonged to the one true church—was more the result of having been born into a "true-church" family and a nation that was nominally Christian than anything else.

While questions about the religions of the world assaulted my sense of certainty about much that I believed, more devastating still was my belated discovery that the Church of Christ did not spring full-blown from the biblical text. As bizarre as it may seem, I did not discover that my church actually had a human founding and a human history in the United States until I was roughly twenty years old.

But what was that history? What were our roots? What were the cultural and religious forces that had produced this tradition and, by extension, the forces that had shaped me?

These questions were hardly academic. These were questions that assaulted my very sense of self since my sense of self was so completely bound up with my church's claim to be true and right while others were false and wrong.

Those questions tugged at my heart and mind with such urgency that during the twenty-second year of my life, I made a crucial decision: I would become a historian and focus my work on those deeply troubling questions for which, at the time, I had no answers.

Over the years, the answers I discovered led me to turn my back on true-church mythology. But I have not turned my back on the Church of Christ. Somehow, I knew that turning my back on this tradition would amount to turning my back on myself. So instead of rejecting it, I have spent a lifetime seeking to understand it. And that decision has served me well.

The questions that prompted this journey strike me now as a gift of grace. Deeply troubling at the time, they opened for me a vocation that has enriched my life with good books, with good students, and yes, with even more questions that have set me on the journey of discovery time and time again.

THE APOCALYPTIC ORIGINS OF CHURCHES OF CHRIST AND THE TRIUMPH OF MODERNISM

The origins of the American-born Churches of Christ are exceedingly complex. While most historians have argued that Churches of Christ separated from Alexander Campbell's Disciples of Christ late in the nineteenth century, the genesis of Churches of Christ was not a matter of separation from the Disciples at all. Rather, Churches of Christ grew from two early nineteenth-century worldviews that coalesced and intertwined with one another in ways that often defy disentanglement. The first was the apocalyptic perspective of Barton W. Stone; the second was the radically sectarian mentality of the young and brash Alexander Campbell of the *Christian Baptist* period (1823–30). As early as the 1830s, these two perspectives wed, brought together in part by the match-making power of poverty, marginality, and social estrangement.[1] Together, they clearly shaped a portion of the Stone-Campbell movement that, in due time, would come to be

---

[1] Poverty was not the defining factor in the 1830s, but it was important. Later, in the South, the Civil War helped enhance the sectarian outlook, as David Edwin Harrell has amply documented. See Harrell, "The Sectional Origins of Churches of Christ," *Journal of Southern History* 30 (Aug. 1964): 261–77.

known as a denomination separate and apart from the Disciples—namely, the Churches of Christ.

While the perspectives of Stone and the early Campbell intertwined in the lives and thoughts of many in the early nineteenth century, and while the one rarely existed without the other, it is nonetheless possible to identify particular leaders and to discern particular streams of tradition that carried either the Stoneite or the early Campbellian perspective in especially powerful ways. Thus, for example, Campbell's sectarian perspective, which many of his early followers interpreted to mean that Churches of Christ constituted the one true church outside of which there was no salvation, fed through several influential editor/preachers. Most notable among these were Tolbert Fanning and John R. Howard of Tennessee, Arthur Crihfield of Ohio and Kentucky, and Benjamin Franklin and Daniel Sommer of Indiana.[2] Since this tradition is relatively well known, I will not trace it here.

This essay will focus, instead, on the worldview embraced by Barton W. Stone and the sizable corps of preachers he inspired in the Cumberland region of Tennessee in the early nineteenth century, and on the ways in which that worldview helped define a sizable segment of Churches of Christ. This worldview could best be described, quite simply, as *apocalyptic*, embracing a radical sense of estrangement and separation from the world and its values and a keen allegiance to a transcendent vision these people described as "the kingdom of God." That kingdom had manifested itself in the earliest days of primitive Christianity, perpetually stood in judgment on the kingdoms of this earth, and would finally triumph over all things. Because Stone and his people identified so strongly with that kingdom, they typically refused to fight in wars, to vote, or otherwise to participate in the political process.

The apocalyptic worldview, however, should not be confused with premillennialism. There were those, as we shall see, who followed the

---

[2] While Alexander Campbell never claimed, even during the *Christian Baptist* period, that the movement he led comprised the one and only true church, much of his early rhetoric pointed in that direction. By the late 1830s, Crihfield and Howard, in particular, were defending the Church of Christ as the one true church. For Crihfield and Howard, see Richard T. Hughes and C. Leonard Allen, *Illusions of Innocence: Protestant Primitivism in America, 1630–1875* (Chicago: University of Chicago Press, 1988): 128–31.

apocalyptic perspective into a full-blown premillennial outlook. This, however, was not always the case. Indeed, on the Stone side of the movement, there were some who embraced the apocalyptic worldview but stoutly resisted premillennial thinking. On the Campbell side of the movement, there were some who arrived at premillennial convictions out of sheer biblical literalism with no reference whatever to what we here describe as an "apocalyptic worldview."

The irony here is that while many in the movement uncritically fused the Stoneite and early Campbellian perspectives, in significant ways these perspectives were simply incompatible. For if Stone's worldview was predominantly apocalyptic, Campbell's outlook even during the sectarian days of the *Christian Baptist* was fundamentally optimistic regarding this world, progressive, and postmillennial. Further, the intellectual split between Campbell and Stone in this regard reflected a major split in American intellectual life at that time, the split between the "party of memory" and the "party of hope."

In the twentieth century, in the interest of modernization, key leaders of Churches of Christ literally drove from the church both the memory and the reality of the separationist and apocalyptic vision inspired by Barton W. Stone. Discredited and forgotten, this tradition therefore has played no meaningful role in the historiography of Churches of Christ.

Historiography, Cultural Setting, and Backgrounds

In 1906, the US Bureau of the Census recognized for the first time a division in the ranks of the Stone-Campbell restoration tradition and listed two separate denominations: Churches of Christ and Disciples of Christ. Until 1964, most historians rooted this division in a late nineteenth-century dispute over missionary societies and instrumental music in worship, with the emerging Churches of Christ coalescing around the negative position on both these issues. In this view, the Disciples represented the mainstream of this tradition throughout the nineteenth century and even into the twentieth. On the other hand, Churches of Christ departed from that mainstream, as well as from the parent denomination, the Disciples, over these issues and, therefore, possessed little theological identity apart from their resistance to these "innovations."[3]

However, in 1964, David Edwin Harrell took sharp exception to this interpretation and rooted the division in social forces related to the Civil War. Noting that Churches of Christ in the early twentieth century resided overwhelmingly in the upper South and that Disciples in the same period centered in the Midwest, Harrell concluded that the genesis of Churches of Christ as a denomination separate from the Disciples must have been sectional. Thus poverty versus affluence, rural versus urban biases, and deep sectional feelings were all tensions that divided the movement and helped produce Churches of Christ as a separate and distinct denomination. Thus, he concluded, "the twentieth-century Churches of Christ are the spirited offspring of the religious rednecks of the postbellum South."[4]

There is considerable truth both in the traditional reading and in Harrell's revisionist interpretation. At the same time, neither of these interpretations recognizes the pivotal role played by the separationist and apocalyptic tradition of Barton W. Stone in shaping Churches of Christ, much less the cultural split that undergirded the differences between the Campbellite and the Stoneite perspectives.

How might one describe that "cultural split"? On the one hand, the dominant outlook of antebellum America was a postmillennial perspective that celebrated unbounded human potential and unrestrained progress into the modern world. Those who held this viewpoint comprised the

---

[3] This historiographic perspective has been shaped chiefly by historians writing from within the Disciples of Christ side of this movement: i.e., W. E. Garrison and A. T. DeGroot, *The Disciples of Christ: A History* (St. Louis: The Bethany Press, 1948), 404-6; and William E. Tucker and Lester G. McAllister, *Journey in Faith: A History of the Christian Church (Disciples of Christ)* (St. Louis: The Bethany Press, 1948), 251-54. Most major histories of American religion rely on precisely this interpretation: i.e., Sydney E. Ahlstrom, *A Religious History of the American People* (New Haven: Yale University Press, 1972), 822-23; Edwin S. Gaustad, *A Religious History of America*, rev. ed. (New York: Harper and Row, 1990), 258; and Winthrop S. Hudson, *Religion in America*, 4th ed. (New York: Macmillan, 1987), 260n25. Interestingly, the only text to date whose chief interest is a synthetic history of Churches of Christ employs the same interpretive assumptions but for opposite purposes. Thus Earl I. West argues that "by 1906, ... the 'Christian Churches' or 'Disciples of Christ,' as they preferred to be called, took their instruments and their missionary societies and walked a new course." See *The Search for the Ancient Order*, vol. 2 (Indianapolis: Religious Book Service, 1950), 448.

[4] Harrell, "Sectional Origins," 264 and 277. See also Harrell, *Quest for a Christian America: The Disciples of Christ and American Society to 1866* (Nashville: Disciples of Christ Historical Society, 1966); and *The Social Sources of Division in the Disciples of Christ, 1865-1900* (Atlanta: Publishing Systems, 1973). Bill J. Humble shared the view that the Civil War, with its attendant social factors, played a significant role in dividing the Disciples into two separate communions. Humble, "The Influence of the Civil War," *RQ* 8 (4th Quarter 1965): 245.

"party of hope," perhaps best epitomized by Ralph Waldo Emerson. Further, many who held this position were primitivists who took their bearings from a mythic, primordial age—a point underscored by Major L. Wilson in a seminal essay published in 1961. As Wilson put it, "the politics of restoration was not . . . a conservative flight to the past," but instead a vision of primordial perfections that "made further progress possible."[5] Those who took this view were confident that, through their own efforts, they could recover the perfections of that primal age and project those perfections into the American future. They would therefore recreate, in their own time, the kingdom of God on earth.[6]

Those Americans who embraced the minority position, on the other hand, placed themselves in radical opposition to this perspective and generally affirmed a pessimistic and antimodern worldview that frequently turned out to be profoundly apocalyptic. Often Calvinists convinced of the radical sinfulness of humankind, these Americans comprised the "party of memory" of which Emerson so loudly complained. Many of these also were primitivists, but their skepticism regarding human potential and progress prevented them from easily projecting the perfections of the first age into an American future. Instead, these Americans often proclaimed their allegiance to a "kingdom of God" that they saw manifest in the primordium and that they anticipated would manifest itself again in the millennium, but only at God's initiative. They simply had no confidence that the kingdom of God could appear between those end times

---

[5] Major L. Wilson, "Paradox Lost: Order and Progress in Evangelical Thought of Mid-Nineteenth-Century America," *CH* 44 (Sep. 1975): 352-54. R. W. B. Lewis made the same point when he argued that "the more intense the belief in progress toward perfection, the more it stimulated a belief in a present primal perfection" (*The American Adam: Innocence, Tragedy, and Tradition in the Nineteenth Century* [Chicago: University of Chicago Press, 1955], 5). Richard Hofstadter concurred in *The Progressive Historians: Turner, Beard, Parrington* (New York: Vintage Books, 1970), 7, arguing that American progress often was progress backward to "the primitivist sense of the ideal human condition." There was by no means consensus in antebellum America on the specific content of the primordial age.

[6] Clearly, many of the Transcendentalist communal experiments reflected this outlook. Thus, Bronson Alcott saw America as the site of "the second Eden" in which humankind might be restored to "rightful communion with God in the Paradise of Good." See Clara E. Sears, *Bronson Alcott's Fruitlands, with Transcendental Wild Oats by Louisa Alcott* (Boston: Kessinger Publishing, 1915). And John Humphrey Noyes imagined that the millennial age in which he lived, patterned after the perfections of the primitive church, would sustain not only social relationships free from selfish pride but even the scientific breeding of the perfect human being. See Maren Lockwood Carden, *Oneida: Utopian Community to Modern Corporation* (New York: Harper and Row, 1971), 12-13. Similarly, the humanitarian crusade aimed at nothing less than the complete elimination of evil from the social fabric of American life.

of God-directed, primal perfections. For these Americans, primitivism often took on distinctly antimodern dimensions.[7]

The division that finally produced Disciples of Christ on the one hand and Churches of Christ on the other, while rooted in a variety of factors, had its oldest and deepest roots in this ideological polarization. Indeed, the Disciples of Christ are the legitimate children of the postmillennial, modernizing progressivism of the mature Alexander Campbell—a man who represented the "party of hope" as fully as any man of his age. Churches of Christ, on the other hand, ultimately descend, at least in part, from the separatist, antimodern perspective of Barton W. Stone, who stood squarely in the "party of memory."[8]

Yet it must be said that for all their mutual enmity, the party of hope and the party of memory shared significant common ground. The fact that nineteenth-century Americans often rooted progress in the perfections of the primal past helps us understand how the Campbell and Stone movements, embracing as they did such radically differing worldviews, could unite in 1832. Indeed, most in both groups were convinced that they shared common restorationist presuppositions. How different those presuppositions really were became evident as the nineteenth century wore on, slowly revealing the existence of two denominations, not one: the Disciples and the Churches of Christ.

Indeed, recognition of these two divergent traditions helps account for the North/South sectional alignment of Disciples and Churches of Christ. While Professor Harrell's "sectional origins" thesis helps account to a great degree for the sectional alignment of these traditions, that thesis

---

[7] Why, in an age dominated by postmillennial dreams and anticipations, would this minority voice exist at all? In the first place, Calvinism—with its emphasis on the sovereignty of God and the fallenness of humankind—led some to view with profound suspicion the assumption that human beings might create, through their own efforts, the Kingdom of God on earth. In the second place, many who embraced such skepticism were people estranged from the progress and optimism of the age by social and economic circumstances. Thus, many found in William Miller's prediction that Christ would return in 1843 meaningful compensation for economic losses occasioned by the depression of 1837.

[8] Almost alone among historians, Martin Marty recognized that the division between Disciples and Churches of Christ was finally a division between modernism and primitivism. *Modern American Religion*, vol. 1: *The Irony of It All, 1893-1919* (Chicago: University of Chicago Press, 1986), 163-64. Marty's account does not recognize, however, that this ideological split was rooted in the differing worldviews of Alexander Campbell and Barton W. Stone.

still leaves much unexplained.[9] In the first place, if the identity of Churches of Christ was principally defined by Southern sectional prejudices, why did these churches thrive only in a relatively small region of the South in Tennessee, southern Kentucky, and northern Alabama, but hardly at all in the Deep South and the Southeast? Even more important, when the two major terms of the Stone-Campbell movement's agenda, unity and restoration, finally broke apart, why did the restoration ideal make its home chiefly among Churches of Christ in the upper South, while the unity theme made its home chiefly among Disciples in the Midwest?

On the other hand, taking seriously the differences between Stone and the mature Campbell helps clarify answers to these questions. From the earliest years of the nineteenth century, a major strand of the movement that would become Churches of Christ centered in the Cumberland Plateau of Tennessee, an area where the leadership of Barton W. Stone was pronounced. R. L. Roberts, in fact, has compiled a list of approximately two hundred preachers in the Cumberland area, all influenced either directly or indirectly by Barton W. Stone, who were actively establishing Churches of Christ long before the mid-1820s, when Campbell was first known in that region. From that time on, Campbell made occasional visits to middle Tennessee, but he preached mainly in cities and towns, leaving the sizable corps of Stoneite preachers to dominate the rural countryside.[10]

On the other hand, Campbell's visits to Kentucky—an early bastion of the Stone movement—were far more frequent than his visits to Tennessee, and his long-term influence centered therefore especially in Kentucky and points further north. It is hardly any wonder, then, that the strength of Disciples of Christ is especially pronounced to this day

---

[9] Professor Harrell does speak of the "divided mind" of the movement. Thus, he writes, "two distinct emphases emerged. One group conceived of Christianity in the denominational framework of practical religion, social and political activism, and, often, a nationalistic postmillennialism. A second group emphasized the sectarian tradition of Biblical legalism, a fanatical disposition, and uncompromising separation from the world" (Harrell, *Quest for a Christian America*, 66). However, Harrell does not recognize that among the various roots of the sectarian side of the movement, the Stoneite tradition played a prominent role; nor does he emphasize the apocalyptic dimensions that often accompanied the sectarian phase of the movement, especially in the South.

[10] R. L. Roberts, "Early Tennessee and Kentucky Preachers," Restoration Movement Resources, www.acu.edu /restoration-movement/.

in the original Campbell heartland of Kentucky and the Midwest, while Churches of Christ find their greatest strength in the region bounded by the Cumberland Plateau on the east and Texas on the west.[11]

The story that follows is one of competing perspectives on the values of this world, human progress, and modernity. The story concludes, however, with profound irony, for while Campbell's early, sectarian view of both the church and Scripture dominated Churches of Christ from the 1820s on, his optimistic assessment of this world and of human progress finally came to dominate them as well. This was a slow development, gathering momentum for more than one hundred years. Finally, in the World War I era, Churches of Christ took a decisive turn away from the old Stoneite worldview, increasingly embracing Campbell's optimistic view of human progress. As a result, these churches became agents of modernization as fully as did Campbell's Disciples; the primitivism of Churches of Christ became not a foe of modernization but a pivotal source of support for that process; and the traditional Stoneite insistence on separation from the world finally became little more than sectarian exclusivism, calling only for separation from the surrounding denominations.

Alexander Campbell

Alexander Campbell exerted little or no influence on the sizable Stoneite communities of Kentucky, southern Ohio, and middle Tennessee—communities most often called Churches of Christ—until 1823, when he traveled to Kentucky to debate William L. McCalla. The Stoneites, whose insistence on Christian freedom had left them almost vacuous theologically, found compelling Campbell's clear and detailed exposition of the forms, structures, and practices of primitive Christianity.[12] From that time

---

[11]For delineation of the sectional alignments of Disciples and Churches of Christ in 1906, see Harrell, "Sectional Origins," 263-64. By 1950, Disciples of Christ had their greatest strength in the five states comprising the original Campbell heartland—Kentucky, Ohio, Indiana, Illinois, and Missouri—and in Texas, with slightly lesser strength in Iowa, Kansas, and Oklahoma to the west and in Virginia and North Carolina to the east. See Edwin S. Gaustad, *Historical Atlas of Religion in America* (New York: Harper and Row, 1962), 65. On the other hand, by 1960, Churches of Christ were especially concentrated in middle and western Tennessee, northern Alabama, Arkansas, Oklahoma, and Texas. Gaustad, "Churches of Christ in America," in *The Religious Situation: 1969*, ed. Donald R. Cutler (Boston: Beacon Press, 1969), 1,030-31. By the mid-twentieth century, both Disciples and Churches of Christ had significant strength in Southern California, a phenomenon explained by westward migration patterns.

[12]Hughes and Allen, *Illusions of Innocence*, 115-16.

on, Campbell exercised a growing, and finally decisive, influence over Churches of Christ in that region. Indeed, in January 1832, the Stone and Campbell movements formally united in Lexington, Kentucky.[13]

For almost a decade prior to that union, Campbell had contributed to Churches of Christ a Common Sense view of the Bible drawn directly from Scottish Baconianism,[14] a clear and detailed description of those aspects of the primitive church that ought to be restored, and great confidence that human beings were fully capable of reading Scripture aright, implementing its divine patterns, and restoring in full the grandeur and beauty of the apostolic age.

Campbell's great confidence in human insight and human ability to bring about moral and spiritual reform stood at the intellectual heart of his movement and, more than anything else, distinguished his movement from that of Barton W. Stone. But Campbell also differed from Stone in his understanding of Christian primitivism. For this reason, Campbell's position can be designated *rational, progressive primitivism.* Indeed, restoration for Campbell was not so much a response to the sovereign rule of God, understood in Calvinist terms, as it was a response to the authority of Scripture, understood in some respects as a technical, even scientific, manual for the recovery of primitive Christianity. Clearly, Enlightenment perspectives significantly shaped Campbell's restoration vision that, when all was said and done, focused on *progress toward* the rule of God, aided by rational analysis and technical reconstruction of the first Christian age. Ultimately, a complete restoration of the apostolic institutions would transform human society and launch the millennial dawn.[15]

But Campbell also was convinced that the millennium would be the fruit of rational and scientific progress and simply would not and could not begin until scientific progress had run its course, enlightening all humankind. He made this point abundantly clear in 1858 in response to

[13] Dean Mills, *Union on the King's Highway: The Campbell-Stone Heritage of Unity* (Joplin, MO: College Press, 1987).

[14] Samuel Morris Eames, *The Philosophy of Alexander Campbell* (Bethany, WV: Bethany College, 1966), esp. 19–32; and Robert F. West, *Alexander Campbell and Natural Religion* (New Haven: Yale University Press, 1948), 220–21, 225.

[15] On Campbell's postmillennialism, see West, *Alexander Campbell and Natural Religion*, 163–217; and Carl Wayne Hensley, "The Rhetorical Vision of the Disciples of Christ: A Rhetoric of American Millennialism," PhD diss., University of Minnesota, 1972.

claims that the revival of that year was the harbinger of the golden age. In rebutting this claim, Campbell argued for the following "incomparably paramount" consideration:

> It was but yesterday that the mariner's compass was discovered, that printing was shown to be practicable, that steam power was laughed at as an absurdity, and the electric telegraph ridiculed as the hobby of a vagarian's brain. . . . We have too much faith in progress . . . to subscribe to the doctrines of these theological gentlemen who hint the last days are at hand.[16]

But there was no exchange that more clearly illumined Campbell's postmillennial principles than his quarrel in 1833–34 with Samuel M. McCorkle. Profoundly pessimistic regarding human progress, McCorkle challenged Campbell's most fundamental presupposition regarding the possibility of recovery of a golden age. "The present cannot be renovated," McCorkle complained. "No means on earth can bring or restore the administration back to primitive rectitude; it grows worse yearly in despite of all the efforts that can be made to heal."[17] Writing under the pseudonym "A Reformed Clergyman," Campbell was incredulous. Had not Bacon, Locke, and Newton inspired tremendous progress in politics and science? And what of the noble contributions of Luther, Calvin, and Zwingli? Beyond this, "the invention of gunpowder, the mariner's compass, the printing press, the discovery of America, the American Revolution—what have they wrought!!" Even Campbell's own movement might well launch "a restoration" that would "bless the world in ten thousand ways." A millennium would dawn, to be sure, and its driving force would be "knowledge, scientific, political, and religious."[18] To Campbell, the conclusion of the entire matter was clear: "This is, of all ages and of all generations, the most unpropitious for the assertion of the dogma that moral and intellectual means can benefit society in no very valuable nor

---

[16] Campbell, "The Millennium," *MH* (June 1858): 335–36.

[17] S. M. McCorkle, "Signs of the Times," *MH* (Oct. 1833): 483.

[18] A Reformed Clergyman, "The Millennium—No. 3," *MH* (Oct. 1834): 549; "The Millennium—No. 7," *MH* (Mar. 1835): 105; and "The Millennium—No. 8," *MH* (Apr. 1835): 148.

permanent way. Almost every common newspaper presents insuperable difficulties to such a preposterous opinion."[19]

By 1844, McCorkle found refuge not in Campbell's *Millennial Harbinger* but in Barton W. Stone's *Christian Messenger*. Indeed, Stone opened to McCorkle the pages of the *Messenger* for a lengthy series of articles in which McCorkle launched a massive counter-attack on Campbell's views. "'*Restoration* of *ancient order*,' is a pleasing *dream*—a brilliant phantom," McCorkle began in July, and he specifically called on Campbell to show how the "man of sin" might be destroyed by merely "moral means." By August, McCorkle took the gloves off and came out swinging:

> Great names in the Christian church have vetoed the doctrine of a personal reign of Messiah, and our credulous brethren following in the perilous *wake*! . . . Half inebriate with the *fumes* of Babylon, . . . [editors] are harping upon, "Christianity restored," when we are approaching a *time of trouble*, such as never was. . . . Will they counteract by the "Ancient Order" the strong delusion that God has promised to send . . . ?[20]

Barton W. Stone

It is significant that McCorkle chose to publish these strictures in Stone's *Christian Messenger* and that Stone chose to print them. Perhaps even more significant was McCorkle's confession to Stone: "With the exception of yourself, I have the editorial corps [of the movement] against me." For while Stone did not approve of all that McCorkle wrote,[21] he was profoundly sympathetic with McCorkle's pessimistic outlook on human potential and progress. Indeed, in spite of their rejection of Calvinist theories of conversion, Stone and his followers—most of whom came from Presbyterian or Baptist backgrounds—continued to nurture for many years a Calvinist assessment of human nature.[22] Stone typified most when he wrote, "That

---

[19] A Reformed Clergyman, "The Millennium—No. 3," *MH* (Oct. 1834): 549–50.

[20] S. M. McCorkle, "Conversion of the World, No. 4," *CM* 14 (July 1844): 70–71; and "Conversion of the World—No. 4 [*sic*]," *CM* 14 (Aug. 1844): 97–98.

[21] S. M. McCorkle, "The Laymen [*sic*]," *CM* 13 (Mar. 1844): 349.

[22] See Newell D. Williams, "Barton W. Stone's Calvinist Piety," *Encounter* 42 (Autumn 1981): 409–17; and Hughes and Allen, *Illusions of Innocence*, 112–16.

mankind are depraved, is a lamentable truth, abundantly attested by the word of God, and confirmed by universal experience and observation. . . . All are in want of what they were made to enjoy, which is God; and have a propensity to satisfy that want with meaner things."[23]

Stone's followers generally joined to their Calvinist appraisal of human nature an experience of poverty and deprivation. John Rogers, one of the early Stone preachers in Kentucky, later recalled that the pioneers "were mostly men of small means" who "knew nothing of the luxuries and refinements of modern society." Isaac Jones recalled that all the preachers in middle Tennessee and south-central Kentucky early on were "poor men, (some having no homes of their own) having but little education."[24] While Campbell preached in meeting houses, Stone's early preaching is described as largely itinerant, being "done under an Elm and Oak" and "under a Beech Tree, covered with a summer grapevine." And if Campbell moved among the cultured and the sophisticated, the work of Stone and his colleagues was among rustic and unlettered frontier people whose religious practices were often both primitive and emotional.[25] Further, the Stoneites typically idealized poverty as a Christian virtue—a fact that stands in stark contrast to Alexander Campbell, who died the wealthiest man in West Virginia, having plowed an inheritance from his father-in-law into farming, land speculation, book publishing, and educational enterprises.

Finally, the Stoneites were every bit as utopian and restorationist as Alexander Campbell, but for them, restoration had less to do with the forms and structures of the primitive church and more to do with lives of simple holiness.

These features, taken together, nurtured in Stone and his people a distinctly antimodern bias and helped sustain their apocalyptic outlook. That outlook, in turn, expressed itself in three specific ways: their insistence on

[23] B. W. Stone, "A Compendious View of the Gospel," in Stone, *The Biography of Eld. Barton Warren Stone, Written by Himself*, ed. John Rogers (Cincinnati: J. A. & U. P. James, 1847), reprinted in *The Cane Ridge Reader*, ed. Hoke S. Dickinson (Paris, KY: Cane Ridge Preservation Project, 1972), 191–92.

[24] John Rogers, "Funeral Discourse on Elder H. Dinsmore," *American Christian Review* 6 (Sep. 17, 1863): 181; and Isaac N. Jones, "The Reformation in Tennessee," included in J. W. Grant, "A Sketch of the Reformation in Tennessee," c. 1897, typescript, 35 (manuscript housed in Center for Restoration Studies, Abilene Christian University).

[25] J. W. Grant, "A Sketch of the Reformation in Tennessee," 9–10; Isaac Jones, "The Reformation in Tennessee," in Grant, "Sketch of the Reformation," 31–32; and Joseph Thomas, *The Life of the Pilgrim Joseph Thomas* (Winchester, VA: Jonathan Foster, 1817), 124, 160, 162–63, and passim.

a radical separation from the world, an eschatology that often manifested itself in premillennial terms, and their disdain for political involvement of any kind.

The theme of separation from the world abounds on almost every page of fourteen volumes of Stone's *Christian Messenger*, which ran from 1827 through 1844. Stone himself is a case in point. Aiming originally at a career in law, Stone abandoned that for a career in preaching. Then, when he and four other dissidents left the Presbyterian church in the aftermath of the Cane Ridge Revival, Stone voluntarily relinquished all salary and committed himself to a life of poverty in the interest of the kingdom of God. If Stone had a creed, he surely expressed it in 1841 when he admonished his readers "that you must not mind earthly things, nor set your affections on them—not to be conformed to the world. . . . Here you have no abiding place, but are as strangers and pilgrims seeking a better country."[26]

All this stands in remarkable contrast to the world Martha Wilson, a mountain girl from North Carolina, found at Campbell's Bethany College in 1858. Having accompanied her husband to Bethany, Martha wrote home to her Aunt Julia in Yadkinville that she and Virgil, her husband, had "had invitations to tea at Mr. Campbell's and most of the *Professors*. They are all very sociable and friendly but there are rather more grades and circles in society than I think ought to be in a Christian community." In another letter she complained: "I do not like to visit here—the people visit too fashionably." Yet, her husband was awed with the prospects facing Bethany graduates. He wrote, "Tell Uncle that a great many young men go out from college to teach, but owing to the reputation of Bethany for its instruction, they command enormous prices never less than $800. One young preacher has been offered $1500 in S. Virginia to preach for three churches."[27] Without a doubt, the issue of orientation toward the world was a clear line of demarcation that separated the basic worldviews of the Stone and Campbell movements.

The Stoneites' radical sense of separation from the world grew quite naturally from their apocalyptic orientation, an outlook that often gave

[26] Stone, *Biography*, 49–50; and "Christian Union. Lecture III," *CM* 11 (May 1841): 316–17.

[27] Martha Wilson, "Letter to Aunt Julia, Bethany, Virginia," (personal letter) July 21, 1858, in Jones Family Papers, Southern Historical Collection, Wilson Library, University of North Carolina, Chapel Hill; Martha Wilson, "Letter to Aunt Julia, Bethany Virginia," (personal letter), September 11, 1858, and postscript to letter from Martha Wilson to Aunt Julia, Bethany, Virginia, July 21, 1858.

expression to an explicitly premillennial eschatology. Indeed, millennial excitement was central to the Stone movement from its inception at the Cane Ridge Revival of 1801. John Dunlavy recalled after the revival that many thought "the day of the Lord, or Millennium, was at hand, and that that revival would never cease until that day should commence." Levi Purviance remembered that, during the revivals, "many were fully persuaded that the glorious Millennial Day had commenced, and that the world would soon become the Kingdom of our Lord Jesus Christ."[28]

Due to the paucity of sources, however, it is difficult to trace the progress of Stone's millennial thought between the revivals and 1827 when he launched the *Christian Messenger*. But by the early 1830s, no one could doubt where he stood on the millennial question. One sample of his thinking—a reply to an Elder William Caldwell—will suffice: "The second coming of Christ is at the commencement of his millennial reign on earth— here on earth he will reign till the 1000 years be finished—nor will he cease to reign on earth till he has raised from death the wicked, and judged them according to their works."[29] While the Millerite excitement of the early 1840s exacerbated Stone's interest in this theme,[30] his convictions regarding the premillennial kingdom of Christ predated those events by many years.

It is precisely here, tucked away in the union of separationism and apocalypticism, that one finds the origin of a third theme central both to Stone and to a major stream in Churches of Christ for over a century. This tradition held that civil government—including American democracy— was both demonic and illegitimate, and that Christians should refuse all active participation in government and politics, including voting. In fact, the Stoneites generally thought, following Daniel's vision in the second chapter of Daniel, that the kingdom of Christ would, in the last days, fill the entire earth, destroy every human government—democracies along

---

[28] John Dunlavy, *The Manifesto, or a Declaration of the Doctrine and Practice of the Church of Christ* (1818; repr., New York: Edward O. Jenkins, 1847), 437; and Levi Purviance, *The Biography of Elder David Purviance* (Dayton: B. F. & G. W. Ells, 1848), 248–49. See also B. W. Stone et. al., *Observations on Church Government, by the Presbytery of Springfield*, 1808, in Dickinson, *The Cane Ridge Reader*, 12.

[29] B. W. Stone, "To Elder William Caldwell," *CM* 8 (May 1834): 148; see also Stone, "The Millennium," *CM* 7 (Oct. 1833): 314; and Stone, "Reply," *CM* 7 (Dec. 1833): 365–66.

[30] See B. W. Stone, "The Signs of the Last Days," *CM* 12 (Aug. 1842): 301–6; Stone, "Signs of the Last Days—Continued," *CM* 12 (Oct. 1842): 363–67; and Stone, "The Coming of the Son of God," *CM* 12 (Apr. 1842): 166–70.

with monarchies—and rule the earth along with Christ for a thousand years. Once again, Stone is a case in point.

> The lawful King, Jesus Christ, will shortly put them [human governments] all down, and reign with his Saints on earth a thousand years, without a rival. . . . Then shall all man made laws and governments be burnt up forever. These are the seat of the beast. . . . We must cease to support any other government on earth by our counsels, co-operation, and choice.[31]

Based on this fundamental presupposition, the Stoneites time and again admonished one another to total noninvolvement in civil government other than paying taxes and obeying civil law—but only those laws that did not conflict with the kingdom of God.[32]

In this connection, it should be noted that the Stoneites' rejection of ecclesiastical societies (missionary, Bible, temperance, etc.) grew out of the same apocalyptic vision that governed their refusal to participate in civil government. God had ordained none of these societies, and his coming kingdom would destroy them, along with all human governments and institutions devised by men's wits. On this point, the Stoneites stood once again in marked contrast to the Campbell movement. Campbell also stood opposed to ecclesiastical societies during the early years of his career, but he based his opposition not on apocalypticism but on the biblical pattern. Further, Campbell abandoned his opposition in the 1840s and became president both of the American Christian Bible Society (1845) and the American Christian Missionary Society (1849).

Finally, since Daniel, chapter 2, was such an important text for the apocalyptic visions of Stone and his people, it is interesting to note that Campbell tamed that passage and placed its meaning squarely in the context of human history and progress. For Campbell, the little stone that would fill the entire earth was not the coming kingdom of God but rather

---

[31] Stone, "Reflections of Old Age," *CM* 13 (Aug. 1843): 123–26. See also Stone, "Civil and Military Offices Sought and Held by Christians," *CM* 12 (May 1842): 201–5; letter to T. P. Ware and letter from T. P. Ware, *CM* 14 (Oct. 1844): 163–71; and "An Interview between an Old and Young Preacher," *CM* 14 (Dec. 1844): 225–300.

[32] See James M. Mathes, "Number III," *CM* 10 (May 1836): 65–66; and Jn. T. Jones, Jno. Rigdon, M. Elder, and D. P. Henderson, Committee, "Report," *CM* 9 (Nov. 1835): 250–51.

the Protestant Reformation, and the image that the stone destroyed was not human government but the Roman Catholic Church.[33]

The contrast between Campbell and Stone with reference to the restoration vision can now be sharpened. If Campbell's vision can be called "rational, progressive primitivism," it is equally proper to name Stone's vision "apocalyptic primitivism." This designation points to his apocalyptic worldview that undergirded and sustained his premillennial perspective and that, in turn, reflected his Calvinist sense of the sovereignty of God. This meant Stone was not so much interested in the church as in the *kingdom*, that is, the rule of God over all human affairs. That rule, he felt, was manifest preeminently in the restored church but would be consummated only in the premillennial second coming of Jesus Christ. Between the times, Stone felt, the kingdom of God was a countercultural reality that stood in judgment on all rational, scientific, and technical progress and, indeed, on all human creations whatsoever.[34] More than anything else, this conviction formed the basis for Stone's antimodern bias. Further, this apocalyptic and countercultural perspective provided the mainspring not only for Stone but also for a sizable segment of Churches of Christ until well into the twentieth century, even when that mainspring joined itself to the biblicism of Alexander Campbell.

David Lipscomb

The man who more than anyone else carried this tradition into the twentieth century was David Lipscomb. Clearly the most influential person

---

[33] Alexander Campbell, "American Christian Missionary Society. President's Address," *MH* (Mar. 1852): 124.

[34] Most contemporary historians have not come to grips with the profound difference between Stone and Campbell regarding the restoration ideal. This is not surprising, for they also have failed to take seriously the apocalyptic worldview of Stone. David Edwin Harrell's work is a case in point. Harrell argued that Stone and Campbell alike were committed to a "spirit of moderation" and to postmillennial visions of social progress (*Quest for a Christian America* [Nashville: Disciples of Christ Historical Society, 1966], 36, 41, 45). Indeed, "prior to 1830, both [men] ... linked their religious reform efforts with the eventual spiritual and social regeneration of the world." Interestingly, the one passage from Stone that Harrell cited to support this claim finds Stone arguing just the reverse, vehemently criticizing the postmillennial vision and contending that "God would *overturn, and overturn, and overturn,* till Messiah shall reign alone, and all submit to his government" (*Quest for a Christian America*, 41). (The passage Harrell cites from Stone is from "Remarks on Liberty of Conscience," *CM* 3 [Feb. 1829]: 91.) Harrell did recognize that "the sectarian emphasis of nonparticipation in civil government centered around the influence of Barton Stone in the early years of the church," but he never connected that emphasis either with Stone's apocalyptic, countercultural worldview, or with the very same perspective one finds later in both Tolbert Fanning and David Lipscomb (*Quest for a Christian America*, 54–55).

among Churches of Christ from the close of the Civil War until his death in 1917, Lipscomb edited the immensely influential *Gospel Advocate*, based in Nashville, Tennessee, for most of those years.

There is no question that Lipscomb was, in many ways, a Campbellite, holding a profoundly rational view of Scripture and even turning Campbell's biblicism toward legalism. As editor of the *Advocate*, Lipscomb inevitably stood at the heart of the fights between Churches of Christ and Disciples of Christ over missionary societies, the propriety of instrumental music in worship, the role of women in the church, and basic attitudes toward Scripture. Further, it was Lipscomb who responded to S. N. D. North, Director of the Federal Census of 1906, who thought he detected a major rupture in the Stone-Campbell movement. North was right, Lipscomb responded, and he urged him to list Churches of Christ completely separate from Disciples of Christ.[35]

Yet, if Lipscomb was a Campbellite who turned Campbell's own biblicism toward legalism, he also stood squarely and profoundly in the Stone tradition of separationism, apocalypticism, and apoliticism. It is difficult, if not impossible, to know all the sources for this emphasis in Lipscomb's thought. Given the pervasiveness of the Stone movement in Middle Tennessee, Lipscomb could have been influenced by any one or combination of a number of Stoneite preachers. Undoubtedly, however, the critical link between Stone, a first-generation leader, and Lipscomb, a third-generation leader, was Tolbert Fanning, founding editor of several journals, including the *Gospel Advocate*, and the most powerful second-generation leader among mid-South Churches of Christ. He also was a mentor to David Lipscomb. Fanning had been deeply influenced in his youth by three Stoneite preachers in northern Alabama: Ephraim D. Moore, James E. Matthews, and Ross Houston. From these men, especially from Ephraim D. Moore, Fanning learned that "the Church of God is . . . destined, finally, . . . to triumph over all the powers of the earth."[36]

---

[35] David Lipscomb, "The 'Church of Christ' and the 'Disciples of Christ,'" *GA* 49 (July 18, 1907): 457.

[36] On Fanning, see James R. Wilburn, *The Hazard of the Die: Tolbert Fanning and the Restoration Movement* (Malibu: Pepperdine University Press, 1980). On Fanning's debt to Moore, Matthews, and Houston, see Wilburn, *Hazard*, 13–16, and Fanning, "Obituary," *GA* 6 (Jan. 1860): 31. On Fanning's early apocalypticism, see Fanning, "Ministers of Peace in the World's Conflicts," *GA* 7 (Nov. 1861): 347–48.

While apocalyptic in his thinking, however, Fanning was not premillennial. He did not expect the literal rule of Jesus on this earth, nor did he expect any sort of divine rule for a literal thousand years. Nonetheless, he did expect God's rule to be realized on this earth when the kingdom of God would finally triumph over the kingdoms of this world. Accordingly, Fanning—like Stone before him—advised his people not to vote and espoused a consistently pacifist position.[37]

However, Fanning's apocalyptic worldview was different from that of Stone in other ways, for Fanning had absorbed the rational and technical perspectives of Campbell in a way that Stone had not. The kingdom of God remained for Stone a transcendent reality, never fully actualized in the present world, always standing in judgment on human creations and institutions, and destined to be realized completely in this world only at the end of time. Fanning's extreme Common Sense rationalism, however, led him to particularize the transcendent in ways that had been foreign to Stone. In Fanning's view, the kingdom of God was, in fact, the Church of Christ of his own temporal experience in Tennessee and the mid-South, and he wrote numerous articles explaining and defending this church to outsiders.[38]

The countercultural dimensions of Stone, therefore, while still alive in Fanning at one level, gave way at another level to sectarian exclusivism. Indeed, while it may appear that the increasingly dominant influence of Alexander Campbell in the Cumberland region simply obscured the old Stoneite worldview, this is not the case. Instead, Tolbert Fanning and his comrades, beginning in the late 1830s and 1840s, reshaped the Stoneite vision to make it more compatible with the sectarian vision of the early Alexander Campbell. Separation from the world, therefore, increasingly came to mean for Fanning and many of his generation simply opposition to the surrounding denominations.[39] For the remainder of the nineteenth

---

[37] See Fanning, "Reply to Brethren Lillard, Harding, and Ransome," *GA* 7 (Sep. 1861): 265–76; "The Church of Christ in Prophecy No. 2," *Religious Historian* 2 (Feb. 1873): 40–44; "Political Strife amongst Christians," *Christian Review* 1 (Aug. 1844): 184–85; "'The Kingdom of Heaven' A Spiritual Empire," *Christian Review* 3 (May 1846): 101; and "Peace," *Christian Review* 3 (Mar. 1846): 65.

[38] Fanning, for example, ran an entire series of fourteen articles entitled simply, "The Church of Christ," in the *Gospel Advocate* from October 1855 through December 1856.

[39] Most notable among Fanning's colleagues in the 1840s who employed an apocalyptic worldview to undergird their sectarian exclusivism were Arthur Crihfield and John R. Howard. On both, see Hughes and Allen, *Illusions of Innocence*, 128–31.

century, more and more members of Churches of Christ conformed themselves to this sectarian understanding, lost their apocalyptic orientation, and reconciled themselves to participation in the American political system. In this way, Fanning helped subvert the antimodern impulse in Stone and opened the way for the full-blown acceptance of modernity and modernization that would occur among Churches of Christ in the early twentieth century.

There were some, however, who kept alive the original Stoneite vision, and none were more important in this regard than David Lipscomb. In part because he had been mentored by Tolbert Fanning, Lipscomb stood squarely in the two worlds of Alexander Campbell and Barton Stone. He therefore embraced in his own person both the drive toward modernization and a distinctly antimodern impulse.

Nonetheless, his success in combining the Campbell and Stone perspectives into a single outlook is a major reason for his tremendous power and influence throughout the increasingly heterogeneous fellowship of Churches of Christ. Had Lipscomb focused exclusively on the rational and legal side of Alexander Campbell, he would have alienated those whose roots ran deeply into the separationist piety of Barton Stone. And had Lipscomb focused only on the apocalyptic, separationist heritage of Stone, he would have alienated the legalists whose roots reached into the rationalism and biblicism of Campbell. Lipscomb's genius lay in the way he coherently combined these two perspectives into one. Further, Lipscomb was the last major leader in the history of Churches of Christ to combine these two perspectives successfully. Following his death in 1917, the mainstream of Churches of Christ increasingly relegated the apocalyptic and antimodern perspectives of the Stone movement to the status of heresy and built their house instead on the world-affirming foundation laid by Alexander Campbell, buttressed by the rational, legal, and technical themes that grew from Campbell's biblicism. Lipscomb stands, therefore, as a pinnacle in the history of Churches of Christ, looking backward to both Stone and Campbell and forward to a monolithic Church of Christ that would expel Stone's apocalyptic antimodernism from its agenda.

Nonetheless, in his lifetime, Lipscomb was an articulate proponent of the Stoneite worldview. In the years immediately following the Civil War, Lipscomb published a series of articles on the Christian's relation to the world and especially to civil government and, in 1889, gathered these articles into a small book that received wide circulation among Churches of Christ. He called the book *Civil Government*, and a year after its publication, he judged that "nothing we ever wrote so nearly affects the vital interests of the church of Christ and the salvation of the world as this little book."[40]

Lipscomb began with the Stoneite conviction that the Christian belongs to a kingdom ruled by God, not to the kingdoms ruled by humankind.[41] From this basic premise flowed the same themes that had characterized Stone: separation from the world, apocalypticism, and apoliticism.

Separation from the world meant for Lipscomb, first of all, reliance on the sovereign power of God. It was here that he found human institutions so objectionable. Indeed, the very existence of human institutions and governments represented for Lipscomb a profound departure from God's primordial design. In *Civil Government*, Lipscomb argued that from the beginning, God intended to be sovereign over all the earth. His sovereignty, in fact, formed the very essence of the Garden of Eden before the fall. But "the act [by Adam and Eve] of . . . disobedience culminated in the effort of man to organize a government of his own, so that he himself might permanently conduct the affairs of earth, free from . . . God's government." This rejection of God's sovereignty meant for Lipscomb that humanity had transferred its allegiance from God to Satan. This, for him, was the meaning of Satan's statement to Jesus that all the kingdoms of earth "were delivered to me." For Lipscomb, then, human government was nothing less than Satan's dominion in rebellion against God.[42] Ever since humanity's rejection of God's government, Lipscomb claimed, God's intent had been to restore his sovereignty over the earth. This was the point of the Jewish wars against the Canaanites tribes. "The work to which they were called was a war of extermination against all people maintaining a human government." Again, God attempted a restoration with the advent of Jesus

---

[40] Lipscomb, *GA* (1890): 199.

[41] Lipscomb, *Civil Government* (hereafter *CG*), 13–14, 16–17, 88–89, 91, 92, 128, 145.

[42] Lipscomb, *CG*, 8–9, 48, 9–10.

Christ into the world. At one level, Jesus's mission succeeded because he conquered "death and hell and the grave." At another level, however, Jesus's mission failed because it ultimately failed to destroy sin and rebellion.[43]

Precisely here Lipscomb introduced the same apocalyptic themes that characterized both Barton Stone and Tolbert Fanning before him. The day would come, Lipscomb claimed, when God would reestablish his sovereignty over all the earth and destroy all human governments, the best along with the worst. Like Stone and Fanning, Lipscomb also rooted this vision in Daniel, chapter 2:

> The end of all the conflicts and strifes of earth, will be the complete and final destruction, the utter consuming of the last vestige of human governments and institutions, and the giving of the dominion, and power, and authority of the whole earth to the people of the saints of the Most High. . . . All these kingdoms are to be broken in pieces, and consumed . . . but the little stone cut out of the mountain without hands is to become a great mountain, and fill the whole earth.

Further, these themes for Lipscomb were the very "key notes . . . of the Old and New Testaments." Without them, the Bible was "without point or meaning."[44]

At this point, Lipscomb differed significantly, however, from his mentor, Tolbert Fanning, who had particularized the transcendent and had virtually identified the eschatological kingdom of God with the Church of Christ. Lipscomb agreed that when God established the church, he also reestablished his kingdom, rule, and authority. However, the kingdom of God in its church form was by no means the same as the eschatological kingdom that would break in pieces all the kingdoms of the earth. Lipscomb made this point abundantly clear in a key article he wrote in 1903 on "The Kingdom of God": "The kingdom in its present stage is not called 'the everlasting kingdom,' but it will grow into it. It is the same kingdom in a lower stage of growth and development." In *Civil Government*, he spoke

---

[43] Lipscomb, *CG*, 14, 46-47; "The Kingdom of God," *GA* 45 (May 21, 1903): 328; and *CG*, 51-53.

[44] Lipscomb, *CG*, 25, 27-28 (see also 83-84), and 96.

of the church as the present manifestation of the coming kingdom of God. Like Stone before him, Lipscomb could not imagine final human perfection between the times of primordium and millennium.[45]

Clearly, Lipscomb's apocalypticism embodied a profound eschatological expectation that governed his worldview. But was Lipscomb also premillennial? This question is important since premillennialism became such a pivotal issue for Churches of Christ during the first half of the twentieth century, and since Lipscomb's position on that issue was so hotly disputed following his death.

If by premillennial one means that when Jesus returns, he will reign on the throne of David in Jerusalem for a literal thousand years, then Lipscomb apparently did not fit the description. In the first place, Lipscomb displayed little or no interest in the role of Israel and the throne of David in the millennial age. In the second place, Lipscomb always spoke of the kingdom of God "fill[ing] the whole earth, and stand[ing] forever."[46] The millennium for Lipscomb, therefore, was not a thousand-year interlude but rather the eternal rule of God on this earth.

However, if one means by premillennial simply that Jesus's return to earth will precede and inaugurate this final golden age, then Lipscomb clearly advocated a premillennial position. One finds glimpses of this position in an assortment of articles Lipscomb wrote for the *Gospel Advocate* over a period of years. For example, in 1878, Lipscomb commented favorably on the First American Bible and Prophetic Conference, convened at the Holy Trinity Episcopal Church in New York City in October of that year.[47] The speeches of the conference, he noted, focused on "the idea of the re-appearance of the Savior before and preparatory to the advent of the millenium [*sic*]," and he commended those speeches as doing "honor to the word of God." While Lipscomb was not then certain whether Christ's "coming precedes or succeeds the conversion of the world to God," he urged his readers to acquire copies of the speeches by writing to the New York *Tribune*, cautioning only that no one make this topic "a hobby to disturb

---

[45] Lipscomb, "The Kingdom of God," *GA* 45 (May 21, 1903): 328; *CG*, 60.

[46] Lipscomb, *CG*, 28.

[47] For this conference, see Timothy P. Weber, *Living in the Shadow of the Second Coming: American Premillennialism, 1875-1925* (New York: Oxford University Press, 1979), 28.

the peace of churches."[48] Later in the century, Lipscomb spoke explicitly of a "reign of Jesus on earth" and declared that "'the times of restoration of all things' must be when Jesus returns again to earth—the restoration of all things to their original relation to God."[49]

Further, there can be no doubt that the millennium Lipscomb envisioned was a literal kingdom on this earth. Thus, for example, he spoke clearly of "the glorious millennial morn" in connection with "the re-establishment [of] the kingdom of God on earth." Again, he wrote, "the one purpose of God was to re-establish his authority and rule on earth." Or again, "This earth in the material, moral and spiritual world must become a garden of God's own planting." Further, to those who asked regarding God's rule on earth, "How would the mails be carried? How could the affairs of Railroads, Manufactures, and the many large corporations . . . be managed?" Lipscomb simply replied, "We will cheerfully commit the adjustment and management" of these things to God.[50]

Many in Lipscomb's circle shared these basic positions, though with differences in emphasis. James A. Harding, cofounder with Lipscomb of the Nashville Bible School, first president of that institution, and coworker with Lipscomb on the *Gospel Advocate*, candidly and explicitly advocated a view much more in keeping with classic premillennialism:

> When the saints are caught up to meet him, Christ comes with
> them to earth. . . . Satan is then caught, chained and cast into
> the abyss . . . [where] he is confined for one thousand years . . .
> [while] Christ and his saints reign; but the rest of the dead live
> not until the thousand years have expired. This, the resurrection
> of the righteous, is the first resurrection.

Others in Lipscomb's circle revealed time and again, often in an off-handed way, their premillennial assumptions. For example, when answering a question from a reader of the *Gospel Advocate*, E. G. Sewell

---

[48] Lipscomb, "The Prophetic Conference," *GA* 20 (Nov. 21, 1878): 725.

[49] Lipscomb, "Queries," *GA* 37 (June 23, 1898): 397; and Lipscomb, *Queries and Answers*, ed. J. W. Shepherd (Cincinnati: F. L. Rowe, Publisher, 1918), 360.

[50] Lipscomb, *A Commentary on the New Testament Epistles: Ephesians, Philippians, and Colossians*, ed. J. W. Shepherd, vol. 4 (Nashville: The *Gospel Advocate* Co., 1939), 76; Lipscomb, *CG*, iii, 28 (see also 12–13); and Lipscomb, *CG*, 136.

simply assumed a millennium bounded by a "first resurrection" of the righteous and a "second resurrection" when "the thousand years of peace are finished." Phillip S. Fall, contemporary of Stone in Kentucky, close friend of Campbell, relative of Tolbert Fanning, and preacher for the Church of Christ in Nashville from 1858 to 1877, wrote to Mrs. Alexander Campbell: "In regard to the pre-millennial advent, . . . the New Testament . . . impresses me with the hope that this earth . . . is to be the home of the righteous. . . . I can conceive of no higher ideal of heaven than that [we] . . . will dwell together with him . . . in this renovated spot."[51]

Finally, Lipscomb and those in his circle strongly resisted elaborating on their premillennial perspectives and engaging in speculation regarding "what the millennium is or when it begins or ends."[52] They refused to speculate on the millennium because they did not wish to press beyond what they viewed as the bounds of Scripture. Further, they did not argue or debate the premillennial question simply because it was not an issue. Rather, it was a working assumption, one that characterized many in the Tennessee, Kentucky, and Alabama Churches of Christ from the days of Stone throughout the nineteenth century. In spite of all this, historians generally have failed to see that Lipscomb was premillennial at all.[53]

---

[51] James A. Harding, "The Kingdom of Christ versus the Kingdoms of Satan," *The Way* 5 (Oct. 15, 1903): 929–31; E. G. Sewell, "Queries," *GA* 37 (July 11, 1895): 437; and P. S. Fall, "Interesting Reminiscences" [letter to Mrs. Alexander Campbell], *GA* 21 (May 15, 1879): 310.

[52] See Lipscomb, "Queries," *GA* 40 (June 23, 1898): 397; and E. G. Sewell, "Queries," *GA* 37 (July 11, 1895): 437.

[53] Three factors help account for this oversight. First, the tendency of Disciple historians to understand their movement principally in terms of Alexander Campbell's faith in progress has obscured not only the premillennial sentiments of Stone but those of Lipscomb as well. Second, the fervent refusal especially of Lipscomb and his circle to speculate on the second coming has led some to assume that he simply had little or no interest in millennial themes. Thus, for example, David Edwin Harrell argued that Lipscomb was "persistently unwilling to discuss the subject," something Harrell attributes to the general decline of interest in premillennial themes dating from before the Civil War (Harrell, *Quest for a Christian America*, 44, esp. n. 68). Third, beginning with World War I, Churches of Christ launched a frontal attack on premillennialism that lasted fully one-third of a century. When that attack had run its course by the mid-1940s, most mainstream Churches of Christ had come to view premillennialism as a heresy. Historians working within the context of the church, therefore, might well have little inclination to discern the significance of such views among revered leaders such as Stone and Lipscomb. Thus both of Lipscomb's biographers—Earl West and Robert Hooper—simply ignore the premillennial theme in Lipscomb. West identifies the "kingdom" with the "church," and simply fails to see the apocalyptic dimension in Lipscomb's thought. (West, *The Life and Times of David Lipscomb* [Henderson, TN: Religious Book Service, 1954], 97–99.) And Hooper spiritualizes Lipscomb's notion of the kingdom, suggesting that a "perfect kingdom," in Lipscomb's view, "could not be attained in this world" but only "in the world to come." (Hooper, *Crying in the Wilderness: A Biography of David Lipscomb* [Nashville: David Lipscomb College, 1979], 110–22, esp. 121.)

The third component in Lipscomb's antimodern outlook was his rigorous pacifism and his refusal to vote or otherwise participate in civil government.[54] "The mission of the kingdom of God is to break into pieces and consume all these kingdoms, take their place, fill the whole earth, and stand forever," Lipscomb declared. "How [then] could the individual citizens of the kingdom of God found, enter into, and become part and parcel of—upbuild, support, and defend, that which God's kingdom was especially commissioned to destroy?" In this, Lipscomb stood by no means alone, for many premillennialists of his era embraced the same antipolitical posture and for precisely the same reasons. The Presbyterian dispensationalist James Brookes, for example, suggested that "those who are dead to the world and alive to Christ should avoid the polling place, because 'dead men do not vote.'"[55]

On the other hand, in perpetuating the old Stoneite worldview, Lipscomb stood fundamentally at odds with the Disciples of Christ of the late nineteenth century who perpetuated the Campbellian assessment of the world, modernity, and human progress. If Lipscomb had thought that the kingdom of God would "break into pieces" all the kingdoms of this earth, the editor of the Disciples-oriented *Christian Oracle* argued for "a very intimate relation between the advancing influence of Christian nations and the advancement of the kingdom of God." J. C. Tully typified the Campbellite/Disciples faith in progress when he asked, "Will the earnest desire in the hearts of men for freedom from the shackles of the past ever fade away and die?" and then rejoiced,

> Never, never, no never. The forces are going forward, not
> back. . . . So rapidly has the spirit of the age come upon us, that

[54] Johnnie A. Collins has argued that Lipscomb's pacifism was principally a function of Southern, post-Civil War sectionalism ("Pacifism in the Churches of Christ, 1866–1945," PhD diss., Middle Tennessee State University, 1984). That claim, however, is only partly true. In the first place, Lipscomb claimed that he arrived at these conclusions "early in life," long before the Civil War (*CG*, iii). In the second place, to ascribe Lipscomb's position only to the War is to diminish the importance of a long intellectual tradition that began with Stone and of which Lipscomb was heir. On the other hand, it is clear that the Civil War drove Lipscomb to take the Stoneite tradition seriously in a way he had not before. Indeed, Lipscomb cast his vote in 1860 for John Bell, the presidential candidate of the Constitutional Union Party (*GA* 1912: 953). But he never voted again after the War.

[55] Lipscomb, *CG*, 28 (cf. also 83–84 and iv); and James Brookes, "Gentile Dominion," *The Truth* 6 (1880): 536, cited in Weber, *Living in the Shadow of the Second Coming*, 92–93. See J. J. Robinson, "Is Social Service Part of the Apostasy?" *Christian Workers Magazine* 14 (July 1914): 729–32, also cited in Weber, *Living in the Shadow*, 92–93.

it may be affirmed of a truth: We are not in the same world, although on the same planet, with those who lived in the last century. We live in the age of progress in civilization and in all things which, in human judgment, minister to its perfection.[56]

These two opposing worldviews stood, in many ways, at the heart of the debates over missionary societies and instrumental music in the late nineteenth century and finally contributed to the emergence of two well-defined denominations: Churches of Christ and Disciples.

Indeed, when one understands Lipscomb's commitment to "the kingdom of God," one then can understand the genius of Lipscomb's restoration vision and why he took the positions he did on music, societies, and a host of other issues. If one imagines Lipscomb as simply a legalist, committed only to restoring the forms and structures of the primitive church, then one has missed the heart of David Lipscomb. Lipscomb was a legalist, to be sure, but his legalism pointed beyond itself in two directions. First, it pointed to Eden before the fall, when God's sovereign rule prevailed in sublime perfection. Second, it pointed to God's inevitable, final, and future rule over all the earth, when the perfections of Eden would be restored.[57] In between these times of perfection, the church was the finite manifestation of God's kingdom on earth. Moreover, because the restoration of the primordial and Edenic rule of God was absolutely certain, Christians must therefore live their lives and order their churches according to God's law in its every detail. In this sense, Lipscomb's efforts to restore biblical forms of worship and biblical patterns of church organization all pointed beyond themselves to the restoration of the kingdom of God in "the glorious millennial morn."

When this becomes clear, one also begins to see how Lipscomb could hold together in a single movement the modernizing heirs of Alexander Campbell and the antimodern heirs of Barton W. Stone. The heirs of Stone

---

[56] J. C. Tully, "The Divine Law of Expansion," *Christian Oracle* 16 (Jan. 18, 1899): 2; and Tully, "Responsibility of the Disciples of Christ to the Present Age," *Christian Quarterly Review* 4 (1885): 581–82. For a brief discussion of the doctrine of Anglo-American progress among Disciples at century's end, see Harrell, *Social Sources of Division*, 23–25. Harrell also notes that some Disciples leaders joined a postmillennial faith in American progress to prophetic themes.

[57] Lipscomb, *CG*, 136–37, 53–56.

fully understood the apocalyptic context of Lipscomb's legalism and his ethics. For them, rejecting instrumental music in worship and refusing to vote were two sides of the same apocalyptic coin. On the other hand, those who rooted their legalism in the biblicism of Alexander Campbell could simply ignore Lipscomb's apocalyptic thrust as well as his position on civil government. If Lipscomb wanted to refuse to vote, that was an idiosyncrasy they could tolerate. For them, it was enough that Lipscomb railed against departures from the "ancient order" among the emerging Disciples of Christ.

During Lipscomb's lifetime, however, more and more of his people exchanged the antimodern, apocalyptic vision of Stone for the rational, progress-oriented outlook of Alexander Campbell. Symptomatic of this shift was Lipscomb's lament in 1880 that a majority of the readers of the *Gospel Advocate* did not share his antipolitical position.[58] Those who made this shift would form the vanguard of Churches of Christ in the twentieth century. On the other hand, those who continued to hold the apocalyptic, antimodern, and apolitical perspectives of Stone, Fanning, and Lipscomb would be cast from the mainstream as heretics. But that is another story for another time.[59]

---

[58] Lipscomb, "Withdrawal," *GA* 22 (Sep. 16, 1880): 597.

[59] This "story for another time" is the story of the war that most of the leaders among mainstream Churches of Christ made on R. H. Boll, proponent of both premillennialism and the apocalyptic sentiment, from roughly 1915 through 1945. That story is told in detail in the article from which this essay is adapted, "The Apocalyptic Origins of Churches of Christ and the Triumph of Modernism," *Religion and American Culture: A Journal of Interpretation* 2 (Summer 1992): 181–214; and in even greater detail in Richard T. Hughes, *Reviving the Ancient Faith: The Story of Churches of Christ in America* (Grand Rapids: Eerdmans, 1996), 137–67.

it may be thought of a truth. We belong to the same world, although on the same planet, with those who lived in the last century. We live in the age of progress in civilization and in all things which, in human judgment, minister to its perfection.

These two opposing worldviews stood at, in many ways, at the heart of the debate over missionary societies and other doctrinal music in the late nineteenth century and finally contributed to the emergence of two well-defined denominations: the Churches of Christ Disciples.

Tolbert apostolic eschatology was a cornerstone to the kingdom of God. One the one hand it revealed the appeal of apostolic restoration. It's why he paid attention to church and its practices, and a host of other issues. Moreover, since Lipscomb was simply a legalist committed only to restoring the forms and structures of the primitive church, then he has missed the heart of Lipscomb's work. Lipscomb was a legalist, to be sure, but his legalism pointed beyond itself in two directions. First, it pointed the believer to the past, which God's sovereign rule prevailed in sublime perfection. Second, it pointed to God's inevitable final and future rule over all the earth, when the perfect order of Eden would be restored. In between these two ancient perfection, the church was the finite manifestation of God's kingdom on earth. Moreover, because the restoration of the primitive and future rule of God was absolutely certain, Christians then there conformed their lives and order their churches according to God's law in its eternal will. In this sense, Lipscomb's efforts to establish biblical forms of worship and biblical patterns of church organization all pointed beyond themselves to the restoration of the kingdom on earth in the glorious millennial morning.

When this becomes clear, one also begins to see how Lipscomb could hold together in a single movement the modernizing heritage of Alexander Campbell and the apocalyptic temper of a people whom he called "Sons in the House of Stone

TWO RESTORATION TRADITIONS

Mormons and Churches of Christ in the Nineteenth Century

I n the spring of 1841, only eleven years after Joseph Smith and his colleagues had organized the Church of Jesus Christ of Latter-day Saints, four men met for a debate at the Ridge Meetinghouse in Smith County, Tennessee, in the foothills of the Smoky Mountains, just east of Nashville. Those four were John DeLee and Alfonso Young, representing the Mormons, and Abraham Sallee and Samuel Dewhitt, representing the Churches of Christ. The second proposition for debate defined the critical difference between these two traditions. That proposition read: "Are the gifts and offices of the ancient Apostolic Church of Christ, necessary in this age, in order to constitute a perfect church or body?"[1] The Mormon preachers affirmed; the Church of Christ preachers denied.

---

[1]Debate between Mormons and Church of Christ in *Crihfield's Christian Family Library* and *Journal of Biblical Science* 1 (July 18, 1842): 210. This journal published the proceedings of the debate in the issues of July 18, 1842; July 25, 1842; August 1, 1842; and August 15, 1842. In addition, John D. Lee provides a record of the debate in his diary, contained in the entry dated May 28 and 29, 1841. I am grateful to Mr. Verne R. Lee of Loomis, California, who provided me with a typescript of the appropriate sections of this diary.

In spite of their very fundamental differences, one finds in this debate two upstart Christian movements that, in many ways, shared far more in common with each other than they shared with any of the older denominations. Indeed, Mormons and Churches of Christ alike rejected the surrounding denominations, which they viewed as "man-made churches," and based their authority instead on their respective understandings of the ancient church of the primitive era.

Historiographic Presuppositions

To come to terms with these two traditions in the nineteenth century, then, we first must assess the intellectual heart and soul of each of these traditions, namely, their restorationist orientation. In this task, however, we will find little help from most social and economic historians who write of Mormons and/or Churches of Christ, for most of those historians typically fail to take the restoration ideal seriously as a powerful and pervasive theme in its own right. Often, if they acknowledge this ideal at all, they explain it simply as a function of various social factors without which, one presumes, the restoration sentiment would collapse and disappear.

Thus Rhys Isaac, speaking of the profoundly restorationist Separate Baptists of Virginia, altogether missed the power of the restoration ideal and interpreted Separate Baptists simply "as a popular response to a mounting sense of social disorder." Likewise, Gordon Wood ascribed the popularity of several restorationist traditions in the new Republic, including Baptists, "Christians," and Mormons, to "a social disintegration unequalled in American history."[2]

Again, Nathan O. Hatch explained the genius of both the "Christian" movement and the Latter-day Saints in terms of a populist, democratic revolt against their social betters. He viewed the "Christians" or Churches of Christ especially in terms of a "pervasive collapse of certainty within popular culture."[3] And Mormons he understood chiefly in terms of poverty and social estrangement. Thus he wrote:

[2] Rhys Isaac, *The Transformation of Virginia* (Chapel Hill: University of North Carolina Press, 1982), 168; and Gordon Wood, "Evangelical America and Early Mormonism," *New York History* (Oct. 1980): 365.

[3] Nathan O. Hatch, "The Christian Movement and the Demand for a Theology of the People," *Journal of American History* 67 (Dec. 1980): 561, 546. Also see Hatch, *The Democratization of American Christianity* (New Haven: Yale University Press, 1989), 68–81.

the Book of Mormon is a document of profound social protest, an impassioned manifesto by a hostile outsider against the smug complacency of those in power and the reality of social distinction based on wealth, class, and education. . . . The single most striking theme in the Book of Mormon is that it is the rich, the proud, and the learned who find themselves in the hands of an angry God.[4]

Or again, David Edwin Harrell, who has written eloquently and perceptively of the restoration theme within the history of Churches of Christ, has nonetheless explained that theme and the peculiar directions it has taken within this fellowship, largely in terms of social forces. Thus, in attempting to explain the theological genius of Churches of Christ, he focused especially on the Civil War and argued that "social force, class prejudice, sectional bitterness, and theologies shot through with economic presuppositions were the base upon which doctrinal debates were built." He therefore judged that the sectarian theology of the largely Southern Churches of Christ in the years following the Civil War often amounted to little more than "a thinly veiled appeal for backing to the supporters of the lost cause."[5]

Such judgments, I suspect, may often reveal more about the materialistic and scientific biases of those of us who inhabit the modern academy than they do about the spiritual struggles and insights of ordinary Americans some two hundred years ago. To the modern mind, steeped in the conviction that material reality is the only reality there is, and convinced that spiritual concerns are but reflections of more fundamental material issues, the nineteenth-century search for the kingdom of God almost inevitably becomes a search for social and economic standing.

I would be the last to suggest that the arguments of the historians I have cited are without merit, for they hold substantial merit, so long as one does not imagine that they take us to the center of these traditions. Likewise, I would be the last to suggest that social and economic factors

---

[4] Hatch, *Democratization*, 116–17.

[5] David Edwin Harrell, *The Social Sources of Division in the Disciples of Christ* (Athens: Publishing Systems, 1973), ix; and "The Sectional Origins of the Churches of Christ," *Journal of Southern History* 30 (Aug. 1964): 270.

play no role in shaping religious perspectives, for they clearly do. Further, it is obvious that the methods and presuppositions of social history are especially productive when one studies movements that clearly are driven by social rather than by intellectual or spiritual concerns. But it may well be that the presuppositions and methods of social and economic history are ill-equipped to uncover in a meaningful way the driving power behind such religious movements as Mormons and Churches of Christ.[6]

Indeed, the historian who instinctively places social and economic issues front and center will almost inevitably miss the genius of restorationist movements in America—for most restorationist movements in antebellum America struggled with a profoundly spiritual crisis that one simply cannot explain in terms of social, economic, and military pressures. That spiritual crisis typically revolved around the quest for the true church, for the kingdom of God, or for the sacred in the midst of a profane and fallen world. And that is a quest historians should take seriously in its own right.

One begins to grasp the immense dimensions of that spiritual crisis when one recalls how central had been the concern for the "true, apostolic church" among Puritans on both sides of the Atlantic.[7] Further, as Dan Vogel recently pointed out, this concern bedeviled a host of British and American Seekers from the seventeenth through the nineteenth centuries, including Lucy Smith, the mother of Joseph.[8] Moreover, this concern stood at the very center of American restorationist traditions like Mormons and Churches of Christ.

Religious pluralism in the United States, however, compounded the problem beyond measure for those who began with this concern. Joseph Smith tells us that he found himself "in darkness and confusion" over this very issue. Accordingly, the crisis that stood at the very heart and soul of the Mormon experience in the early nineteenth century was not an economic

---

[6] Clearly there were some restorationist movements that were virtually driven by social and economic considerations. A case in point was Elias Smith's "Christian" movement in New England in the early nineteenth century, as Nathan Hatch accurately points out. Hatch, however, is on far less solid ground when he finds central to Alexander Campbell and Barton Stone—also leaders of nineteenth-century "Christian" movements—the same social and economic motives he finds in Smith (Hatch, *Democratization*, 68–81).

[7] See Theodore Dwight Bozeman, *To Live Ancient Lives: The Primitivist Dimension in Puritanism* (Chapel Hill: University of North Carolina, 1988).

[8] Dan Vogel, *Religious Seekers and the Advent of Mormonism* (Salt Lake City: Signature Books, 1988).

issue or a social issue but a spiritual issue, captured in the question Joseph put to the Lord in the spring of 1820: "which of all the sects was right and which I should join."[9] John DeLee echoed this same concern in his debate with the Church of Christ preachers at the Ridge Meetinghouse in 1841. "We now see six hundred and sixty sects," he lamented, "all professing to be the Church of Christ. Each sect contending for its own infallibility—and each contending that every other one is wrong." Then DeLee asked that simple but penetrating question that lay at the heart of the spiritual crisis that ultimately defined both Mormons and Churches of Christ in the nineteenth century: "Why is this?"[10]

This question, however, seems both quaint and irrelevant to most Americans in the waning years of the twentieth century when tolerance and pluralism have become an accepted way of life. Accordingly, historians with little sense of the spiritual urgency of that question, and schooled in the scientific methods and materialistic presuppositions of modern social history, often find lurking beneath such a question overtones of social and economic deprivation.

Such presuppositions not only miss the spiritual core of many restorationist traditions; they also tend toward a variety of conclusions unsupported by the evidence. Thus several recent studies have simply overturned, in many instances, the conventional wisdom that Mormon primitivism reflects social and economic deprivation. These studies have pointed out that the Kirtland Saints in the mid-1830s stood far closer to the economic mainstream of their neighbors than generally has been supposed.[11] After exploring the evidence in this regard, Grant Underwood finally concluded that "if Mormon millenarians wished to see the world destroyed, it was because it had deprived them of spiritual, not economic, opportunity."[12]

---

[9] Joseph's "First Vision," in *History of the Church of Jesus Christ of Latter-day Saints*, ed. B. H. Roberts, 2nd ed. (Salt Lake City: Deseret Book Co., 1964), 1, 4–6.

[10] Debate, *Crihfield's Christian Family Library* 1 (Aug. 15, 1842): 238.

[11] See Mark R. Grandstaff and Milton V. Backman Jr., "The Social Origins of Kirtland Mormons," *BYU Studies* 30 (Spring 1990): 47–66; and Marvin S. Hill, C. Keith Rooker, and Larry T. Wimmer, "The Kirtland Economy Revisited: A Market Critique of Sectarian Economics," *BYU Studies* 17 (1977): 391–472.

[12] Grant Underwood, *The Millenarian World of Early Mormonism* (Urbana: University of Illinois Press, 1993), chap. 6.

All of this suggests that intellectual history, not social history, may be the path that will lead us into the center and core of most of the restoration-ist movements of the antebellum United States.

The Spiritual Core of the Restoration Vision

If we choose to follow that path, we quickly make several important and highly relevant discoveries. First, we learn that the restoration vision was in no way peculiar to antebellum America, much less to the process of democratization or to social marginality in the new Republic. Instead, this vision in the modern world grew from the bias toward pure beginnings generated by the Christian Humanists in the Renaissance who despaired of the moral and intellectual corruption of their age. Through the influence of the universities, this theme quickly dominated the Reformed side of Protestantism, especially in Zurich, from the very outset of the sixteenth-century Reformation. We learn as well that Reformed leaders like Heinrich Bullinger and Martin Bucer exerted powerful influences on the English to find in the restoration theme the center and core of the Christian faith. It is little wonder, then, that during the Marian Exile, the commitment to primitive Christianity became a defining characteristic of the Puritan party.[13]

From there, the restoration vision took two routes in its journey to America, one route important for Mormons, the other route important for Churches of Christ. The first route took the Puritans across the Atlantic to the New World, where the restoration vision would become fundamental to their task. Here in New England, then, one finds the intellectual tradition that would eventually inform and mould a young seeker by the name of Joseph Smith. Indeed, the ways in which both Puritans and Mormons virtually reenacted the sacred dramas from both Old and New Testaments were strikingly similar—and that was not coincidental.

The second route to America—the one that would become particularly important for Churches of Christ—was far more circuitous, and involved an extensive layover in Scotland. Indeed, John Knox carried the

---

[13]This history is spelled out in more detail in Richard T. Hughes, "Christian Primitivism as Perfectionism: From Anabaptists to Pentecostals," in *Reaching Beyond: Chapters in the History of Perfectionism*, ed. Stanley Burgess (Peabody, MA: Hendrickson Publishers, 1986), 213-23.

restoration vision from England to his native land, where it became central to Scottish and later to Scotch-Irish Presbyterianism. Thousands of those Presbyterians would later settle in the Middle Colonies, in the American South, and in northern Appalachia. Among those Presbyterians were the earliest leaders of Churches of Christ, namely Thomas and Alexander Campbell in northern Virginia and Barton W. Stone in Kentucky and Tennessee. Especially in the South, Baptists and Methodists also shared the vision of the primitive Christian faith. Little wonder, then, that Churches of Christ would find in that region an especially fertile soil for their appeal to "the ancient order of things."

Clearly, then, by the time of the American Revolution, restorationist thinking had become an important fixture in American intellectual life, from New England to Georgia. Yet this vision proliferated and thrived, especially between the Revolution and the Civil War. There are several social and cultural factors that prompted this proliferation, and indeed, it is precisely in this context that the work of the social historians is especially valuable.

First, there can be no doubt that the radically democratic and populist qualities of American life in the early nineteenth century rendered the restoration vision especially urgent. Here, the work of Nathan Hatch is especially helpful. Indeed, if Americans had abolished the tyrannies of princes and kings in the political realm, Christian primitivists now sought to do the same in the religious realm by declaring the jurisdiction of Christian history null and void.

Second, to Americans in the new Republic, the American political system seemed radically new, altogether discontinuous with any political system that had ever gone before. The Great Seal of the United States captured this perception with the phrase *novus ordo seclorum*, or a "new order of the ages." But if the American political system was new, it was also ancient, even primeval, and descended as Thomas Paine told us over and again from God himself, at the beginning of the world.[14] This means that this new democratic order stood outside human history, derived from the primordium, and now had been restored in the American millennial dawn.

---

[14] Philip S. Foner, ed., *The Complete Writings of Thomas Paine* (New York: Citadel Press, 1945), 1:376, 1:273–75.

Such a powerful cultural myth would inevitably quicken and heighten the centuries-old restoration vision that a variety of English dissenters had brought to these shores.

But of all the social and cultural factors that facilitated the restoration vision, none was more important than the bewildering array of churches that competed on the American frontier. This was the problem that prompted Alexander Campbell to seek to unify American churches by pointing them to the apostolic faith. And this was the problem that prompted Joseph Smith to ask the Lord which of all the churches was his own. Indeed, this was the source of the spiritual crisis that demanded an answer. That answer came, both to Mormons and to Churches of Christ, in the form of the old, venerable restoration heritage, now quickened and heightened by democratic expectations and by the radical newness of the American experience.

This means that Walter Scott, one of the early leaders of Churches of Christ, was simply mistaken when he ascribed the success of the early Mormons to principles he thought Mormons had learned from the Campbellites. Indeed, he charged, Sidney Rigdon "filched from us" the notion of immersion for the forgiveness of sins, and this accounted, Scott surmised, "for the success of the ministers of Mormonism."[15] This myth has been a powerful theme among Churches of Christ from the 1830s until the present day.

Nothing, in fact, could have been further from the truth. Mormons succeeded for the same reason Churches of Christ succeeded: each inherited a restoration vision that spoke in powerful and urgent ways in the cultural climate of antebellum America.

Differences between Mormons and Churches of Christ

Yet, for all their similarities, Mormons and Churches of Christ were radically different. The most striking difference obviously involved the Book of Mormon and a Latter-day prophet on the Mormon side of the ledger—developments Churches of Christ rejected. Indeed, those two developments have dominated anti-Mormon rhetoric on the part of Churches of Christ

---

[15] Walter Scott, "The Mormon Bible," *The Evangelist*, New Series, 7 (July 1, 1839): 160.

for more than a century and a half. Yet to focus on the Book of Mormon and the Prophet obscures both the fundamental similarity and the fundamental differences between these two traditions.

The fundamental similarity that must be recognized is the profoundly restorationist quality of both churches. Churches of Christ, however, find it difficult to discern in Mormonism any restorationist dimension whatsoever. A restorationist, according to most in Churches of Christ, is one whose restorationist efforts concentrate exclusively on the New Testament. Thus one of several who took me to task for involving Latter-day Saints in the 1991 Pepperdine University conference on "Christian Primitivism and Modernization" complained, "I am asking you to explain what rationale was used in including the Mormons in a conference such as this. Is it your view . . . that the Mormon church is seeking to restore primitive Christianity?"[16] That, of course, is precisely my view, but to understand the crucial difference between Churches of Christ and Latter-day Saints in this regard, we must resort once again to intellectual history.

First, we must recognize that the restoration vision is, in a fundamental sense, a vacuous vision. It is finally nothing more than a method, a perspective that looks backward to what one discerns as the first and therefore normative time. In this context, to say that one focuses on the Bible is hardly adequate, for there are many ways of reading and interpreting the Bible, each shaped and informed by one's intellectual presuppositions. This means that to understand Mormonism and Churches of Christ, we must first understand the intellectual traditions that shaped and molded these two movements.

What we find, however, is not at all straightforward or simple to unravel, for both Mormonism and Churches of Christ drew on intellectual traditions that in many ways competed with one another and that pointed in very different directions.

Churches of Christ

In the case of Churches of Christ, the two competing traditions were apocalyptic revivalism and Enlightenment progressivism.

---

[16] A conference on "Christian Primitivism and Modernization: Coming to Terms with Our Age," Pepperdine University, Malibu, California, June 6–9, 1991.

The apocalyptic, revivalistic perspective belonged to the earliest leader of Churches of Christ, Barton W. Stone. A man who carried out the bulk of his ministry in Kentucky and Tennessee, Stone's thought bore the indelible imprint of Calvinism, on the one hand, and revivalism on the other. Indeed, by virtue of his teachers, Stone stood squarely in the heritage of the Great Awakening and then, in 1801, emerged as a pivotal leader of the Great Kentucky Revival at Cane Ridge.

Revivalism and Calvinism together bred in Stone an apocalyptic outlook that became the cornerstone of his life, which often expressed itself in an explicitly premillennial eschatology, and which virtually defined his restoration vision.[17] Convinced that the kingdom of God would finally triumph over all human governments and institutions, Stone and his considerable band of followers remained fundamentally pessimistic about human progress.

Further, they exhibited far less interest in the formal structures of the church than in the rule of God over human affairs. They therefore conceived of primitive Christianity chiefly in terms of biblical ethics. As a result, they refused both to serve in the military and to vote, since all human governments, they imagined, stood squarely under the judgment of God. Further, they time and again summoned one another to abandon themselves in the interest of the poor, to free their slaves, and to reject both fashion and wealth.

This apocalyptic/ethical emphasis, with its negative assessment of human progress and human culture, comprised the earliest understanding of primitive Christianity among Churches of Christ. Indeed, long before Churches of Christ in Kentucky and Tennessee had even heard of Alexander Campbell, Stone had gathered a corps of some two hundred preachers and a membership of perhaps twenty thousand.[18] It is little

---

[17] By "apocalyptic," I do not mean "premillennial." By "apocalyptic," I mean the conviction that one belongs not to the kingdoms of this world but to the kingdom of God, which finally will triumph over all human institutions. Premillennialism, on the other hand, points to how God's kingdom will come, namely, through the premillennial second coming of Jesus Christ. As it turns out, Stone was both apocalyptic and premillennial in his outlook, but his apocalyptic perspective was the fundamental term in his thought.

[18] R. L. Roberts, "Early Tennessee and Kentucky Preachers," Restoration Movement Resources, www.acu.edu/restoration-movement/.

wonder, then, that his pessimistic, apocalyptic orientation prevailed among many Churches of Christ, especially in their Middle Tennessee heartland, until World War I, when those churches embarked on the process of modernization and acculturation.

In the meantime, however, the second intellectual tradition—that of the Enlightenment—increasingly came to dominate Churches of Christ, especially through the leadership of Alexander Campbell, whose restoration vision I choose to call rational, progressive primitivism. A Scotch-Irish immigrant who settled in Bethany, Virginia (later West Virginia), Campbell arguably became the most influential first-generation leader among Churches of Christ over the long term.

Steeped in Lockean empiricism and the "Baconian" perspective of the Scottish "Common Sense" Realists, Campbell rejected the apocalyptic outlook of Stone and embraced instead a robust, postmillennial optimism about the world in which he lived. Indeed, Campbell imagined that through a rational and scientific reconstruction of primitive Christianity, he and the movement he led would unify a fragmented Christendom and, as a consequence, raise the curtain on the millennial dawn.

In keeping with his rational vision, Campbell concerned himself not so much with biblical ethics as with the forms and structures of the ancient church. He viewed the New Testament almost as a divinely inspired, scientific text that supplied precise directions for admission into the church, for church organization, for proper worship, and for a variety of other details pertaining to church life. Further, just as a scientific experiment carried out in the same way under the same conditions would yield the same results time and again, in the same way, Campbell imagined, faithful attention to biblical directions would produce the same church today that it produced in the days of the apostles.

With such a scientific perspective, and in the political climate of antebellum America, it was inevitable that Campbell's followers would increasingly view the New Testament as a veritable constitution for the church. Indeed, this was the central metaphor the Church of Christ preachers used against their Mormon opponents in the Tennessee debate of 1842. Accordingly, Samuel Dewhitt argued that the New Testament is perfect, and . . . all which is necessary to constitute a perfect church or body is obedience to that law. The Apostles were lawgivers acting by divine authority. The Elders were only executive officers whose business it was to see these laws enforced. If the laws, given by the Apostles, were sufficient to constitute churches in their day we having the same laws, need nothing more.[19]

Dewhitt also urged:

when the framers of the Constitution of the United States of America had formed that instrument their work was accomplished, and that duty ceased and can never be resumed until the Constitution is abolished and it becomes necessary to make another. Now Jesus Christ and his Apostles made the laws for his government on earth, and the overseers of the Church now have nothing to do but to see those laws executed.[20]

Here, in these statements, one finds the very heart and soul of the restorationist perspective, conformed to the contours of Enlightenment thought that dominated Churches of Christ under the influence of Alexander Campbell.

It is important to recognize, however, that both Abraham Sallee and Samuel Dewhitt began their careers as Stoneite preachers, only later embracing the more rational and more progressive primitivism of Alexander Campbell. This point is instructive since Campbell's Enlightenment optimism eventually buried Stone's apocalyptic influence in virtually all quarters of the movement and, in so doing, paved the way for extensive modernization and acculturation among Churches of Christ in the twentieth century.

Latter-day Saints

When one turns from Churches of Christ to the Latter-day Saints, one enters a radically different world, though it must be said a world that was

[19] Debate, *Crihfield's Christian Family Library* 1 (Aug. 15, 1842): 236–37.
[20] Debate, *Crihfield's Christian Family Library* 1 (Aug. 15, 1842): 237.

no less restorationist. The restoration vision among Latter-day Saints conformed itself both to apocalypticism and to the Enlightenment, and in this
they shared with Churches of Christ. But Romanticism quickly emerged
as the defining intellectual influence on Latter-day Saints, and this was the
difference that made all the difference.

Though he never spelled it out, Harold Bloom hinted at this point when
he praised the imaginative genius of Joseph Smith and consistently placed
Smith in the company of Ralph Waldo Emerson. Indeed, Bloom confessed,
"I myself can think of not another American, except for Emerson and
Whitman, who so moves and alters my own imagination."[21]

While American Romanticism shared with the Enlightenment a profound celebration of human potential, it stood starkly opposed to the
scientific constrictions and materialistic biases of Enlightenment ideology.
Indeed, Romantics of practically every stripe—including both spiritualists and Transcendentalists—sought to shed their earthly constraints, to
enlarge the boundaries of the human spirit, and to touch in some meaningful way that spiritual realm that transcended the merely rational structures
of the here and the now.

When we understand the genius of American Romanticism, we draw
near to the genius of the restoration vision as articulated by Latter-day
Saints—for Latter-day Saints cared little for the forms and structures of
primitive Christianity, rationally perceived and reconstructed as ends in
themselves. Instead, they hungered for communion with the divine and
valued forms and structures only insofar as they facilitated that communion. They longed for the heavens to open and for God himself to descend
once again to humankind, just as he had done in the days of Adam, Moses,
David, John, and Paul. Moreover, they were convinced that no restoration
could occur apart from immediate, divine authority, which would come
as contemporary and continuous revelation.

Further, Romanticism served Mormons as the grand, eclectic umbrella,
which allowed them to draw from Judaism, Christianity, Masonry, and
the American experience, and to fuse them into a grand perspective that

---

[21] Harold Bloom, *The American Religion: The Emergence of the Post-Christian Nation* (New York: Simon and Schuster, 1992), 102, 127.

pointed beyond itself, and beyond all its singular components, to the Infinite that embraced them all.

Mormons, from their distinctly romantic perspective, occasionally lampooned and scorned the rationalist and materialist biases of their own age as grossly inferior to their own romantic vision. Perhaps no passage in all of early Mormon literature more effectively captured this contrast than the following from Parley P. Pratt:

> Witness the ancients conversing with the Great Jehovah, learn-
> ing lessons from the angels, and receiving instructions by the
> Holy Ghost, . . . until at length the veil is taken off and they
> are permitted to gaze with wonder and admiration upon all
> things past and future; yea, even to soar aloft amid unnumbered
> worlds. . . . Compare this intelligence with the low smatterings of
> education and worldly wisdom that seem to satisfy the narrow
> mind of man in our generation; yea, behold the narrow-minded,
> calculating, trading, overreaching penurious sycophant of the
> nineteenth century who dreams of nothing here but how to
> increase his goods, or take advantage of his neighbor, and whose
> only religious exercises or duties consist of going to meeting,
> paying the priest his hire, or praying to his God, without expect-
> ing to be heard or answered, supposing that God has been deaf
> and dumb for many centuries, or altogether stupid and indiffer-
> ent like himself.[22]

Indeed, for Latter-day Saints, the fall of the church from its perfect original occurred not in the loss of material forms and structures, which might now be rationally perceived and restored, but rather in the loss of divine rev-elation and the wonder-working power of the Holy Spirit. In the absence of immediate revelation, human beings had taken it upon themselves to interpret the Bible through human wisdom and human rationality, and to erect a myriad of denominations that were miserable substitutes for the true church of Christ, founded on the wonder-working power of God. Even Campbell, Mormons claimed, for all his restorationist rhetoric, had

---

[22] Parley P. Pratt, *A Voice of Warning* (1837; repr., Salt Lake City: Deseret Book Company, 1978), 88.

acted without immediate, divine authority, and therefore had founded yet another man-made sect.[23]

This was precisely the point the Mormons made in their debate with Abraham Sallee and Samuel Dewhitt in 1842. Thus, when John DeLee inquired into the reasons for religious pluralism in the United States, he quickly answered his own question. "We answer," he affirmed, "because they have lost the spirit which was possessed by the primitive Christians, and they lack the gifts which were originally and still are necessary to create a perfect church or body."

Alfonso Young concurred. "The church was once perfect and united," he declared, "and why is it not so now? I answer, because the professed Christians of the present day deny spiritual influences. In short, because they neither possess nor seek the gifts which the apostles and primitive Christians possessed."[24]

In short, the debate at the Ridge Meetinghouse in Middle Tennessee in 1841 featured two religious movements that shared a common restoration heritage but that had conformed said heritage to radically different intellectual molds: the Enlightenment and Romanticism. Perhaps in no single exchange was the difference between these two molds more effectively illumined than in the exchange over the relation of faith to miracles. The Church of Christ preachers, following John Locke and Alexander Campbell, claimed that miracles functioned as empirical evidence which in turn produced faith. John DeLee, however, turned this conception virtually upside down. "I will not only contend that miracles do not produce faith," he argued, "but that faith is necessary for the production of miracles." Later in the debate, he elaborated on this very point:

> If Christians of the present day would exercise the same mea-
> sure of faith and obedience as did the primitive Christians, they
> would receive the same blessings which were enjoyed by the first
> disciples of Christianity. They spake with tongues and wrought
> miracles. And so would Christians of the present day if they

---

[23] See Parley P. Pratt, "Grapes from Thorns, and Figs from Thistles," reprinted from *Millennial Star*, in *Writings of Parley Parker Pratt*, ed. Parker Pratt Robison (Salt Lake City: Parker Pratt Robison, 1952), 303.

[24] Debate, *Crihfield's Christian Family Library* 1 (Aug. 15, 1842): 238, 236.

possessed the same faith and exercised the same degree of obedience and holiness.[25]

When one discerns the power of the romantic vision in antebellum
America, one is hardly surprised to learn that disillusioned members of
the Church of Christ in Mentor, Ohio, abandoned Alexander Campbell
for Joseph Smith and thereby comprised the first corps of converts to the
Latter-day Saints. At one level, those conversions are easily understood, for
the converts simply moved from one restoration tradition to another. Yet,
on another level, the conversions are puzzling. Why the disillusionment
with Campbell and why the attraction to Joseph Smith? And even more
puzzling, why would these converts begin with a church rooted in the
Enlightenment, then abandon that church for one more in tune with the
Romantic mood of the time?

In effect, to ask that question is to answer it. Elizabeth Ann Whitney in
many ways spoke for all the converts when she reported that "my husband,
Newel K. Whitney, and myself were Campbellites. We had been baptized
for the remission of our sins, and believed in the laying on of hands and the
gifts of the spirit. But there was no one with authority to confer the Holy
Ghost upon us." Or, as John Murdock, an 1830 convert from Churches of
Christ to the Latter-day Saints, reported, "finding their principal leader,
Alex Campbell, with many others, denying the gift and power of the Holy
Ghost, I began to think of looking me a new home."[26] Indeed, Whitney
and Murdock were essentially Romantics whom Campbell initially
attracted by virtue of his restoration vision. But when they discovered the
Enlightenment dimensions of Campbell's vision, they began, as Murdock
put it, "to think of looking me a new home."

This Romantic thirst for a direct encounter with the Spirit of God
turned the restoration vision among Mormons in several directions, which
the rationalistic Churches of Christ would find incomprehensible. First,
it meant that Latter-day Saints viewed as normative the entire Bible, not

---

[25] Debate, *Crihfield's Christian Family Library* 1 (Aug. 15, 1842): 217, 236.

[26] Edward Wheelock Tullidge, *The Women of Mormonism* (New York: Tullidge and Crandall, 1877), 41–42; and John Murdock, "Abridged Record of the Life of John Murdock, Taken from His Journals by Himself," 4–10; typescript copy courtesy of Milton V. Backman, Brigham Young University.

the New Testament alone, for the entire Bible contained the records of a God who routinely broke into the orbit of human affairs to commune with humankind. For this reason, Latter-day Saints found no compelling reason to distinguish between Old and New Testaments as did Alexander Campbell. For his part, on the other hand, Campbell thought simply absurd the Book of Mormon idea that "the Nephites . . . were good Christians, . . . preaching baptism and other Christian usages hundreds of years before Jesus Christ was born!"[27]

Second, Latter-day Saints had little interest in mere obedience to biblical commands and replication of biblical data. Indeed, they never viewed the Bible as data at all. Instead, they viewed the Bible as story, as drama in which they themselves were participants along with Adam, Enoch, Moses, and Paul. As Philip Barlow recently observed, Joseph Smith "placed himself inside the Bible story" and put "endings . . . on stories that had their beginnings in the scriptural text." Or, as Jan Shipps has pointed out, Mormon restorationism involved far more than mere replication of events of the biblical long ago. It involved instead a ritual re-creation of those events in the here and now.[28] To the rational mind of Alexander Campbell, such an agenda seemed sheer nonsense. But to one who approached the restoration task from the perspective of Romanticism, as many did in antebellum America, such an agenda was irresistibly compelling.

Third, the Romantic dimensions of the Mormon restoration led Latter-day Saints to place enormously more importance on the experience of God than on the Bible itself. Indeed, for Mormons, the Bible simply pointed beyond itself to divine power and authority that manifested itself not only in the first age but continued to manifest itself in the here and now. This clearly accounts for the fact that Joseph Smith felt comfortable revising the Bible—an act that would have horrified Alexander Campbell. Yet, precisely here, in that act of revision, one finds abundantly proclaimed the Romantic dimensions of the Mormon faith. For as Barlow again points out, Smith never sought to determine "the intent of the ancient authors."

---

[27] Alexander Campbell, "Delusions," *MH* 2 (7 Feb. 1831): 87.

[28] Philip L. Barlow, *Mormons and the Bible* (New York: Oxford University Press, 1991), 21; and Jan Shipps, *Mormonism: The Story of a New Religious Tradition* (Urbana: University of Illinois Press, 1985), 53–65.

Instead, he "used the Bible less as a scholar than as a poet," or as Barlow finally concludes, as "a prophet."[29]

Fourth, if the heart of Churches of Christ was their appeal to a fixed and permanent first-century norm that would never change, the principle of continuing revelation meant that the heart of Latter-day Saints was change and adaptation, guided by a latter-day prophet. This difference would have enormous implications for the way in which these two restoration traditions would adapt themselves to the modern age.

Finally, if Romanticism provided the intellectual underpinnings for the restoration vision of Latter-day Saints, and thereby dramatically separated Mormons from Churches of Christ, there is a sense in which the inner dynamics of Mormons and Churches of Christ in the early nineteenth century were fundamentally similar. For if early Churches of Christ split on their assessment of human progress, so did the Latter-day Saints. Indeed, like the followers of Barton W. Stone, Latter-day Saints were profoundly apocalyptic and even premillennial, and therefore deeply suspicious of human potential apart from the divine initiative.[30] This theme dovetailed nicely with their peculiar brand of Romanticism, for the Saints looked not to human reason but to the Spirit of God to open the heavens and speak to humankind, to establish his people in Zion, to defeat their enemies, and to renew the earth.

At the same time, however, Latter-day Saints shared profoundly in the spirit of optimism that characterized Alexander Campbell. And yet there was a difference. For if Campbell exuded optimism over human progress and the larger culture, the optimism of the Saints pertained not so much to the larger culture, but rather to the Saints themselves.

One finds this optimistic strand especially in Mormon soteriology, perhaps classically expressed in Joseph's King Follett discourse of 1844: "God himself was once as we are now, and is an exalted man, and sits enthroned in yonder heavens!" Lorenzo Snow later summarized the point, "As man now is, God once was; as God now is, man may become." Whatever one makes of this passage, it clearly expressed enormous confidence in

---

[29] Barlow, *Mormons and the Bible*, 73; see also 70.

[30] See Underwood, *Millenarian World of Early Mormonism*.

human potential. Further, as the nineteenth century wound on, that confidence became more and more central to Mormon thought.[31]

There is no reason to ascribe the optimism expressed here to the Enlightenment, for it squares well with the exuberance over human potential that characterized many Romantics. At the same time, however, Mormon optimism inevitably absorbed Enlightenment characteristics. Thus one finds this familiar statement in a revelation of 1833: "The glory of God is intelligence" (*D&C* 93:36). By 1889, Orson F. Whitney combined that theme with the notion of eternal progression: "So says Joseph Smith. Intelligence is the glory of God. It is his superior intelligence that makes him God. The Gospel . . . is nothing more or less than a ladder of light, of intelligence, or principle, by which man, the child of god, may mount step by step to become eventually like his Father."[32] Little wonder, then, that Brigham Young could praise education "in every useful branch of learning" and urge his people "to excel the nations of the earth in religion, science, and philosophy."[33]

The fundamental question regarding Latter-day Saints, therefore, has to do with the relation between the pessimistic, regressive strands of Mormon thought, on the one hand, and the optimistic, progressive strands of Mormon thought on the other. In the case of Churches of Christ, Enlightenment optimism finally triumphed over apocalyptic pessimism, and thereby paved the way for full-scale modernization. My sense is that precisely the same has been true with Latter-day Saints.

Conclusion

Finally, we conclude where we began, with a consideration of the scholars. Klaus Hansen's work is relevant here in a back-handed kind of way since his reading of Mormonism stands precisely opposite to my own. Indeed, Hansen found Mormonism essentially a reflection of Enlightenment optimism and order, standing in radical opposition to Romanticism.

---

[31] O. Kendall White Jr., *Mormon Neo-Orthodoxy: A Crisis Theology* (Salt Lake City: Signature Books, 1987), esp. chap. 3.

[32] White, *Mormon Neo-Orthodoxy*, 83.

[33] White, *Mormon Neo-Orthodoxy*, 79.

He drew this conclusion because he interpreted the restoration vision as an Enlightenment phenomenon, virtually antagonistic to the Romantic mind, and because he imagined that few in antebellum America had much interest in such a peculiar, restorationist worldview. Thus he spoke of Joseph's question, "which of all the sects was right," and then observed:

> Most American Protestants had been sufficiently influenced by the romantic mood so that the question simply never occurred to them. Conversion was an individual experience that could happen to a Baptist as well as a Methodist or a Presbyterian. All of them had a pathway to heaven; as long as they got there, it did not matter very much how. In the literal mind of Joseph, however, there had to be one church that was objectively true.[34]

It is manifestly the case that Joseph searched for a church that was objectively true. But objectivity for Joseph—and for Latter-day Saints in antebellum America—was not a matter of rational and scientific precision as it was for Alexander Campbell and the Churches of Christ, and as it is for the modern mind today. It rather was a matter of the immediate power of God, which carried for Latter-day Saints fully as much objective truth as the Bible carried for Alexander Campbell.

When all is said and done, that was the critical difference between Mormons and Churches of Christ in nineteenth-century America.

---

[34] Klaus J. Hansen, *Mormonism and the American Experience* (Chicago: University of Chicago Press, 1981), 70-71.

SECTION TWO

CALLED BY A BOOK—MAKING SENSE OF THE RESTORATION VISION

CALLED BY A BOOK

A t its core, the question of vocation—if we are Christians—has everything to do with living one's life as a disciple of Jesus, hearing his summons, embracing his call. And the life to which he calls us, if we have ears to hear, is a life of solidarity with those he called "the least of these"—the hungry, the thirsty, the naked, the stranger, the sick, the marginalized, the oppressed, and those in prison.

In a word, Jesus calls us to become fully human—to see through the facades of power, fame, and success, to burst the artificial barriers that separate us from people less fortunate than ourselves, and to claim our common humanity. As William Stringfellow observed many years ago, this profoundly Christian vocation can be lived out through any number of professions or careers.[1]

When I arrived at Abilene Christian University in the fall of 1966 as a first-year graduate student, I understood none of this. Frankly, I had the cart before the horse. I had already made the decision to become a historian, but I had never considered how that decision related to Jesus's summons to live as his disciple. In fact, I had never given much thought to Jesus's summons at all. I had fixed my gaze instead on lesser things—questions

---

[1] William Stringfellow makes this point as well as anyone I have read. See his *A Keeper of the Word: Selected Writings of William Stringfellow* (Grand Rapids: Eerdmans, 1994), 30–31.

about the one true church and whether it existed, and where it existed over the long course of Christian history. Those were the questions that took me to Abilene Christian where I would pursue an MA in Christian history.

And then, by grace, a special book came into my life—a book that brought me face-to-face with Jesus's call to live as his disciple. That book transformed my life, offered a sense of vocation that I found immensely compelling, and set me on a journey radically different from any journey I had ever envisioned for myself.

Some forty years later, in 2006, shortly after we moved from Pepperdine University to Pennsylvania's Messiah College, a school with deep Anabaptist roots, my wife, Jan, reminded me of how radically this book had up-ended our lives. "I believe," she said, "that we've been on a forty-year journey to Messiah College."

Puzzled, I asked what she meant. "It all began," she told me, "when your professor put that book in your hands some forty years ago."

And then I knew. The professor was Everett Ferguson, the noted historian of early Christianity and the man who directed my MA thesis at ACU. One day he performed a simple but profoundly gracious act. He placed a book in my hands and told me to read. That was all—nothing more and nothing less. He could not have known how profoundly that simple act of grace would alter my thinking and change my life, for that book brought me face-to-face with Jesus's summons to live as his disciple.

The book was Franklin H. Littell's *The Anabaptist View of the Church*. Dr. Ferguson asked me to read that book since he knew of my struggles with the idea of restoration and the notion of the one true church. And so I took up the book and began to read.

The further I read, the more captivated I became, for this book told the story of a community of Christians very much like my own, committed—like us—to the ideals of the earliest Christians.

But there was a crucial difference between their vision and ours. In our concern to restore the ancient church, we typically focused on forms and structures. We sought to recover the true form of worship, the correct plan of salvation, the right form of baptism, and the proper organization of the church. We asked how often the Lord's Supper should be celebrated—weekly, monthly, or yearly, for example—and some of us even asked if we should use one cup or many. To each of these questions, we believed we had found the answer in the biblical text.

Out of the entire Bible, our one special book was the book of Acts since Acts was the book that most fully revealed what we believed was the pattern for restoring the primitive church.

But now, as I read *The Anabaptist View of the Church*, I discovered a tradition that also called for the restoration of the most ancient Christian tradition, but that seldom focused on the book of Acts. Instead, these people focused on the Gospels. And they seldom asked the question, "What were the forms and structures of the ancient church that should now be restored?" Instead, they asked, "What does it mean to be a disciple of Jesus?"

As they sought to answer that question, several principles began to emerge. They lived their lives for the sake of others and shared their goods with those in greatest need. They extended love and compassion to all human beings, including their enemies who sought to destroy them. And they refused to take another's life, even if that person had taken the sword against them. As a badge of their commitment to follow Jesus in all these ways, they embraced the baptism of confessing adult believers.

Soon the whole world turned against them. Catholics and Protestants, princes, priests, and reformers—everyone called for their blood and sought to exterminate these gentle people from the face of the earth. When the bloodbath was over, the authorities had executed thousands upon thousands. They drowned them, burned them at the stake, and ran them through with the sword. Their crime? In their zeal to follow the simple but radical teachings of Jesus, they had broken from the state church to which every citizen belonged simply by virtue of being alive, and had erected instead congregations of people who pledged to follow the radical but peaceable Jesus.

I found the Anabaptist vision so extraordinarily biblical and compelling that I wrote my MA thesis on the topic: "A Critical Comparison of the Restitution Motifs of the Campbells (1809–1830) and the Anabaptists (1525–1560)." "The Campbells" were Thomas and Alexander Campbell, the earliest leaders of the Churches of Christ.

That thesis was far more than an academic exercise, for it forced me to ask serious questions about the restoration vision. What, after all, *should* be restored? And that question led to another: What sort of issues stood at the heart of the Christian religion? I had grown up in a world in which forms and structures were terribly important, but I had now discovered a world in which forms and structures played a minor role while allegiance to the radical teachings of Jesus on how we should treat other people—our enemies as well as our friends—moved front and center.

Slowly I began to see that how we treat others, especially the vulnerable and the dispossessed, was more important in the eyes of God than all the forms and structures in the world.

Time and again I have failed in my efforts to respond to Jesus's call. But this I know—I am still a historian, but the vision of the upside-down kingdom that Jesus preached shapes what I read and why I read it. It shapes what I teach and how I teach it. And it shapes what I write and how I write it. In a word, the vocation of following Jesus has transformed my career.

RESTORING FIRST TIMES IN THE ANGLO-AMERICAN EXPERIENCE

W hen J. Hector St. John de Crevecoeur observed that "the American is a new man, who acts upon new principles; he must therefore entertain new ideas, and form new opinions," he was only offering a realistic assessment of American life, labor, and social structures as he perceived them.[1] There were others, however, in Crevecoeur's generation and the next who infused the image of American newness with a mythic dimension. For these interpreters, Americans were new in that they had been cut loose from the constraints of history and time and stood on the threshold of a radically new age that was wholly discontinuous with all previous epochs. Thus, Charles Pinckney argued in 1787 that the American situation was simply "unexampled" in the past, and Gulian Verplanck told students at Union College in 1836 that America was "without a parallel in past history."[2] Three years later, a writer in the *Democratic Review* contended that

---

[1] J. Hector St. John de Crevecoeur, *Letters from an American Farmer* (1782; New York: Penguin American Library, 1981), 70.

[2] Charles Pinckney, address to the Constitutional Convention, June 25, 1787, in *Documents Illustrative of the Formation of the Union of the American States*, ed. Charles Tansel (Washington, DC: Government Printing Office, 1927), 804–5; Gulian C. Verplanck, *The Advantages and the Dangers of the American Scholar: A Discourse Delivered . . . Union College, July 26, 1836* (New York: Wiley and Long, 1836), 5.

America had little connection with the histories of modern nations "and still less with all antiquity, its glories, or its crimes. On the contrary, our national birth was the beginning of a new history, . . . which separates us from the past and connects us with the future only."[3] Poetically, Walt Whitman captured the essence of this sentiment in "Pioneers! O Pioneers!":

All the past we leave behind,
We debouch upon a newer, mightier world, varied world.

And graphically, the great seal of the United States captured the sentiment of radical American newness when it pictured all human history prior to America as a barren and arid wilderness from which emerged the American *novus ordo seclorum* (new order of the ages) in 1776.

That millennial visions are implicit in this understanding is obvious, and anyone even casually acquainted with American religion in this period knows that millennialism of various kinds flourished in America between the Revolution and the Civil War. Intrigued by the various visions of millennial newness and the way those visions related to American purpose and identity during this period, scholars have explored the meaning of nineteenth-century American millennialism in painstaking and minute detail.[4] Most scholars writing on this subject, however, have failed to recognize that generally implicit in the rhetoric of American newness and millennialism was the fundamental theme of recovery—recovery of something primal, ancient, and old. To be sure, most Americans were not concerned to recover their recent past, or even an ancient past that was merely history, fully as corrupt and degenerate as the recent past from which they had sprung. But they were concerned to recover the primordial past that stood behind the historical past. The objective of their recovery was, to use the language of Mircea Eliade, sacred time, not profane time— the time of the gods, not the time of humankind.

Implicit in this conception is the notion of a fall from primal purity and rightness, and it was history—the long duration of human time—that

[3] "The Great Nation of Futurity," *Democratic Review* 6 (Nov. 1839): 426–27.

[4] For a sampling of the extent to which millennialism has been explored, see Leonard I. Sweet, "Millennialism in America: Recent Studies," *Theological Studies* 40 (Sep. 1979): 510–31; and Hillel Schwartz, "The End of the Beginning: Millenarian Studies, 1969–1975," *Religious Studies Review* 2 (July 1976): 1–15.

embodied the disastrous aftermath of that fall. Understood in this way, millennialism was itself a kind of recovery of sacred time. Far from depicting a vacuous, contentless vision of the last age, most millennial visions elaborated a very specific content drawn from a first age whose perfections had been lost or obscured in a fall but that might be recovered or restored in the millennial dawn.

A few scholars have sensed the importance of the notion of recovery in the American experience and have written cogently and suggestively regarding this theme. Fred Somkin, in his book *Unquiet Eagle*, finds it notable that delegates to the constitutional convention looked to the classic world for instruction rather than to the England of the commonwealth. This meant, Somkin argues, that the delegates sought to identify "with a universalism that transcended the mere homeland." Then Somkin makes the crucial point:

> In the classic, archetypal forms of political life were to be
> found the rights of man, as distinguished from the rights of
> Englishmen. Such a point of view argued an American alien-
> ation from the grasp of an organic, efficacious past, as though
> America were itself a kind of rebuke to time. An appeal to the
> nature of man, rather than to his history, evidenced a faith in
> something that had emerged unscathed from the gauntlet of his-
> torical time.[5]

Further, Somkin clearly recognizes that America's newness was predicated precisely on her oldness, that is, on her identification with primordial norms. Thus while writing of America's "unprecedentedness" and of her "utterly new beginning," Somkin also can write that "America . . . , by cleaving to the primitively old, to that which had not grown old through the agency of time, gained the possibility of continuing to be always new."[6] This description comes close to suggesting the image of America straddling the stream of history, with one foot planted squarely in the primordium and the other in the millennial dawn. In this way, America became "a

---

[5] Fred Somkin, *Unquiet Eagle: Memory and Desire in the Idea of American Freedom, 1815–1860* (Ithaca, NY: Cornell University Press, 1967), 57.

[6] Somkin, *Unquiet Eagle*, 57, 61.

providential conspiracy against time, . . . an attempt to outwit time by an evasion of the exigencies of temporal causality." None of this means, of course, that Americans were ahistorical or unhistorical or failed either to know or to appreciate the past. Quite to the contrary. "As record, as deposit, the past undoubtedly existed," Somkin observes, "but Americans contested the extent of its jurisdiction."[7]

Contesting the extent of the jurisdiction of the past is precisely what Sidney Mead had in mind when he wrote of the sense of "historylessness" that American denominations in the nineteenth century so often manifested. Contending with one another in the new free market of souls, created and sustained by religious freedom and pluralism in the new nation, both right-wing denominations and left-wing sects sought legitimacy by claiming to duplicate primitive Christianity more closely than the others. In so doing, Mead observes, sects and denominations in America became both radically new and radically old at one and the same time so that all, to one degree or another, embraced "the idea of building anew in the American wilderness on the true and ancient foundations."[8]

I

One of the chief contentions of this chapter is that recovery of primal norms has been a fundamental preoccupation of the American people. In the quest for identity, both the nation and the nation's religious traditions have employed this perspective with striking regularity.

The concern to identify with pure beginnings is a legacy of the Protestant Reformation, though this legacy survives in the twentieth century in a myriad of forms, some of which are explicitly Protestant and denominational and some of which are broadly cultural and political. One might argue, for example, that American foreign policy, often dominated by redemptive themes, rests ultimately on the conviction that America has restored pure, natural, and primal norms while other nations remain snared in the web of history, tradition, and artificial contrivance. America's

---

[7] Somkin, *Unquiet Eagle*, 60, 57.

[8] Sidney E. Mead, *The Lively Experiment: The Shaping of Christianity in America* (New York: Harper and Row, 1963), 108–13. Mead addressed in considerably more detail the theme of recovery in American life in "The Theology of the Republic and the Orthodox Mind," *Journal of the American Academy of Religion* 44 (Mar. 1976): 105–13.

task, therefore, is redemptive precisely because America, at the level of fundamental identity, transcends the vicissitudes of history and the constraints of finitude. Put another way, American institutions—especially democracy and free enterprise—are simply natural and reflect the way the Creator intended things to be from the beginning.

In the mid-1980s, a spate of pro-American, anti-Soviet films reflected these themes at the popular level. *Rocky IV* was a notable case. When Rocky Balboa trained for his great fight with the Russian giant, Drago, he trained in the Siberian wilderness as a fundamentally natural man. Instead of lifting manufactured weights, Rocky lifted timber and stones. He pulled crude sleds across the Siberian terrain and jogged on mountain tops. He was the American—the natural man. In stark contrast, Drago was contrived and artificial. He trained on the latest scientific equipment and jogged in a modern, scientific gymnasium. If Rocky was the natural man, Drago was preeminently a product of modern science and technology. And when Rocky finally defeated the Russian giant, the Soviet crowd, responding enthusiastically to the compelling attraction of the natural man, began to chant, "Rocky, Rocky, Rocky." The symbolism was clear: America, the natural, primal, and pure nation, once again had defeated the hosts of history, time, and artificial contrivance.

To describe this perspective, I employ in this chapter the terms *primitivism* and *restorationism* interchangeably, for the heart of this perspective is the concern to "restore" what seems to be "primitive" or prior to the mere traditions of history. This American perspective descends ultimately from a sixteenth-century tradition that viewed antiquity, and especially the primitive Christian church, as the standard for all subsequent Christian faith and practice. In England this viewpoint emerged with extraordinary power when Christian Humanism and Reformed theology made it a common cause under the catalytic influence of William Tyndale's covenant theology. The uniqueness of this perspective, at least in Christian history, appears when contrasted with the other dominant tradition of the Reformation, the theology of Martin Luther. Luther had virtually no interest in resurrecting the primitive Christian church as a norm for his own age, and severely chastised Andreas Bodenstein von Karlstadt, who attempted to model the church in Wittenberg after a supposed apostolic pattern. The particular content of Karlstadt's theology Luther viewed as beside the point. It was the theological method itself that Luther viewed as demonic, for it "destroys faith, profanes the blood of Christ, blasphemes the gospel, and sets all that Christ has won for us at nought."[9] Luther was not so much concerned with returning to an earlier time as he was with finding a place to stand, a ground of being (*ontos*), in his own time.

Noting the radical difference between Luther's theological method and that of Christian Humanism and much of the Reformed tradition, Gordon Rupp and George Yule prefer to speak of "patterns of Reformation" rather than Reformation per se. Both distinguish between the overriding *sola gratia* theology of Luther and the other major way of doing theology in the Reformation period, a method Rupp describes as "plans of salvation" and Yule describes as "reformation by biblical precedent."[10] In our view, a workable and suggestive way of distinguishing between Luther's theological method and the theological method of much of Reformed Christianity is to distinguish between *ontological reform*, where the primary question is "How can I find a merciful God, or a place to stand?," and *primordial reform*, where the primary question is "What was the ancient tradition?" It was this latter question that dominated both the worldview and the theological method of Christian Humanism, the Reformed tradition, and the Puritans. When Rationalism finally revolted against Puritan dominance and intransigence in England, it was able to extricate itself from Puritan preoccupation with the primitive church and apostolic practices, but it did not extricate itself from the basic question of primordial reform—namely, the question concerning some kind of ancient or primitive norm.

II

Before sketching briefly the historic development of primordial reform, and its manifestations in both Puritanism and the Enlightenment, we need to view primordial reform from a phenomenological perspective. Here the works of Mircea Eliade regarding sacred and profane time in primitive religions

---

[9] Martin Luther, "Against the Heavenly Prophets," in *Luther's Works: American Edition*, vol. 40: *Church and Ministry*, ed. Conrad Bergendoff (Philadelphia: Fortress Press, 1958), 90–91.

[10] Gordon Rupp, "Patterns of Salvation in the First Age of the Reformation," *Archiv für Reformationsgeschichte* 57 (Heftland 2, 1966): 60; George Yule, "Continental Patterns and the Reformation in England and Scotland," *Scottish Journal of Theology* 18 (1969): 305.

prove helpful. Eliade argues that for the primitive person, the only real time, and therefore "sacred time," was primordial time; that "profane time" was "the 'unreal' *par excellence*, the uncreated, the nonexistent: the void"; and that primitive man sought, through periodic rituals and festivals, to repeat the paradigmatic activities of the gods, thus making primordial time or real time contemporary. Through the restoration of sacred, primordial time, primitives transformed profane chaos into sacred cosmos—a world possessing reality and wholeness.[11] This epitome of Eliade's argument makes clear what we mean by primordial reform: *chronos* is reversed until profane history is transcended and the believer stands squarely in the first age.

In applying such a construction to the Christian tradition, the critical question is, of course, How is it possible to apply essentially nonhistorical categories to a historical religion? The answer lies in recognizing that any human history, if that history has more than a formal and factual significance, bears mythical and symbolic power. To the degree that the factual history outweighs the power of the myth, and a certain distance is maintained between the particular history that is normative and the believer's own time, then we may speak of a particular religious tradition as being historical. In such cases, a certain objectivity remains. But when the normative history is swallowed up in myth to such an extent that the believer loses the clear distinction between his or her own time and the primal time, then that historic tradition has lost its historicality. At that point, the particular time that was merely normative now has become the eternally repeatable primordium within which the believer lives and moves and has his or her being and apart from which life itself has no meaning or significance.

A classic illustration, drawn squarely from the American situation, is the Church of Jesus Christ of Latter-day Saints, which contends that the church established during the apostolic primordium but subsequently lost from the face of the earth was restored once and for all by the prophet Joseph Smith. All efforts by Mormons to verify the facts of this historical norm (the primordium) or the facts of its recovery (the restoration) are beside the point, because efforts to verify are not for the sake of the believer but rather for the sake of the outsider. The power of the myth

---

[11] Mircea Eliade, *The Sacred and the Profane* (New York: Harcourt, Brace, 1959), 20–113.

emanating from the particular history has already grasped the believer, and no amount of verification or lack of verification can possibly make any difference. Put another way, whether the history has any objective reality is beside the point; the myth carries existential reality and that alone is sufficient. Only as the power of the myth diminishes does the history require repeating, and this repetition occurs only for the sake of reinforcing the myth. In this case, history enlarges the myth, rather than the myth being constrained and refined by the facts of history. Moreover, Mormons, while fond of repeating their own particular history, typically do not repeat the larger history that lies behind their own. They typically either ignore or dismiss as an aberration from the primordial norm the eighteen centuries of Christian history that precede. Mormons are utterly ahistorical in taking this approach, and yet they are part of a historic tradition—the Judeo-Christian faith. In their case, however, the power of the myth outweighs and even obscures the facts of the history that produced them.

The student of Christian history, therefore, should be aware that a historical religion quickly may become ahistorical when its adherents either deny or attempt to transcend the particular history that produced them. Once one perceives this possibility, it becomes difficult to dismiss the insights of Eliade for a study of certain aspects of Christian history. Indeed, the concept of the primordium may be far more applicable to certain dimensions of Christian history than is immediately apparent. For, as Eliade describes it, the primordial event was precisely whatever the believer understood to be primordial. Eliade's treatment of Walt Whitman's *Homer* helps us understand this conception of the relativity of primordial time: "Whitman expressed with force and glamour the obsession with the primordial, the absolute beginning. He enjoyed 'reciting *Homer* while walking beside the Ocean' because *Homer* belonged to the *primordium*; he was not a product of history—he had founded European poetry."[12] Similarly, for many strands of the Reformed and English Protestant traditions, the examples of Israel, Jesus, the apostles, and the primitive church belonged to the primordium; they were not products of history—they had founded the

---

[12] Mircea Eliade, *The Quest: History and Meaning in Religion* (Chicago: University of Chicago Press, 1969), 101.

only real history there was, Christian history now understood as the primitive church and the Protestant era. All intervening history was profane.

Eliade himself makes it clear that the notion of a primordial norm is not universally applicable to Christianity and that it would be faulty to apply it to theologies like that of Luther. Utilizing the rubric "Christianity" but describing a Christianity dominated by a radical conception of *sola fides* and *sola gratia*, Eliade contends that

> in Christianity . . . the *basileia tou theou* [kingdom of God] is already present "among" those who believe, and . . . hence the *illud tempus* [former or first time] is eternally of the present and accessible to anyone, at any moment, through *metanoia*, [repentance]. Since what is involved is a religious experience wholly different from the traditional experience, since what is involved is faith, Christianity translates the periodic regeneration of the world into a regeneration of the human individual.[13]

Primordial reform, however, differs significantly from what Eliade describes here. We turn now to a brief history of this tradition.

III

The primordial dimension of the English Reformation and Puritanism drew essentially from three sources: Christian Humanism, the Reformed tradition of the Continent, and the covenant theology of William Tyndale. Christian Humanism, through its concern to restore both the source documents of primitive Christianity and the morals of Christian antiquity, provided the springboard for primordial thinking in the Reformation period. The writings of Desiderius Erasmus, for example, reflect a deep reverence for the ancient Christian writings over against the scholastic theology of his own age, and a concern that people learn to live according to the *philosophia Christi*. The following passage from the *Paraclesis* typifies the Erasmian emphasis:

---

[13] Mircea Eliade, *The Myth of the Eternal Return* (Princeton: Princeton University Press, 1954), 129.

Why devote the greater part of life to Averroes rather than to the gospels? Why spend nearly all of life on the ordinances of men and on opinions in contradiction with themselves? . . . Let us all, therefore, with our whole heart covet this literature [the Scriptures], let us embrace it, let us fondly kiss it, at length let us die in its embrace, let us be transformed in it, since indeed studies are transmuted into morals.[14]

Erasmus, to be sure, never suggested that the apostolic church provided a model for the church of the sixteenth century. As Abraham Friesen has pointed out, Erasmus was prohibited from taking that step, on the one hand, by his commitment to the traditions of Christendom and, on the other hand, by his Neoplatonic conception of Christ by which Christ's perfection could only be reflected, not duplicated.[15] But at the same time, the basic structural presuppositions of chronological reform were present in his thought—the supremacy of Christian antiquity and the preeminence of the *philosophia Christi*.

It is critical at this point to note that Christian Humanism influenced practically every sixteenth-century reformer who embraced primordial reform. The early English Catholic reformer John Colet, whose humanism was beyond question, provides a notable case in point. William Clebsch has demonstrated that Colet's conception of reform, while predicated on the Pauline corpus, nevertheless differed radically from the posture of Luther. As Clebsch puts it, "that which is particularly Coletian . . . is the fastening . . . upon the Pauline writings as descriptive of the pure primitive Church, for a model of individual and corporate Christianity."[16] Nowhere in the sixteenth century is Eliade's conception of the transformation of chaos into cosmos through the repristination of the primordial norm more thoroughly typified than in the thought of Colet. According to Colet, the Edenic state of nature had been reestablished in primitive Christianity

[14] Cited in John C. Olin, ed., *Christian Humanism and the Reformation: Desiderius Erasmus* (New York: Harper and Row, 1965), 104–5.

[15] Abraham Friesen, "The Impulse toward Restitutionist Thought in Christian Humanism," *Journal of the American Academy of Religion* 44 (1976): 40–45.

[16] William Clebsch, "John Colet and Reformation," *Anglican Theological Review* 37 (1955): 172.

and thus restoring apostolic life and teachings also meant restoring the primordial norm in the most objective sense possible.

> It was the purpose of Christ, himself the author of nature, to express nature herself among men, and to bring back to the order and beauty of nature what had diverged from order, and to reform the human race, all deformed as it was, and disfigured and abominable. . . . This could not be done without some mighty living force, which, being in all its fulness in one, might be poured out from that one upon the many; which might go forth, and recall, restore, win back and re-establish for mankind their pristine state.[17]

Colet's theology epitomized the recovery of the primordial norm. The sources of that norm were twofold: nature and revelation—the same two traditions that would converge, now in this way and now in that, to shape the contours of the Anglo-American primordium for generations to come.

The notion of primordial reform, however, was not popularized by Colet and had to await the Marian Exiles for its full-blown development. But when at last the Exiles developed this theme, they did so with a profound sense of urgency rooted in the covenant theology of William Tyndale. For Tyndale, England was a "new Israel," and just as God had smitten ancient Israel for covenant-breaking, so God would smite England with "hunger, death, murrain, pestilence, war, oppression, with strange and wonderful diseases, and new kinds of misfortune and evil luck" if England failed in her covenant duties.[18] But, Tyndale wrote in the preface to his 1534 New Testament, "If we meke oure selves to god, to kepe all his lawes, after the ensample of Christ: then God hath bounde his selfe vnto vs to kepe and make good all the mercies promysed in Christ throwout all the scripture."[19]

The implications of Tyndale's covenant theology for primordial reform were obvious, especially given the milieu of Christian Humanism present in England during the early and mid-sixteenth century. But what was

---

[17] John Colet, *An Exposition of St. Paul's Epistle to the Romans,* cited in Clebsch, "Colet and Reformation," 175.
[18] *The Whole Works of W. Tyndale, John Frith, and Doct. Barnes* (London, 1573), 10.
[19] "W. T. to the Reader," in *The New Testament* (Antwerp, 1534), 4. Michael McGiffert, "William Tyndale's Conception of the Covenant," *Journal of Ecclesiastical History* 32 (1981): 167–84.

merely an implication became clear during the first year of Edward's reign when injunctions were issued ordering every pastor to obtain Erasmus's *Paraphrases* on the New Testament as a study guide to the New Testament. Significantly, a strong dose of Tyndale's covenant theology was appended to Erasmus's *Paraphrases* in the prefaces written by Nicholas Udall and Thomas Key. This joining of Erasmus and Tyndale in the same volume clearly implied that England could fulfill the covenant through a return to the sources and morals of Christian antiquity. This volume circulated so widely that by the time the primitivist impulse from the Continent began shaping English theology later in the reign of Edward VI, a unique blend of Tyndalic deuteronomism and Erasmian Humanism had already prepared the ground.

The continental influences on England during Edward's reign came from a host of sources, to be sure, but principally from the Reformed theologians of Zurich and Strassburg. While the Zurich theologians Huldreich Zwingli and Heinrich Bullinger both upheld a profound doctrine of justification by faith, both also were Christian Humanists who strongly advocated primordial reform. Bullinger, for example, was quite explicit that "the church should hold tightly to no other form than that transferred and established by the Lord and the Apostles and should remain unchanged," and he even sought to approximate the primitive traditions in his rejection of musical instruments in the Great Minster: "The organs in the churches are not a particularly old institution, especially in these parts. Since they do not agree with the apostolic teaching (1 Cor. 14) the organs in the Great Minster were broken up on the 9th of December in the year 1527. For from this time forth neither singing nor organs in the Church was wanted."[20] Zwingli and Bullinger profoundly influenced the English theological scene through letters, commentaries, Bullinger's *Decades of Sermons*, and the proto-Puritan John Hooper. Further, their influence was sufficiently extensive as to prompt King Edward himself to write the senate

---

[20] Heinrich Bullinger, "Zuschrift an Frau Anna Roist," cited in Bernard Verkamp, "The Zwinglians and Adiaphorism," *CH* 42 (1973): 495; *Heinrich Bullingers Reformationsgeschichte*, 1 (Frauenfeld, 1838–40), cited in Charles Garside, *Zwingli and the Arts* (New Haven: Yale University Press, 1966), 61.

of Zurich on October 20, 1549, regarding the "mutual agreement between us concerning the Christian religion and true godliness."[21]

The Strassburg influence on England came primarily from Peter Martyr Vermigli and Martin Bucer, though it is Bucer who demands our attention in this context. Bucer, in his *De Regno Christi* presented to Edward VI in 1550, clearly called for primordial reform, but his chief contribution lies in the fact that he placed his call for primordial reform squarely within the context of the national covenant. Thus, for the first time in England, the presuppositions of Tyndalic deuteronomism and Erasmian Humanism had been combined to create an explicit and urgent demand that England— the entire *corpus christianum*—become the primordial kingdom of Christ, lest England be afflicted with the wrath of God.[22] Bucer, in other words, called for a Christian civil religion. Consistent with this appeal, Bucer's model was not the apostolic church of the first century but rather the Constantinian church and society, which was for him the Christian primordium that should be replicated in his own time.

The appeal to a Christian priordium within the context of a national covenant—a phenomenon that would become common in America— became commonplace within the early Puritan movement as it grew up among the Marian Exiles. But more to the point, this primordial appeal became the basis for a powerful dissenting tradition that emerged at this time. The Geneva Bible, produced by the Exiles, provides an important case in point. The preoccupation of the translators with the national covenant is well known. Within that context, the advancing of true religion meant to the Exiles the faithful reproduction of the primitive church revealed in the Word of God. Thus in the dedication to Queen Elizabeth, the translators charged her to build up the church

> according to the word of God. . . . For if it was not lawful for
> Moses to build the material Tabernacle after any other sort
> than God showed him by a pattern, . . . how can it be lawful

---

[21] Cited in John Opie, "The Anglicizing of John Hooper," *Archiv für Reformationsgeschichte* 59 (Heft 2, 1968): 155.

[22] Martin Bucer, "De Regno Christi," in *The Library of Christian Classics*, vol. 19: *Melanchtnon and Bucer*, ed. Wilhelm Pauck (Philadelphia: Westminster Press, 1969), 194, 196, 209–11, 224, 225ff.

to proceed in this spiritual building any other way, than Jesus Christ the Son of God, who is both the foundation, head and chief corner stone thereof, hath commanded by his word?

Dan G. Danner, who has analyzed carefully the theology of the Geneva Bible, has summarized this theme: "No man has the authority to exceed the bounds of scripture, either to add to, or take from. . . . Whatever is not commanded by God's Word 'touching his service, is against the word.' Only the Bible is God's authority which contains norms for worship and piety."[23] The recovery of the biblical pattern was at one and the same time the recovery of a primordium that had been lost in the previous years of darkness and ignorance. The Exiles believed, therefore, that

> it hath pleased [God] to call us into this marvelous light of his Gospel, & mercifully to regard us after so horrible backsliding and falling away from Christ to Antichrist, from light to dark-ness, from the living God to dumb and dead idols, & that . . . we are . . . received again to grace with most evident signes and tokens of God's especial love and favor.[24]

These Exiles had a keen awareness of stepping, as Eliade would put it, from profane time into sacred time, from the present as present into the present as primordium, and it was this awareness that propelled their dissent.

It is within this context that John Knox's controversy with Richard Cox in Frankfurt makes sense. Knox developed his well-known covenant theology in response to Mary Tudor's accession to the throne in 1553, an event that the proto-Puritans among the Exiles typically interpreted as God's scourge on England for failing to sufficiently reform the church. In *An Admonition or Warning*, completed in 1554, Knox summarized the covenant: "This is the league betwixt God and us, that He alone shall be oure God, and we shall be his people: He shall communicate with us of his graces and goodness; We shall serve him in bodie and spirit: He shall

---

[23] Dan G. Danner, "The Theology of the Geneva Bible of 1560: A Study in English Protestantism," PhD diss., University of Iowa, 1969, 67–68. See also Judah J. Newberger, "The Law of the Old Testament in Tudor and Stuart England," PhD diss., New York University, 1976, esp. 127–32.

[24] "To our Beloved in the Lord, the Brethren of England, Scotland, Ireland, &c.," in *The Geneva Bible*, iii.

be oure safeguard from death and damnation; We shall seek to him, and shall flee from all strange Gods."[25] Thinking in covenantal terms, Knox argued with Richard Cox in Frankfurt that the Anglicans failed to exercise godly discipline. The real issue, which Knox failed to articulate but which Richard Vander Molen perceptively observes, was what kind of discipline should be imposed. For Anglicans, any principle of discipline was of necessity historically conditioned. They were willing therefore to accept national church traditions. Knox and his followers, on the other hand, sought to return to a first-century norm for a method of discipline uncontaminated by subsequent historical and cultural influences. Cox strongly suggested to Knox that such an ideal was illusory and that even his concern to approximate a first-century norm was historically and culturally conditioned.[26]

Following the Exile, the compulsion to duplicate the Christian primordium in the present time became a central feature of Puritan dissent. Sixteen years after Knox's *Admonition*, Thomas Cartwright argued, in his Cambridge lectures on Acts (1570), that the government of the first Christian church in Jerusalem was presbyterian and that therefore, ipso facto, presbyterian church government should be employed in the present age. Indeed, so insistent was Cartwright that the church of his own day replicate the primitive church that, taking his cue from Tertullian, he found the very silence of Scripture prohibitive.

As Cartwright put it, "The scripture denieth that, whiche yt noteth not." Moreover, Cartwright was convinced that the further one moved in time from the first apostolic communities, the more corrupt the church became, so that by the end of the first five hundred years of Christian history the true church hardly existed at all.[27] Indeed, Donald McGinn has argued that the heart of the entire controversy surrounding Cartwright's

---

[25] Cited in Richard L. Greaves, "John Knox and the Covenant Tradition," *Journal of Ecclesiastical History* 24 (1973): 24.

[26] Richard Vander Molen, "Anglican against Puritan: Ideological Origins during the Marian Exile," *CH* 42 (1973): 49–56.

[27] *The Second Replie of Thomas Cartwright: Agaynst Maister Doctor Wbitgiftes Second Answer Touching the Churche Discipline* (1575), 81; John K. Luoma, "Who Owns the Fathers? Hooker and Cartwright on the Authority of the Primitive Church," *Sixteenth Century Journal* 8 (1977): 48–50. See Luoma, "The Primitive Church as a Normative Principle in the Theology of the Sixteenth Century: The Anglican-Puritan Debate over Church Polity as Represented by Richard Hooker and Thomas Cartwright," PhD diss., Hartford Seminary Foundation, 1974.

famous *Admonition to Parliament* was the question of the primitive church. Two years after the Admonition was published, Walter Travers published what B. R. White calls "the most systematic exposition of presbyterian churchmanship during this period for English Puritans," *De Disciplina Ecclesiastica*, translated that same year by Cartwright into English and entitled *A full and plaine declaration of ecclesiasticall discipline*. Travers there argued the same point, namely, that the Bible provided a perfect pattern for ecclesiastical discipline "which is common and general to all the church and perpetual for all times."[28]

Other and later Puritans repeated this basic argument almost ad nauseum. Although agreed on the fact of a perfect ancient pattern, they disagreed continually on its features. The Separatist Henry Barrow, for example, judged the Marian Exiles, for all their primordialist sentiments, to have missed the mark. But, generously, he excused them.

> It can be no wonder that those godly men so unexpert and
> unexercised in this heavenly work, never having lived in, seen,
> or heard of any orderly communion of saints, any true estab-
> lished church upon earth of so many hundred years, ever since
> the general defection under Antichrist so much foretold of in
> the Scriptures, no marvel, I say, if they erred in setting up the
> frame. But what then? Should we therefore justify or persist
> in their errors? Especially should we reject the true pattern of
> Christ's Testament which reproveth our works, and showeth us a
> better course?[29]

And the Separatist turned Congregationalist John Robinson put his case in a classic form that illustrates well the phenomenological perspective of Eliade. "We do believe, by the word of God," he wrote, "that the things we teach are not new, but old truths renewed; so are we not less persuaded, that the church constitution in which we are set, is cast in the

---

[28] Donald McGinn, *The Admonition Controversy* (New Brunswick, NJ: Rutgers University Press, 1949), 49–63; B. R. White, *The English Separatist Tradition* (Oxford: Oxford University Press, 1971), 38–40. See James Spalding, "Restitution as a Normative Factor for Puritan Dissent," *Journal of the American Academy of Religion* 44 (1976): 47.

[29] Leland H. Carlson, ed., *The Writings of Henry Barrow, 1587–1590* (London: Allen and Unwin, 1962), 126.

apostolical and primitive mould, and not one day nor hour younger, in the nature and form of it, than the first church of the New Testament."[30]

In New England, the primordial theme was equally as pronounced. The great tutor of the New England Puritans, William Ames, had affirmed that Scripture was "not a partial, but a perfect rule of Faith and manners," and within that context the New England Puritans perpetuated the venerable primordialist tradition.[31] *The Cambridge Platform* of 1648 argued, for example, that church government is "exactly described in the word of God . . . so that it is not left in the power of men, officers, Churches, or any state in the world, to add, diminish or alter anything in the least measure therein." This clearly was a way of urging conformity to the once-for-all-ness of the primordial norm and rejecting merely historical traditions as of any value whatsoever. Likewise William Bradford, in *Of Plymouth Plantation*, recalled how Satan had opposed the truth in England, reluctant that "his kingdom should go downe, the trueth prevaile; and the churches of God reverte to their anciente puritie; and recover their primitive order, libertie, and bewtie."[32] Bradford here was recalling the time when primordial theology was a tool for dissent.

But in New England what once was the basis for dissent became the basis for an established church. Nowhere is this shift more apparent than in John Cotton's affirmation that the New England Way was as close as could be to what "the Lord Jesus [would erect] were he here himselfe in person." The shift appears in Cotton Mather's smug proclamation that "the Churches of New England are [not] the most *regular* that can be; yet I do say, and am sure, that they are very like unto those that were in the first ages of Christianity." Not surprisingly, Edward Winslow wrote in 1646 that the Bay churches had not borrowed from the Plymouth churches or vice versa. Rather, the Bay churches "advised with us," and we "accordingly shewed them the Primitive practice for our warrant. . . . So that here also thow maist see they set not the Church at Plimouth before them for

---

[30] Robert Ashton, ed., *The Works of John Robinson, Pastor of the Pilgrim Fathers* (Boston: Jonathon Cape, 1851), 2:43.

[31] William Ames, *The Marrow of Sacred Divinity Drawne Out of the Holy Scriptures* (London, 1642), 150.

[32] Williston Walker, ed., *The Creeds and Platforms of Congregationalism* (New York: Charles Scribner's Sons, 1893), 203; William Bradford, *Bradford's History of Plymouth Plantation, 1606–1646*, ed. William T. Davis (New York: Charles Scribner's Sons, 1908), 1:23.

example, but the Primitive Churches were and are their and our mutuall patterns and examples."[33]

Later in the seventeenth century, a major shift took place in English religious thought, a shift from Puritanism to the Enlightenment. Puritanism was credited with causing bitter societal divisions, war, bloodshed, the fragmentation of English society, and finally, regicide. The Puritans' efforts to construct a newly established order in England by returning to the ancient Christian primordium now seemed a failure, and sober and reasonable men and women sought diligently for a new theological glue that might once again bind their world together. Lord Herbert of Cherbury first adumbrated this new theology that sought to reduce religion to a set of essentials on which all reasonable persons could agree. The source for this new theology was not something highly particular, knowable only to a few, but rather highly universal, knowable to all: the source was nature.

IV

For all the theological changes involved in the shift from orthodoxy to the Enlightenment, however, one thing did not change, and that was the theological method. The quest for the primordium persisted; the rationalists simply substituted one book—the book of Nature—for another and exchanged the primordium of the early church for the primordium of Eden. The basic theological question continued to be, What is truth? And the old assumption that truth resided in antiquity continued to prevail. The basic difference was that the rationalists carried their quest for truth to an antiquity far older than the Christian antiquity they were rejecting. As one Enlightenment thinker put it, the antiquity they sought was as old as creation.

The appeal to antiquity was especially strong among the Jeffersonians in the American Enlightenment. No one made the point more clearly than Thomas Paine in *Rights of Man*, where he argued that human rights are rooted in the original creation and can be justified by appealing only to the original creation.

---

[33] Cotton Mather, *Magnalia Christi Americana: or, the Ecclesiastical History of New England, from Its First Planting in the Year 1620 unto the Year of our Lord, 1698* (London, 1702), 1:26–27. Edward Winslow, *Hypocrisie Unmasked*, cited in Perry Miller, *Orthodoxy in Massachusetts* (New York: Harper and Row, 1970), 136.

The error of those who reason by precedents from antiquity, respecting the rights of man, is that they do not go far enough into antiquity. They do not go the whole way. They stop in some of the intermediate stages of an hundred or a thousand years, and produce what was then done, as a rule of the present day. This is no authority at all . . . but if we proceed on, we shall at last come out right; we shall come to the time when man came from the hand of his Maker. . . . We have now arrived at the origin of man, and at the origin of his rights.[34]

The Jeffersonians could argue that all men were created equal because the created order of things, they supposed, had remained virtually unchanged since the creation itself. Thus to study the creature was to study the creation, and to attend to nature was to attend to Eden. Again, Paine made the point well:

All men are born equal, and with equal natural rights, in the same manner as if posterity had been continued by creation instead of by *generation*. . . . Consequently every child born into the world must be considered as deriving its existence from God. The world is as new to him as it was to the first man that existed, and his natural right in it is of the same kind.[35]

From an Eliadian perspective it might well be said that, for Paine, the birth of a human being was a sort of sacred festival making contemporary the primordial, creative activity of the gods. But if this were true, then why had so many human governments denied the God-given rights of man? Here Paine sketched a theory of the fall:

because there have been upstart governments, thrusting themselves between, and presumptuously working to *un-make*

---

[34] Philip S. Foner, ed., *The Complete Writings of Thomas Paine* (New York: Citadel Press, 1945), 1:273. Henry F. May notes the primordialist dimensions of both the Jeffersonians and other participants in the phase of the Enlightenment that May terms "the Revolutionary Enlightenment": "Since the new order would be a natural order, there was usually some element of primitivism in adherents of the Revolutionary Enlightenment: the enlightened future would reproduce some golden age of simple goodness." *The Enlightenment in America* (New York: Oxford University Press, 1976), 153.

[35] *Complete Writings of Thomas Paine*, 1:274.

man. . . . It is not among the least of the evils of the present exist-
ing governments in all parts of Europe that man, considered as
man, is thrown back to a vast distance from his Maker, and the
artificial chasm filled up with a succession of barriers, or sort of
turnpike gates, through which he has to pass.[36]

Paine described these barriers erected between human beings and
the original creation as kings, parliaments, magistrates, priests, nobility,
and Peter. But lo, in these latter days, Paine argued, the barriers had been
destroyed and a restoration had occurred. The creative activity of the gods
had been made contemporary in the eighteenth century with the founding
of the American republic and the recovery of the primordial rights of man.

> In viewing this subject, the case and circumstances of America
> present themselves as in the beginning of a world; and our
> inquiry into the origin of government is shortened by referring
> to the facts that have arisen in our own day. We have no occa-
> sion to roam for information into the obscure field of antiquity,
> nor hazard ourselves upon conjecture. We are brought at once to
> the point of seeing government begin, as if we had lived in the
> beginning of time. The real volume, not of history, but of facts,
> is directly before us, unmutilated by contrivance, or the errors
> of tradition.[37]

It is significant that Paine did not regard history as the real volume
of facts. History, for Paine, had been transcended, and the facts of the
matter were to be found in nature. Given these peculiarly primordialist
presuppositions, it is hardly surprising that Daniel Boorstin should write
that "the Jeffersonians reasoned that man . . . had no significant past. . . .
By merging man into the whole natural universe, the Jeffersonians had in
fact alienated themselves from the humanistic past."[38] Methodologically,
though not theologically, the Jeffersonians were at one with the Puritans.

---

[36] *Complete Writings of Thomas Paine*, 1:274–75.

[37] *Complete Writings of Thomas Paine*, 1:376.

[38] Daniel Boorstin, *The Lost World of Thomas Jefferson* (Boston: Beacon Press, 1960), 169.

Thus when Jefferson, like Herbert of Cherbury, sought to transcend real or potential religious combustions, he did so by appealing to a faith common to all humankind since it could be learned from nature. Deploring the fruits of Christian orthodoxy, which he described as "castes of inextinguishable hatred to one another," Jefferson sought to transcend both theological particularities and the social repression that insistence on those particularities created. Indeed, he sought, as he put it, to unite people "in those principles only in which God has united us all," namely, the principles that "there is only one God, . . . that there is a future state of rewards and punishments, [and] that to love God with all thy heart and thy neighbor as thyself is the sum of religion," formulations all derived from the primordium of nature.[39] The primordial qualities of these doctrinal statements are made explicit in the Declaration of Independence, which specifically identifies God as "Nature's God" and describes the moral order as an endowment from this God and thus "unalienable." But this theme became even more explicit in Jefferson's earlier draft of the Declaration, which read, "We hold these truths to be sacred & undeniable; that all men are created equal & independent, that from that equal creation they derive rights inherent & inalienable."[40] The rights to life, liberty, and the pursuit of happiness were therefore, to borrow a phrase from the Puritan John Robinson, "not new, but old truths renewed . . . and not one day nor hour younger, in the nature and form of it" than the original creation.

To be sure, this effort to push behind primitive Christianity to the original creation was the difference that made all the difference, theologically, between Puritanism and the Enlightenment. For in spite of the primordial qualities of Enlightenment thought, this new theology was not concerned with restoring finite forms and structures, as had been the case with Puritanism. It rather was an effort to go behind the finite forms and structures to the one universal reality that all people could confess—the sovereignty and providence of God.

---

[39] Thomas Jefferson (personal letter), "To Benjamin Waterhouse, June 26, 1822," in *Jefferson's Extracts from the Gospels: The Philosophy of Jesus and The Life and Morals of Jesus*, ed. Dickinson W. Adams (Princeton: Princeton University Press, 1983), 404.

[40] Thomas Jefferson, "Original Rough Draught" of the Declaration of Independence, in *The Papers of Thomas Jefferson*, ed. Julian P. Boyd (Princeton: Princeton University Press, 1950), 1:423.

Even the early Mormons, who sometimes despaired of their treatment at the hands of the United States government, readily proclaimed their faith in the primal and therefore universal dimensions of the US Constitution. Parley P. Pratt, one of the original Twelve Apostles of the Latter-day Saints who suffered brutal imprisonment in Missouri for his faith, unequivocally affirmed:

> In the principles of the Constitution formed by our fathers . . . there is no difficulty, that is, in the laws and instruments themselves. They embrace eternal truths, principles of eternal liberty, not the principles of one peculiar country, or the sectional interest of any particular people, but the great, fundamental, eternal principles of liberty to rational beings.[41]

In one sense, the theology of the Enlightenment was similar to the theology of Luther, for it stripped away human intermediaries between human beings, affirming the sovereignty of the Creator and the finitude of the creation. And, like Luther, the Enlightenment thinkers taught that God could be depicted and known through a variety of theological formulations, and that those formulations should never be taken as absolute or mistaken for God himself. This is what Sidney Mead meant when he wrote that the Enlightenment thinkers "plumbed for the universal which is dressed and disguised in the particularities of doctrine and practice that distinguish one sect from another."[42]

This kind of theology held profound implications, for the effort to transcend finite forms and symbols resulted in the simultaneous transcendence of both civil dissent and civil religion. Civil dissent was transcended because, at least in theory, all particular finite forms would be permitted. And civil religion was transcended because no particular finite form would be regarded as absolute. Henceforth the glue that would bind this commonwealth together would not be common agreement on a particular set of theological assertions, as with the Puritans, but rather common

---

[41] Parley P. Pratt, "Declaration of Independence—Constitution of the United States," in *Journal of Discourses* (Liverpool, 1854), 1:139.

[42] Sidney E. Mead, *The Nation with the Soul of a Church* (New York: Harper and Row, 1975), 60.

agreement on the one assertion that all theological assertions are equally finite but also equally viable ways of plumbing for the universal.

V

Once again, the radical differences between Puritan and Enlightenment theological content should not obscure the fact that Puritans and Enlightenment thinkers shared a common theological method—the quest for the primordium. And it was at least partly due to this common method, and partly due to the pervasiveness of the Puritan heritage to which virtually all Americans of the time more or less had fallen heir, that the primordium of the primitive church and the primordium of nature could become so thoroughly amalgamated in the thinking of so many in this period. One of the earliest to amalgamate these two categories was John Wise. In *Vindication of the Government of the New England Churches* (1717), Wise argued first that "the Churches in New-England; and the Primitive Churches are Eminently parallel in their Government." But if the Congregational government preserved the original Christian primordium, it also preserved the "Original State and Liberty of Mankind . . . found peculiarly in the Light of Nature."[43] Or again, Jefferson provides a case in point. Like the humanist Colet 250 years earlier, Jefferson was convinced that the first age of the Christian faith had repristinated successfully the virtues of the primordium of nature. Thus, he said, "I adhere to the principles of the first age; and consider all subsequent innovations as corruptions of his religion, having no foundation in what came from him [Jesus]." Or again, in 1821, Jefferson wrote to Timothy Pickering that

> when . . . we shall have unlearned everything which has been taught since his day, and got back to the pure and simple doctrines he inculcated, we shall then be truly and worthily his disciples; and my opinion is that if nothing had ever been added to what flowed purely from his lips, the whole world would at this day have been Christian.

[43] John Wise, *A Vindication of the Government of New England Churches* (Boston, 1717), 10, 30. See Catherine Albanese, *Sons of the Fathers: Civil Religion in the American Revolution* (Philadelphia: Temple University Press, 1976), 35–36.

But Jefferson was not without hope. Quite to the contrary, he was "happy in the prospect of a restoration of primitive Christianity," though he admitted that he "must leave to younger Athletes to encounter and lop off the false branches which have been engrafted into it by the mythologists of the middle and modern ages."[44] And significantly, this restoration of primitive Christianity would take place in nature's nation, under the auspices of nature's God, and its theology would be nature's as well. Daniel Boorstin was right in observing that Jefferson "came close to making Jesus a Son of Liberty, and a member of the American Philosophical Society."[45]

Similarly, on the Puritan side of things, an Abraham Keteltas could link the primordium of nature, which heralded civic liberties for all people, with the primordium of the Christian church, which heralded the universal, magisterial rule of Jesus Christ. The Revolution, he told his flock in a sermon of 1777, was not only "the cause of the oppressed against the oppressor [and] . . . the cause of liberty against arbitrary power," but was also "the cause of pure and undefiled religion against bigotry, superstition, and human invention . . . [and] the cause of reformation against popery." In an interesting theological paradox, he admonished his parishioners to pray for the time when "universal love and liberty . . . shall prevail" and when "the kingdoms of this world are become the kingdoms of our Lord and his Christ (Rev. 11: 15)."[46]

This amalgamation of Jesus and Eden had taken place within the relatively short span of fifty years. The millennial fervor that had characterized the Great Awakening had possessed a single focus: "the new and most glorious state of God's church on earth," that is, "a new world in a spiritual respect," as Jonathan Edwards aptly put it.[47] But during the next fifty years, while the colonists fought the Battle of Armageddon on three successive fronts—the Great Awakening, the French and Indian War, and

[44] Thomas Jefferson (personal letter), "To Jared Sparks, November 4, 1820"; Jefferson (personal letter), "To Timothy Pickering, February 27, 1821"; and Jefferson (personal letter), "To Benjamin Waterhouse, July 19, 1822," in Adams, *Jefferson's Extracts from the Gospels*, 401, 403, 407.

[45] Boorstin, *Lost World of Thomas Jefferson*, 245.

[46] Abraham Keteltas, "God Arising and Pleading His People's Cause, a sermon preached October 5, 1777" (Newburyport, MA, 1777), 29–32.

[47] Jonathan Edwards, "Some Thoughts Concerning the Present Revival of Religion in New England," in *The Works of President Edwards* (New York: S. Converse, 1830), 4:128–29.

the American Revolution[48]—the God of Nature stole stealthily into their hitherto undefiled and sacrosanct Christian temples, put on Christian garb, and in that disguise began to receive the homage that previously had been reserved for Jesus Christ alone. Many Americans now celebrated the primordium of nature, with its liberties for all people, as a uniquely Christian phenomenon, and Timothy Dwight could proclaim that "this continent will be the principal seat of that new, that peculiar kingdom, which shall be given to the saints of the Most High."[49] Though Dwight never would have admitted it, a significant shift in outlook had taken place: the Most High had become the God of Nature, though dressed in Christian garb, and his saints were US citizens who more and more assumed that they constituted a Christian nation. What was emerging was a new American faith, one that was neither the religious establishment of the Puritans nor the religionless "theology of the Republic" adumbrated during the Revolution. Rather, the new faith was a unique blend of Christ and nature, of the primordium of the early church and the primordium of the creation. It was, in fact, the beginnings of the civil religion Robert Bellah described years ago.[50]

But more to the point, all the elements of this new civil religion were rooted in the common conviction that America had transcended history and had made the ancient primordium contemporary in the new Republic.

As Americans progressively collapsed Christ and nature into a single, common primordium, they increasingly, though not always consciously, infused the open-ended dimensions of Enlightenment thought with implied particularities. In this way, the primordium as judgment on all particular assertions became instead a primordium marked by highly particularized assertions. This clearly was the case as the new civil religion blossomed into full flower in the mid-nineteenth century in the doctrine of Manifest Destiny. John L. O'Sullivan, who helped popularize the notion in the 1840s with reference to the Oregon Territory, virtually relegated to oblivion any historical tradition that might have cautioned restraint: "We

---

[48] See Nathan O. Hatch, "The Origins of Civil Millennialism in America: New England Clergymen, War with France, and the Revolution," *William and Mary Quarterly* 31 (1974): 407–30.

[49] Timothy Dwight, "A Valedictory Address . . . at Yale College, July 25, 1776" (New Haven, 1776), 521.

[50] Robert N. Bellah, "Civil Religion in America," *Daedalus* 96 (Winter 1967): 1–21; and Bellah, *The Broken Covenant: American Civil Religion in Time of Trial* (New York: Seabury, 1975).

have a still better title than any that can ever be constructed out of all these antiquated materials of old black-letter international law. Away, away with all these cobweb tissues of rights of discovery, exploration, settlement, continuity, &c."[51] Instead of looking to the legal traditions of a profane history to adjudicate the claim, O'Sullivan identified the interests of the Republic with a sacred dimension that stood completely outside the bounds of profane history.

> Our Claim is by the right of our manifest destiny to overspread and to possess the whole of the continent which Providence has given for the development of the great experiment of liberty and federative self-government entrusted to us. It is a right such as that of the tree in the space of air and earth suitable for the full expansion of its principle and destiny of growth—such as that of the stream to the channel required for the still accumulating volume of its flow.[52]

Clearly, America's destiny was "manifest" because it was rooted in the primordium rather than in the "cobweb tissues" of finite human history.

VI

It is hardly surprising that the Puritan legacy and the Enlightenment perspective could amalgamate so thoroughly in the revolutionary and early national periods. For while these two traditions differed profoundly at the level of theological *content*, at the level of theological *method* they both were committed to restoring pure beginnings. The Christian Humanists had heralded the reality of the restoration many years before, but that reality still had not been realized in a broad and massive sense in the Western Christian world. Countless thousands of Western Christians had longed to view, in their lifetimes, a restoration of that pure and primal age but to no avail.

But all those countless thousands of Christians had not lived to view the American Revolution. From the perspective of many who lived during

---

[51] *New York Morning News*, December 27, 1845, cited in Conrad Cherry, ed., *God's New Israel: Religious Interpretations of American Destiny* (Englewood Cliffs, NJ: Prentice Hall, 1971), 128.

[52] Cherry, *God's New Israel*, 129.

and following the Revolution, that event was the infinitely grand, cosmic battle that, now at last in these latter days, had begun the process of making the primordium contemporary. "Behold, all things have become new" was the common sentiment. And so they had. Americans of that time had simply never known freedom to this extent. But what was new also was what was old, for the open-ended quality of life that characterized the new nation appeared to be the same open-ended quality of life that had characterized the first man and the first woman in the Garden.

Because the experience was both new and old at one and the same time, it could be conceptualized in either primordial or millennial terms. The quest for the millennium during the revolutionary period and thereafter, so well understood by historians, was often a quest for the primordium. Advocates of the millennial age frequently derived their vision from the rich panoply of images that filled the mythic accounts of the golden age (or golden ages) that existed when the gods created the cosmos (or its functional equivalent). In other words, the millennium typically constituted a restoration of the primordium, and all profane history that had intervened between these two end times was obscured, ignored, and transcended. As Crevecoeur said, this American was a new man. But he also was a very old man. And it is this old man who, by and large, has failed to receive the attention from historians that he deserves.

Within this early nineteenth-century context, a host of new religious movements, all given to the celebration of the ancient primordium, rapidly gained popularity in the young Republic. Among these new movements were Shakers, Baptists, Disciples of Christ, Mormons, and utopian communes such as Oneida and Hopedale. Significantly, all these movements prospered during the years following the Revolution when the primordial/millennial fervor was at its height. It is certainly worth considering whether William Warren Sweet's thesis—that those churches that prospered on the frontier were those churches that creatively followed the frontier—might profitably stand some emendation to the effect that those churches that prospered in the westward-moving, primordial nation were those churches that depicted most vividly the ancient primordium to a primordial people.

Precisely here lies the significance of so many of the denominations that first emerged in the early years of the new American nation: most were fundamentally American in that they drank deeply of the well-springs of restoration thought at those times when the primordial waters washed over the emerging American soul and shaped the American character. The Puritans, of course, indelibly stamped the American character during the early colonial period and etched there a deep and abiding concern for pure beginnings. Reinhold Niebuhr in fact observed that "the New England conception of our American virtue began as the belief that the church which had been established on our soil was purer than any church of Christendom."[53] And then, when the nation was born, the Jeffersonian Enlightenment, first, and then the Scottish Common Sense tradition deposited fresh and lasting layers of primitivist thought on the already powerful Puritan concern for first times. When one adds to all this the radical newness of the American political experiment and the millennial fervor that characterized so many Americans at that time, one has the key ingredients that contributed to a profound sense of history-lessness in the early national period.

The point is simply this: Mormons and "Christians" came to birth—and Baptists experienced significant growth and popularity—precisely when numerous factors converged to make the appeal to pure beginnings a powerful dimension of American popular culture. In this context, and in the face of a bewildering array of Christian denominations, sectarians found that the appeal to pure beginnings was the surest way to cut through the confusion of religious pluralism. To proclaim one's own sect a reproduction of the ancient, apostolic order was to anoint one's sect the one, true church while all others were merely historic, tradition laden, and therefore false. Further, while we can adduce various reasons for the popularity of each of these movements, one point we surely must consider is that each reflected primordial concerns to a primordial people and even offered the hope of hastening the realization of America's promise in a microcosmic community of faith. In this sense, these three groups were fundamentally unlike the old, established churches of Europe that

---

[53] Reinhold Niebuhr, *The Irony of American History* (New York: Charles Scribner's Sons, 1954), 25.

had been imported to America's shores. Those older denominations were America's adopted children who, by living in the parent's house for many years, gradually took on the parent's traits. But Mormons and "Christians" were genetic children, nurtured in the parent's womb, born in the parent's house, and inheriting the spiritual and mental characteristics of the one who gave them birth. Baptists, while adopted, were adopted in early childhood and, further, were the natural children of close relatives. Thus they absorbed the spiritual characteristics of their foster parent with little difficulty. For these reasons, Baptists, Mormons, and "Christians" are significant, in a way that many other denominations are not, for what they can tell us about the shape and texture of American life and culture in the early national period. We have focused primarily on these three groups precisely because they offer such telling clues to the character of the American people.

VII

Beyond the question of parent-child relations, however, lies the more fundamental issue of the interaction between restoration and liberty in the American experience. The primitivism embraced by the founders of this Republic was broad and open-ended, avoiding the particular in the interest of what seemed to them the universal. In this conceptual milieu, liberty would flourish. But time and again, zealots of one faith or another would particularize and even absolutize the primordium, elevating one conception of the primordium to standard and authoritative status. On these terms, liberty was possible only for those who conformed themselves to the particularized and absolutized norm.

At times American patriots, totally identifying the primal state of things with America itself, Americanized the primordium. Here, for example, was Thomas Paine, who supposed that by viewing the birth of the nation he also was gazing on the creation, or John L. O'Sullivan who so Americanized the primordium that neither history nor law had any bearing on territorial claims. As a result of such thinking, the British lost Oregon, but far more disastrous were the losses in life and property sustained by Mexicans, Native Americans, and Blacks. While virtually identifying the new American nation with the primordium, primitivists in this nation consigned Mexicans, native people, and Blacks to the finite sphere of human history and proceeded to extinguish not only their liberties but, in many instances, their lives.

Undeniably the issue here was cultural pluralism, and it was ironic that a nation committed to pluralism within its own boundaries, at least for people of light skin, would resist so strenuously the ways and traditions of people of color and in nearby regions. Even more ironic was the fact that primordial theology, employed by the founders to secure liberty, could be particularized so that those not sharing in the "primal particularities" were simply excluded from the blessings of freedom.

In this tendency, however, the nation was not unique, for these patterns were repeated over again by numerous religious groups in America, themselves struggling with the issue of pluralism. For some, such as Puritans and Mormons, identifying themselves with the ancient order of things was the most effective way of blunting the religious legitimacy of others. For others, such as Roger Williams, the early Baptists, and the early "Christians," the appeal to pure beginnings was the very basis for their claim to religious liberty, both for themselves and for others. But once again, irony intruded, and both Baptists and "Christians" finally particularized and absolutized the primordium on their own terms and came to use the primitive church ideal not so much to promote freedom as to define the bounds of the one true church.

Not only have sectarians employed the restoration theme to legitimate their traditions, but patriots have employed the theme to legitimate the nation and/or its ideals. Thus, when Alexander Campbell's followers absolutized their version of the primordium, Campbell began looking more to Protestant America and less to his primitive church as the last, best hope for unity in freedom and diversity. So well rooted was the restoration perspective in the American experience that with the advent of the Civil War, even Southern clerics such as Benjamin M. Palmer employed primitivism to deny freedom to Blacks and to defend both slavery and the Confederacy.

Even in twentieth-century US politics, the restoration theme has persisted with extraordinary vitality. Several presidents constructed foreign policies around its presuppositions, most notably Woodrow Wilson and

Ronald Reagan, and two noted scholars implicitly have described the genius of American ideals in terms of the restoration sentiment. Here, on the one hand, Sidney E. Mead appeals to first times to describe the "theology of the Republic," which, he contends, always stands in judgment on the particular contents of American culture.[54] In this, Mead's vision recalls the prophetic sort of primitivism employed by Roger Williams and Thomas Jefferson. On the other hand, Allan Bloom, in his attempt to reopen the American mind, draws unsparingly on the restoration sentiment but in a way radically different from Mead's use of the theme.[55] Like John Cotton, John L. O'Sullivan, and Benjamin Palmer, Bloom absolutizes particular manifestations of the primordium and, in the interest of opening the mind, ironically provides for its closing. In this, Bloom strikingly illustrates the illusions that the restoration sentiment often generates.

Clearly, the restoration ideal has not been the exclusive property of a few eccentric Christian sects. It has informed the fundamental outlook of preachers and presidents, of soldiers and scholars. Indeed, the restoration perspective has been a central feature of American life and thought from the earliest Puritan settlements, and now continues to exercise a profound influence on the thinking and behavior of the American people. Nowhere can the effect of this perspective be discerned more clearly than in the bounds it has set—and continues to set—on human freedom.

[54] Mead, *Nation with the Soul of a Church*, esp. 48–77; and Mead, *The Old Religion in the Brave New World* (Berkeley: University of California Press, 1977), 157.

[55] Allan Bloom, *The Closing of the American Mind: How Higher Education Has Failed Democracy and Impoverished the Souls of Today's Students* (New York: Simon and Schuster, 1987).

WHY RESTORATIONISTS DON'T FIT THE EVANGELICAL MOLD

F or the most part, American Protestants on both sides of the aisle—evangelicals as well as mainline Protestants—have little or no comprehension of the meaning of the "restoration vision." Whether one employs the term "restorationism" or "primitivism," most find the very concept foreign if not incomprehensible, eccentric, and odd.

Yet there have always existed in American religious life communities of faith that can only be described as restorationist. Though rooted in the Protestant Reformation, these people generally have denied that they were Protestants at all, claiming instead the more universal label of "Christian." And when American Protestantism fractured into modernism and fundamentalism as the twentieth century dawned, restorationists often refused to identify themselves with either camp. Instead, they were loyal to what they perceived as the most ancient forms of Christian faith and practice reflected in Christian Scripture. From their perspective, liberals and evangelicals alike had courted the world's favor, and restorationists therefore judged them both as severely compromised versions of the Christian faith and, in many ways, mirror images of one another.

Mainline Protestants, Evangelicals, and the "Restoration Vision"

What might we say of the mainline Protestant assessment of the restoration vision? The noted Methodist churchman and historian Albert Outler typified that assessment when he chanced to witness, some years ago, on a church building in Sweetwater, Texas, a cornerstone that read,

THE CHURCH OF CHRIST
FOUNDED AT JERUSALEM
A.D. 33
ORGANIZED IN SWEETWATER
A.D. 1882
THIS BUILDING ERECTED, 1907

Outler was dumbfounded. The following summer, he shared this story with friends at the Third World Conference of Faith and Order in Lund, Sweden, but the story drew only "quizzical smiles and, occasionally, polite incredulity."

Over the next several years, Outler repeatedly told his wife about this curious stone, but she responded with utter disbelief. Finally, Outler determined to show her the evidence. The two of them made the two hundred–mile trek west from Dallas to Sweetwater, only to discover that the old building with the curious cornerstone was gone. A new building now stood several miles away, but the old cornerstone was nowhere to be found. Increasingly desperate to show his wife the hard, tangible evidence for this implausible artifact, Outler located the minister and politely asked him what had happened to the stone. A majority in the church, the minister explained, did not wish the old stone in the new building, and the stone now rested in the yard of the local stone mason. Delighted, Outler located the stone, photographed it from every possible angle, then arranged for a flat bed truck to haul the stone from Sweetwater to the university museum at Texas Christian University in Fort Worth, just in case, as Outler explained, "posterity is ever interested."[1]

---

[1] Albert Outler, "Church History by the Cube," *Mission Journal* 20 (Mar. 1987): 30–31.

Though this stone reflects a worldview that characterizes all restorationist traditions to one degree or another, Outler's response of disbelief that such a stone and such a perspective could exist typifies the fundamental failure of mainline Protestants to comprehend what the restoration vision is all about.

One might think that evangelicals understand the restoration ideal better than do their counterparts in mainline Protestantism, but that plainly is not the case. For many years, I indulged myself in the supposition that modern evangelicals bear a strong and special kinship to restorationists. I imagined this was true since evangelicals share with restorationists an intense allegiance to the Bible as the one and only source of Christian truth, and especially since so many evangelical historians have claimed Churches of Christ, Mennonites, and other restorationist traditions as part of the evangelical alliance.[2]

Recently, however, I determined to rethink my assumptions regarding the relation between evangelicals and restorationists. I began that process by reflecting on the history of my own tradition, the Churches of Christ. Before we explore that relationship in the context of the Churches of Christ, a brief introduction to the history of that tradition is in order.

Born on the American frontier in the early nineteenth century, the Churches of Christ were originally part of a wide-ranging movement that sought to unify all Christians by appealing to the Bible alone and to the simplicity and the ethical power of the early Christian communities. In those early years, they answered to the label "Churches of Christ" but also to the terms "Disciples of Christ" and "Christian Churches."

In that founding period, for leadership they looked especially to two men: Barton W. Stone and Alexander Campbell. In many ways, Stone bore the earmarks of a genuine evangelical. A child of the revivals, he stood in debt to the Great Awakening in several ways and then, in 1801, played a key role in the Cane Ridge Revival that helped ignite the Second Great Awakening. He fraternized with the evangelical denominations and recognized their members as brothers and sisters in Christ. And yet Stone was

---

[2]See George Marsden, *Understanding Fundamentalism and Evangelicalism* (Grand Rapids: Eerdmans, 1991), 5; and James Davidson Hunter, "Operationalizing Evangelicalism: A Review, Critique & Proposal," *Sociological Analysis* 42 (1981): 370.

also profoundly restorationist, even countercultural, in orientation. At the heart of his thought stood a New Testament ethic, which he grounded in the biblical promise that the kingdom of God would finally triumph over all the world. Stone took this promise very seriously and believed this ethic could provide the foundation on which all Christians could unite.

Equally ecumenical but less focused on ethics than was Stone, Alexander Campbell believed unity could best be achieved through a progressive, rational reconstruction of the ancient Christian church, based on an almost scientific reading of the biblical text. For a variety of reasons, Campbell's influence slowly eclipsed that of Stone beginning in 1823. Then, in 1832, the Stone and Campbell movements joined forces and soon became the largest indigenous Christian movement in the United States.

By the late nineteenth century, however, this erstwhile ecumenical movement finally divided into two distinct denominations: Disciples of Christ and Churches of Christ. The Disciples carried Campbell's progressive and ecumenical spirit into the twentieth century and finally rejected the restoration vision altogether. At the same time, the Churches of Christ coalesced around the other side of the nineteenth-century platform: the restoration of the ancient Christian faith/church. For them, restoration embodied not only the rational reconstruction of the ancient Christian church, an emphasis they inherited from Campbell, but also a countercultural commitment to biblical ethics, an emphasis they inherited from Barton W. Stone.[3]

This was the tradition in which I was raised and the tradition to which I turned my attention as I began to reflect on the possible relation between evangelicalism and the restorationist heritage.

I began my reflections by reminding myself that for most of my lifetime, Churches of Christ have seldom fraternized with any of the organizations one normally associates with the evangelical world. They have

---

[3] There are several texts that trace the history of this tradition. See Earl Irvin West's four volume *Search for the Ancient Order* (vol. 1: Nashville: *Gospel Advocate* Co., 1964; vol. 2: Religious Book Service, 1950; vol. 3: Religious Book Service, 1979; vol. 4: Religious Book Service, 1987); Robert Hooper's *A Distinct People: A History of the Churches of Christ in the Twentieth Century* (West Monroe, LA: Howard Publishing, 1993); LeRoy Garrett's *The Stone-Campbell Movement: An Anecdotal History of Three Churches*, rev. ed. (Joplin, MO: College Press, 1994); and Richard Hughes's *Reviving the Ancient Faith: The Story of Churches of Christ in America* (Grand Rapids: Eerdmans, 1996; and Abilene, TX: Abilene Christian University Press, 2008).

never sustained a connection to the National Association of Evangelicals and, until recently, none of the dozen or so colleges related to Churches of Christ has ever belonged to the Council for Christian Colleges and Universities.[4] The truth is, in my lifetime, the formal ties that might have connected Churches of Christ to the evangelical world have been virtually nonexistent.

With that in mind, I began reading again George Marsden's book, *Understanding Fundamentalism and Evangelicalism.* I thought it would help if I compared the history of Churches of Christ to Marsden's description of evangelicals at every significant point. Marsden observed first of all that evangelicals trace their American roots to the great revivals of Whitefield, Finney, Moody, Sunday, and Graham.[5] I realized that though I had grown up in Churches of Christ, a denomination Marsden labels "evangelical,"[6] I had never heard of Whitefield, Finney, Moody, or Sunday until I was in graduate school. Until then, I knew little or nothing about the evangelical revivalist tradition.

In that light, I was surprised to find that Marsden identifies Alexander Campbell, one of the nineteenth-century "fathers" of Churches of Christ, as "a revivalist."[7] The truth is, Campbell was not a revivalist in any sense. In fact, Campbell strenuously opposed most of the revivals of his age on the grounds that they substituted emotion for the plain Word of God.

If Campbell was a revivalist, one might rightly expect to find favorable references to Charles Finney in Campbell's *Millennial Harbinger,* which he edited for virtually the duration of Finney's career. Yet, for more than thirty years, only three references appear, and none of them were favorable. Two of the three, in fact, chided Finney on explicitly restorationist grounds: he had substituted "the anxious bench" for baptism and replaced the ancient gospel with his "new measures."[8]

---

[4] Abilene Christian University became the first educational institution related to Churches of Christ to join the Council for Christian Colleges and Universities, having done so on July 26, 1995.

[5] Marsden, *Understanding Fundamentalism and Evangelicalism,* 2.

[6] Marsden, *Understanding Fundamentalism and Evangelicalism,* 5.

[7] Marsden, *Understanding Fundamentalism and Evangelicalism,* 67.

[8] Alexander Campbell, "Elder Finney's Substitute for Baptism," *MH* (Mar. 1841): 141; and Discipulus, "Charles G. Finney," *MH* (Dec. 1841): 591–93.

Campbell, in fact, thought revivals offered little more than "the machinery of 'getting religion' by animal excitement." He complained that

> the doctrine of American Revivals, so rife since the year 1734, has made Methodists of all the Protestants in America, except a few genteel Episcopalians, whose love of good breeding, more than their knowledge of the gospel, has prevented them from screaming, swooning, fainting, jerking, laughing, shouting, under "the influence of the Holy Ghost," as they express it.

Further, Campbell claimed that biblical illiteracy abounded especially among those caught up in the revivals. "I should not be believed," he wrote, "were I to tell half of what I know of the ignorance of the Book in this religious, enthusiastic, and fanatical population."[9]

Again, Marsden notes that three traditions that helped give shape to twentieth-century evangelicalism—dispensationalism, holiness, and pentecostalism—all revered Dwight Moody's lieutenant, Reuben Torrey.[10] What, then, of Churches of Christ? Did they revere Torrey as well? To answer that question, I searched the index to the most powerful paper circulated among Churches of Christ in those years, the *Gospel Advocate*, published in Nashville, Tennessee. Torrey's name never appears.

Or again, Marsden notes that "during the 1950s and 1960s the simplest . . . definition of an evangelical . . . was 'anyone who likes Billy Graham.'"[11] Yet, in my memory, Churches of Christ never much liked Billy Graham for essentially the same reasons Alexander Campbell never much liked Charles Finney. Indeed, the indexes to a variety of journals circulated among Churches of Christ for the past forty years reveal almost no references to Graham at all, and the few that did appear were largely negative.[12]

Most telling of all, Marsden observes that in the evangelical world, "denominational affiliation was ultimately a matter of free choice. . . . If you did not like one church, you could simply leave and go to the one down the

---

[9] Campbell, "Letter to Elder William Jones. No. VI.," *MH* (Aug. 1835): 355.

[10] Marsden, *Understanding Fundamentalism and Evangelicalism*, 43–44.

[11] Marsden, *Understanding Fundamentalism and Evangelicalism*, 6.

[12] See Fred B. Walker, "Billy Graham in the Nation's Capital," *GA* 94 (Feb. 28, 1952): 130–31; and G. K. Wallace, "'My Answer,'" *GA* 117 (Sep. 4, 1975): 565–66.

street."[13] Nothing could be more foreign to the authentically restorationist mind, and certainly nothing could be more foreign to Churches of Christ, at least until recent years.

Restorationists and Evangelicals: The Basic Difference

There are many points at which one might compare restorationists and especially Churches of Christ with the broad evangelical tradition. One might explore worship styles, lifestyles, theology, or a host of other categories. In fact, in another essay, I have compared Churches of Christ with evangelicals from a theological perspective.[14] The present essay, however, focuses on ethics, politics, and culture since, in my view, the genius of the restoration vision finally has more to do with ethics than with theology.

Obviously, the comparisons I have already drawn are not definitive. Instead, they serve as clues to a deeper and wider gulf that separates restorationists from evangelicals. Navigation of that gulf requires a brief assessment of the cultural and political meaning of evangelicalism. We begin with John Calvin, clearly a sixteenth-century hero for most American evangelicals. Though a restorationist of sorts who liked to compare "the ancient church" with what he viewed as Catholic corruptions,[15] Calvin concerned himself chiefly with the sovereignty of God, which he longed to impose over all the earth, beginning with Geneva.

Other Reformed leaders sounded the same refrain. Martin Bucer, for example, dedicated his *De Regno Christi* to Edward VI, King of England, in 1550. Also a restorationist of sorts, Bucer argued in that book that England could become the kingdom of Christ only by restoring the faith and practice of the ancient church. Significantly, however, Bucer defined the ancient church in explicitly Constantinian terms. He described "the period of Constantine and the emperors who followed him" as a period in which "nothing [was] wanting . . . in regard to the happiness of the Church of Christ" and a period "when churches were raised up all over the world

---

[13] Marsden, *Understanding Fundamentalism and Evangelicalism*, 17 and 81.

[14] Richard T. Hughes, "Are Restorationists Evangelicals?" in *The Variety of American Evangelicalism*, ed. Donald Dayton and Robert K. Johnston (Knoxville: University of Tennessee Press, 1991), 109–34.

[15] See John Calvin, "Reply to Sadoleto" (1540), in Hans J. Hillerbrand, *The Protestant Reformation* (New York: Harper and Row, 1968), 154–72.

and flourished in exceptional piety."[16] In this way, Calvin, Bucer, and virtually all Reformed theologians perpetuated the old medieval vision of Christendom, though now in Protestant guise.

Joel Carpenter cast further light on this issue when he wrote that American fundamentalists also were restorationists of sorts. They, too, valued both Scripture and the Christian past. But the past they valued most was not the past of the first Christian age but rather "the past since the Protestant Reformation." Fundamentalists "assumed that primitive Christianity had already been restored at the Reformation and revived several times since then. Their task, then, was not to recover it, but to defend, cultivate, and promote it."[17] Carpenter should have added that the slice of the Reformation that fundamentalists valued most was the magisterial reform of Luther, Calvin, and Zwingli.

This is the context in which we must understand the genius of American evangelicalism: most evangelicals have sought "to defend, cultivate, and promote" the heritage of the magisterial reformation, to Christianize the culture in which they live, and to bring it under the sovereign sway of a distinctly Protestant God. There have been exceptions to this pattern, to be sure. J. Gresham Machen, for example, never fit this mold, as Darryl Hart has pointed out.[18] For the most part, however, evangelicals have never fully abandoned the old Constantinian model, even in the United States. Here one finds the meaning of the title Sidney Mead gave to one of his books: *The Old Religion in the Brave New World.*[19]

Inescapably, this was the cultural significance of virtually all the revivals to which evangelicals trace their identity. In this context, the Second Great Awakening is perhaps the most notable case in point. When evangelical Protestants realized the full implications of the First Amendment to

[16] Martin Bucer, "De Regno Christi," in *The Library of Christian Classics*, vol. 19: *Melanchthon and Bucer*, ed. Wilhelm Pauck (Philadelphia: Westminster Press, 1969), 209.

[17] Joel Carpenter, "Contending for the Faith Once Delivered: Primitivist Impulses in American Fundamentalism," in *The American Quest for the Primitive Church*, ed. Richard T. Hughes (Urbana: University of Illinois Press, 1988), 101.

[18] Darryl Hart, "J. Gresham Machen, Confessional Presbyterianism, and the History of Twentieth-Century Protestantism," in *Re-Forming the Center: American Protestantism, 1900 to the Present*, ed. Douglas Jacobsen and William Vance Trollinger (Grand Rapids: Eerdmans, 1998), 129-49.

[19] Sidney E. Mead, *The Old Religion in the Brave New World: Reflections on the Relation between Christendom and the Republic* (Berkeley: University of California Press, 1977).

the Constitution, they sought to create through persuasion what they no longer could achieve through coercion or force of law, namely, a Protestant America. Further, since the nation's Founders sought to undermine all religious establishments, many evangelicals attacked those Founders as "infidels" whose alleged immorality would inevitably corrupt the nation. In this way, "a great tidal wave of revivalism" virtually drowned the "infidelity" that characterized the nation's founding, as Sidney Mead has pointed out time and again.[20]

Marsden confirms Mead's assessment of these events, but from a distinctly evangelical point of view. Given the nature of its founding, Marsden writes, one might expect that America might well "have adopted a genial democratic humanism, freed from explicitly Christian dogmas and institutions." However,

> the fact that America had not in the nineteenth century followed the course set in the eighteenth by leaders like Franklin and Jefferson was due largely to vigorous evangelical enterprise. The United States had not drifted religiously during the nineteenth century. It had been guided, even driven, by resourceful evangelical leaders who effectively channeled the powers of revivals and voluntary religious organizations to counter the forces of purely secular change.[21]

Those revivals were so successful that Robert Baird, in his 1856 celebration of evangelical Protestantism in America, could describe the United States as "a Protestant empire" and "the most powerful of all Protestant kingdoms."[22] And Marsden concedes that by the time of the Gilded Age, "a Protestant version of the medieval ideal of 'Christendom' still prevailed."[23]

This is the context that illumines the cultural meaning of fundamentalism in the early twentieth century. If fundamentalists were evangelicals

---

[20] Sidney E. Mead, *The Lively Experiment* (New York: Harper and Row, 1963), 53; and *The Nation with the Soul of a Church* (New York: Harper and Row, 1975), 122.

[21] Marsden, *Understanding Fundamentalism and Evangelicalism*, 11–12.

[22] Robert Baird, *Religion in America, with Notices of the Unevangelical Denominations* (New York: Harper and Brothers, 1856), 32.

[23] Marsden, *Understanding Fundamentalism and Evangelicalism*, 10.

who were angry about something, as Jerry Falwell likes to suggest,[24] they were angry precisely because their long-standing domination of American culture was rapidly slipping away as the culture of modernism gained momentum.

This fact, in turn, sheds considerable light on the cultural meaning of the dispensational eschatology that most fundamentalists adopted in those years. Though there were exceptions, most evangelicals prior to the late nineteenth century had proclaimed a robust and highly optimistic *post-millennial* eschatology. America, they believed, was a Protestant empire whose goodness and righteousness would hasten the millennial dawn. Indeed, this conviction had prevailed among American evangelicals for at least 150 years, from the Great Awakening to the close of the nineteenth century. One can only conclude that postmillennial optimism lay at the very heart of American evangelicalism and grew from their long-standing commitment to Constantinian assumptions and their own domination of American life and culture.

Then, suddenly, evangelicals made a radical about-face. They abandoned their optimistic, postmillennial faith and adopted instead its opposite: dispensational premillennialism. Why this sudden change? Clearly, the newfound premillennial theology was not central to historic evangelical thought. Rather it served as a weapon of last resort for fundamentalists who feared that modernism would erode and perhaps even destroy their evangelical empire.

Put another way, fundamentalists would fight modernism first with the weapon of biblical inerrancy. In case they lost that fight and therefore their control of the culture, they had another weapon close at hand. Jesus himself, they believed, would reimpose his control over American life in the coming millennial age, deal the modernists a stunning defeat, and rule with his evangelical saints for a thousand years. This simply means that postmillennialism and premillennialism were but two different ways of expressing the central concern of fundamentalists: the creation and maintenance of a Protestant civilization in the United States. One way or another, the fundamentalists finally would win.

[24] Marsden, *Understanding Fundamentalism and Evangelicalism*, 1.

If this portrayal of American evangelicalism is even remotely correct, then it contrasts dramatically with the historic concerns of restorationists. At the most basic possible level, restorationists are Christians who yearn to return to the first Christian age. Some seek to recover the Pentecost experience of the Holy Ghost, as Grant Wacker, Edith Blumhofer, and Donald Dayton all have pointed out.[25] Others, like many Holiness denominations, seek to recover ancient norms for holy living. Still others, like Alexander Campbell, seek to reconstruct the forms and structures of the primitive church on a rational and scientific basis. Clearly, restorationists of all sorts are especially susceptible to illusions of innocence,[26] especially when they virtually identify themselves with one or another dimension of the first Christian age.

Yet none of these concerns finally exposes the central core of the restorationist vision. That concern is simply this: the world is hopelessly corrupt, and by aligning itself with the world and its values, the church corrupted itself from an early date. There was, however, a golden age when the church had not yet fallen. The church must therefore embrace the values of that golden age when the world and the church had not yet formed their alliance. If this is the heart and soul of the restoration vision, it means that authentic restorationists are inevitably radical and countercultural Christians. This is why, in my judgment, the genius of the restoration vision is fundamentally ethical, not theological.

In this light, authentic restorationists would find themselves bewildered when Marsden explains how "remarkable" it was that "the specifically Christian aspects" of the American heritage did not erode more than they did under the withering "winds of frankly secular ideologies"[27] issuing from the deistic founders of the American nation. Authentic restorationists would find this concept difficult to comprehend, simply because the

[25] See Edith L. Blumhofer, *Restoring the Faith: The Assemblies of God, Pentecostalism, and American Culture* (Urbana: University of Illinois Press, 1993), esp. 1–9; Grant Wacker, "Playing for Keeps: The Primitivist Impulse in Early Pentecostalism," in *The American Quest for the Primitive Church*, ed. Richard Hughes, 196–219; Wacker, "Searching for Eden with a Satellite Dish: Primitivism, Pragmatism, and the Pentecostal Character," in *The Primitive Church in the Modern World*, ed. Hughes (Urbana: University of Illinois Press, 1995); and Donald W. Dayton, *Theological Roots of Pentecostalism* (Grand Rapids: Francis Asbury Press, 1987).

[26] See, for example, Richard T. Hughes and C. Leonard Allen, *Illusions of Innocence: Protestant Primitivism in America, 1630–1875* (Chicago: University of Chicago Press, 1988).

[27] Marsden, *Understanding Fundamentalism and Evangelicalism*, 11.

notions of a "Christian culture" or a "Christian America" make no sense in the context of the restorationist perspective.

For this reason, authentic restorationists of the early nineteenth century were typically not among those who maligned the founders for their alleged immorality and "infidelity." On the contrary, restorationists of that period generally praised the founders for doing what evangelicals had refused to do, that is, for rejecting all attempts to Christianize, much less to Protestantize, the United States. Those actions made it possible for restorationists to thrive in a way that they could not have thrived in a world controlled by evangelical Christians.

Thus N. Summerbell, a spiritual descendant of New England's Elias Smith, criticized in 1847 those evangelicals who had "branded [Jefferson] with *Infidelity, Deism, and Atheism.*" To Summerbell, Jefferson's "religious views . . . [were] as terrible to religious demagogues as were his political views to political tyrants." And when the followers of Barton Stone in Kentucky appealed to "the inalienable rights of free investigation [and] sober and diligent inquiry after [religious truth]," they implicitly praised the founders and condemned those evangelicals who still held out for a Christian establishment in the United States.[28] This suggests that Nathan Hatch's *Democratization of American Christianity* chronicles not so much the thoughts and deeds of antebellum evangelicals as the thoughts and deeds of antebellum restorationists—though, unfortunately, Hatch never made that distinction.[29]

To put all this another way, the fundamental difference between evangelicals and restorationists is this: evangelicals subscribe to a model of Christian history that emphasizes continuity. Christian history, at least since the Reformation, is a seamless piece of cloth. This is why denominational loyalties have always been of small importance for most evangelicals. After all, evangelical Protestant churches of every stripe reflect the essence of the Reformation perspective. Further, to the extent that evangelicals seek to control the larger culture, they embrace a potential continuity between

---

[28] N. Summerbell, "The Religious Views of Thomas Jefferson," cited in Alexander Campbell, "Christian Union—No. XI. Unitarianism," *MH* (May 1847): 258–59; and J. and J. Gregg, "An Apology for Withdrawing from the Methodist Episcopal Church," *CM* 1 (Dec. 25, 1826): 39–40.

[29] Nathan O. Hatch, *The Democratization of American Christianity* (New Haven: Yale University Press, 1989).

the church and the world, if only the world would submit to the sovereign rule of God.

On the other hand, the restorationist vision points to a radical tear in the fabric of Christian history. There is not the slightest possibility of continuity between the church and the world, and to the extent that Christians have made their peace with the world, the fabric of Christian history is badly torn.

Finally, however, we must acknowledge that evangelical *theology* and a restorationist understanding of what it means to live in the kingdom of God are not mutually exclusive perspectives. Surely there is no inherent tension between justification by grace through faith, for example, and Kingdom ethics. On the other hand, the restoration vision and Constantinian assumptions *are* mutually exclusive understandings. Nonetheless, some evangelicals have employed an unmistakable appeal to the first Christian age, not as a tool for resistance and dissent but rather as the basis for creating a Christian political establishment. New England Puritans are perhaps the most notable case in point.[30] Yet we must remember that when the restoration vision first emerged among England's earliest Puritans, it was nothing if not a tool for countercultural dissent. The Separatist Puritan tradition, eventually spawning Baptists, Quakers, and other radical dissenters who lived out of an unmistakably restorationist agenda, provides ample testimony to that dimension of the Puritan enterprise.

At the same time, living as they did when virtually everyone took for granted the notion of a Christian establishment, it was inevitable that some Puritans—most notably the Non-Separating Congregationalists of New England—would eventually employ the restoration vision as a tool for political power and domination. If there is a moral to this brief excursion, it is simply this: while a powerful dimension of nonconformity and dissent always lies at the heart of the restoration vision, restorationists can always employ that vision for precisely the opposite ends. When restorationists behave in this way, however, they have turned their backs on the genius of the vision they have claimed.

---

[30] See Dwight Bozeman, *To Live Ancient Lives: The Primitivist Dimension of Puritanism* (Chapel Hill: University of North Carolina Press, 1988), who convincingly documents the restorationist theme in the New England Puritan experience.

Scott Appleby reached similar conclusions in a recent paper that explored differences between restorationists and fundamentalists, especially in the context of Islam. Fundamentalists, Appleby argued, always seek political power in the modern world. Though their rhetoric often appeals to the founding age, their chief concern is not to conform themselves to the norms of the founding age, but instead to control the modern world. "They are clearly involved," Appleby wrote, "in constructing a synthesis between" ancient norms and the modern world. Yet the results of their efforts "demonstrate that . . . modernity is setting the terms for religious adaptation." For fundamentalists, therefore, appeals to the founding age are rhetorical, not substantive.

Restorationists, on the other hand, care little about political control over the modern world, but care deeply about individual and social moral transformation that takes its bearings from ancient norms. For this reason, Appleby described authentic restorationism as fundamentally prophetic. Restorationists, he argued, maintain a "prophetic stance toward the very kingdoms and nation-states that the fundamentalists seek to conquer." He therefore finally concluded, "The world . . . [restorationists] seek to restore does not sit easily with the ambition of modern world-conquerors," even when those conquerors are fundamentalists.[31]

Restoration Churches: The Attraction of Evangelicalism

The relation between the restoration and evangelical traditions in America, however, is more complex than I have suggested. The picture I have attempted to paint so far is a picture based on the *beginnings* of restoration traditions, when a vision of the primitive faith, undefiled by the world and its culture, still burned brightly. Such a picture would characterize not only the Churches of Christ, but Puritans, Pietists, Methodists,[32] Baptists, Latter-day Saints, Pentecostals, and a variety of holiness advocates in their earliest years. Though often evangelical in their theologies, all these movements began their careers with a distinctly restorationist orientation.

---

[31] R. Scott Appleby, "Primitivism as an Aspect of Global Fundamentalisms," in *The Primitive Church in the Modern World*, ed. Richard Hughes, 17–33.

[32] Franklin H. Littell argues persuasively for the restorationist dimensions of early Methodism. See Littell, "Assessing the Restoration Ideal," in *The Primitive Church in the Modern World*, ed. Richard Hughes, 55–57.

In America, however, primitivist traditions have found it difficult to retain the passion for the purity of first times and the countercultural posture that passion has engendered. The allure of status and respectability in the larger culture has consistently eroded that commitment. When that commitment wanes, however, to whom can these churches go? To ask that question is to underscore the continued power of the two-party system of American Protestantism. To many participants and observers, there seem to be only two places where restorationists might migrate should they drift from their own roots: mainline Protestantism or evangelicalism. For most primitivists, the mainline is not a serious option. Thus the tendency has been for restorationist churches to act as perpetual feeders for the evangelical establishment as they lose touch with their originating visions. Another way of saying this is that authentically restorationist churches are by definition sectarian. As they move away from their sectarian past and adopt a more respectable "denominational" status, they almost invariably tend to adopt evangelical modes of self-definition. Identification with the evangelical world seems to represent the most viable means of locating themselves amid the limited public options that define the symbolic landscape of American religion.

Examples abound. In the late nineteenth century, American Mennonites began a flirtation with evangelicalism that intensified during the early twentieth century when fundamentalist fervor was at its height. For a time, that flirtation did not run a full course to evangelical absorption, thanks chiefly to the Mennonites' historic emphasis on nonresistance. By the early twenty-first century, however, many Mennonites—and even many Amish in places like Lancaster County, Pennsylvania—moved ever more fully into the evangelical orbit, thanks to the allure of evangelical politics, mediated to them via radio.

Similarly, Pentecostals in their earliest years were distinctly restorationist and radically countercultural, but moved quickly into the evangelical orbit, especially during the middle of the twentieth century. In part, this speedy transition doubtless resulted from the pragmatism that accompanied their primitivism (an unlikely pairing of qualities recently demonstrated by Grant Wacker),[33] and in part it was the result of conscious

---

[33] Wacker, "Searching for Eden with a Satellite Dish."

wooing by the emerging National Association of Evangelicals. One might also argue that Mennonites and Pentecostals alike were seduced by the illusion that fundamentalists were distinctly and inherently countercultural Christians like themselves, when in fact they were not.

There is, perhaps, no better example of the transition from restorationist sect to evangelical denomination than the Churches of Christ to whose story we must now return. Unlike the Mennonites, the Churches of Christ did not have a strong sense of history or an established practice of countercultural pacifism to protect them from full colonization by evangelical ideas and ideals. Unlike Pentecostals, they did not have a distinctive, physically manifested form of piety (like speaking in tongues) to give them pause when considering the homogenizing risks of an alliance with evangelicalism. Yet the Churches of Christ did (and to some extent still do) possess a deeply ingrained suspicion of other churches and parachurches that has kept them from full formal membership within the "evangelical" domain. But these institutional quibbles have had little power to fence off the Churches of Christ either from the evangelical marketplace (books, music, magazines, etc.) or from the person-to-person, congregation-to-congregation migration of evangelical spirituality and political ideology, and over the course of time, Churches of Christ, too, transitioned into the evangelical orbit.

Many factors facilitated that transition. First, there is no question that Campbell taught his followers the value of the restoration vision. Yet, like Calvin, Bucer, and other reformers before him, Campbell was only a "restorationist of sorts." After all, his restoration perspective had far more to do with a scientific reading of the biblical text than it did with the creation of countercultural Christian communities. Indeed, Campbell in many ways was a nineteenth-century evangelical who, especially after 1837, sidled up to the evangelical establishment in his various efforts to promote a Protestant nation.[34]

On the other hand, Churches of Christ especially took their countercultural bearings from Barton W. Stone who combined his vision of

---

[34] See "From Primitive Church to Protestant Nation: The Millennial Odyssey of Alexander Campbell," in Hughes and Allen, *Illusions of Innocence*, 170–87.

primitive Christianity with a distinctly apocalyptic perspective.[35] For Stone, the kingdom of God had expressed itself in the primitive church, which was therefore normative for life, faith, and practice. But the kingdom of God would come again soon in all its fullness. When that event transpired, God would rule over all the earth.

This perspective sounds remarkably like that of fundamentalists and evangelicals of the early twentieth century. Yet there was a difference. For fundamentalists embraced an apocalyptic orientation only when they saw the evangelical domination of American life and culture in jeopardy. For them, affirming the expected triumph of the kingdom of God was another way of saying that evangelical Christians would finally win the culture wars of the time and that modernists inevitably would lose. Stone, however, never sought to dominate the culture. Instead, he consistently rejected the values of the larger culture for the duration of his career. If fundamentalists finally threw their full weight behind a Christian America, Stone rejected the notion of a Christian America and even claimed that the kingdom of God, when it manifested itself in its fullness, would finally subvert the United States along with all other political institutions.[36]

There are two notable measures of Stone's countercultural orientation. First, Stone freed his slaves in the aftermath of the revival, "choosing poverty in good conscience," as he put it, "to all the treasures of the world." Soon, other Kentucky Christians loyal to Stone moved to Ohio, where they also freed their slaves. These events transpired long before most Southerners had seriously considered such a course of action.[37] Second, Stone shared with Mennonites an uncompromising commitment to the principles of pacifism and nonviolence. Stone saw clearly the radical tear in the fabric of history that all restorationists discern. He therefore turned his back on the culture of his age and cast his lot with the kingdom of God, both as it was in the ancient church and as he expected it to be when the fullness of the kingdom of God finally arrived.

---

[35] Apocalyptic in this context should not be confused with premillennial. On this point, see Hughes, *Reviving the Ancient Faith*, 3, 92–93.

[36] Barton W. Stone, "Reflections of Old Age," *CM* 13 (Aug. 1843): 123–26.

[37] Barton W. Stone, *The Biography of Eld. Barton W. Stone* (Cincinnati, 1847), 44; and Joseph Thomas, *The Travels and Gospel Labors of Joseph Thomas* (Winchester, VA, 1812), 56.

David Lipscomb was the great third-generation leader of Churches of Christ, whose influence dominated that tradition from the Civil War to the early twentieth century. Lipscomb reflected Stone's countercultural views almost perfectly. Though a man of some means, he identified with the outcast and the poor, resisted racial discrimination in the context of the church, and refused to vote or fight in wars. More importantly, Lipscomb grounded his countercultural behavior squarely in his apocalyptic orientation that prompted him to confidently expect the final triumph of the kingdom of God and "the complete and final destruction . . . of the last vestige of human governments and institutions."[38] More importantly still, Lipscomb thought these convictions reflected the very "key notes . . . of the Old and New Testaments." Without them, he said, the Bible was "without point of meaning."[39]

In that light, it is hardly surprising that when the *Ecclesiastical Almanac* placed Churches of Christ in the evangelical orbit, Lipscomb called the *Almanac's* report both "false and slanderous."[40] But there can be no doubt that Lipscomb's radical posture declined in popularity among Churches of Christ as the nineteenth century wore on. After all, many took their bearings more from Campbell than they did from Stone. These "Campbellites" defined the restoration vision more as a scientific re-creation of the forms and structures of ancient Christianity than as a re-creation of countercultural communities identified with the kingdom of God. Yet Lipscomb's vision persisted with remarkable strength, especially in Middle Tennessee and the surrounding regions.

Over the course of the twentieth century, however, two cataclysmic events turned Churches of Christ away from whatever countercultural moorings they still had left. The first was the First World War and the enormous pressure the US government exerted on church leaders to abandon their pacifist moorings. Once they complied with those demands, the countercultural posture of Churches of Christ was all but gone. Yet, they still remained separate and apart from the broad evangelical movement in the United States.

---

[38] David Lipscomb, *Civil Government* (Nashville, 1889), 25, 27–28.

[39] Lipscomb, *Civil Government*, 25, 27–28 (cf. 83–84), 96.

[40] Lipscomb, "The Question Settled," *GA* 11 (Mar. 11, 1869): 224.

The second cataclysmic event—and the single most important factor that drove Churches of Christ into the arms of American evangelicals—was the social revolution of the 1960s that challenged many of the values that had defined the United States for generations. It rejected White supremacy in the interest of racial equality. It rejected male dominance in the interest of gender equality. It rejected the economic plunder of the earth in the interest of preserving the planet. And through a massive protest against the Vietnam War, it rejected America's military dominance in the world—something many saw as raw imperialism.

At its core, the social revolution of the 1960s was a massive rejection of the values of "Christian America," values that, for the most part, stood far removed from the teachings of Jesus. But most in Churches of Christ, like most in the evangelical world, typically confused the two. And laboring under that confusion, Churches of Christ made common cause with the broad evangelical movement in their defense of the militaristic and White, male-dominated world of "Christian America."

By the mid-1970s, Churches of Christ had completely abandoned any semblance of the countercultural theology that had defined Barton Stone, David Lipscomb, and so many others in the nineteenth century. Indeed, they had become evangelicals with a vengeance. What Dietrich Bonhoeffer called "cheap grace" increasingly displaced any appeal to the ethics of the kingdom of God. A therapeutic gospel coupled with an emphasis on "family values" now dominated Church of Christ pulpits. Worship often verged on entertainment, and many urban congregations adopted "church growth" strategies that had more in common with the Willow Creek Church in Chicago than with the traditional restoration heritage. In all these ways, Churches of Christ were completing a journey they had begun in the early twentieth century—a journey from restorationist sect to evangelical denomination.

Conclusion

So finally we return to the church in Sweetwater, Texas, and to the cornerstone that so amazed Albert Outler. But we must recall that Outler also took note of the fact that a majority in that congregation wanted a new building without the old stone. To Outler, this was nothing less than "rejection of a tradition of rejecting 'tradition.'"[41] But it was more than that. It also symbolized the fact that this congregation—along with Churches of Christ at large—was slowly turning its back on its restoration heritage. While the cornerstone took its place in a museum in Fort Worth, Texas, many Churches of Christ were taking their place in the American evangelical mosaic.

---

[41] Outler, "Church History by the Cube," 31.

CALLED BY THE UPSIDE-DOWN KINGDOM OF GOD

...rejection of a tradition of rejecting tradition." But it was more than that; it also symbolized the fact that this congregation—along with Churches of Christ at large—was slowly turning its back on its restoration heritage. While the cornerstone took its place in a museum in Fort Worth, Texas, many Churches of Christ were taking their place in the American evangelical mosaic.

How a Teacher Heard the Call of Racial Justice

When it comes to understanding race in this country, I have been a very slow learner all my life.

When Martin Luther King wrote his "Letter from a Birmingham Jail," I was twenty years old and a college student in Arkansas, living not far from the great, defining events of the Civil Rights Movement. But I might as well have been on the moon.

What I remember most about those years is that I remember nothing—nothing at all about the Children's March in Birmingham, nothing at all about the police dogs that attacked them, nothing at all about the high-powered water hoses that took the skin off the young marchers, and nothing at all about the paddy wagons and the jails. I didn't read King's "Letter from a Birmingham Jail." I didn't even know he had written it.

Malcolm X was murdered on my birthday in 1965. I didn't even know who Malcolm was.

The fact is, the Freedom Movement passed me by like a ship in the night.

That failure to listen, that failure to hear, and that failure to see defined my world and everything about my world. It even defined the church-related college I attended from 1961 to 1965. In the context of this essay, the most important thing I can say about that college is that my professors—virtually all of them—had dedicated themselves to the work of shaping character—Christian character—in the lives of their students. There can be no question about the purity of their intentions. Still, they did their work in the context of a highly circumscribed, Whitened world that paid no attention and no regard to people of color.

Today I recognize that failure to listen, that failure to hear as the heart and core of what we often call White privilege. The fact is, I was a privileged college student, preparing for a life of greater privilege than even my parents had known. I was living in a bubble we call the American dream. And it was that bubble—that Whitened, all-encompassing bubble—that rendered Martin Luther King and the Black struggle for social justice irrelevant to my concerns.

Not until 1967 did I begin to wake up to the tragic realities of racial injustice in the United States. What woke me up were the protests and the ferment over race and war at the University of Iowa, where I was a doctoral student. Slowly, I began to see and hear what Black people wanted us to know about our nation, our churches, our schools, and, indeed, about ourselves.

But part of me remained in a stupor.

Fast forward now some forty-five years to 2012 when I participated in a panel discussion at the national meeting of the American Academy of Religion. That panel convened around James Cone's important book on the role White Christians played in lynching Blacks in the United States. That book is titled *The Cross and the Lynching Tree*.

As a White man, I knew I couldn't critique a book on "the lynching tree." So I simply told my story in light of Cone's book. As part of my presentation, I explored the five American myths that I discussed in the first edition of *Myths America Lives By*—that America is a chosen nation, a Christian nation, and an innocent nation; that America is also nature's nation, fully in sync with the natural order of things; and the millennial nation, ushering in a golden age for all humankind.

When I concluded my remarks and took my seat alongside the other panelists, the late James Noel, a professor of African American Christianity and American religion at San Francisco Theological Seminary, leaned over and whispered, "Professor, you left out the most important of all the American myths."

"And what might that be?" I inquired.

"The myth of White supremacy," Noel replied.

My initial response to Noel's assertion underscores the subtle power of the myth of White supremacy, on the one hand, and why so many White Americans would likely reject Noel's claim out of hand, on the other. I had spent years thinking about the Great American Myths. I had taught classes and written books and articles on that subject. And while I acknowledged the persistence of racism in American life, not once had I considered the notion of White supremacy as an idea that has been central to the American mythos. I understood that avowed White supremacists stalked the American landscape, but I had always viewed them as standing on the margins of American life. To suggest that White supremacy was a defining American myth struck me as preposterous.

But as I reflected over many months on what Noel had said, I began to see his point. I began to see that even Whites like me—Whites who strongly reject racist ideology—can escape the power of the White supremacist myth only with extraordinary effort, if at all. That is because assumptions of White supremacy are like the very air we breathe: they surround us, envelope us, and shape us, but do so in ways we seldom discern. Put another way, notions of White supremacy are so embedded into our common culture that most Whites take them for granted, seldom reflecting on their pervasive presence or assessing them for what they are.

I have told this personal story to help us discern the powerful ways that White supremacy routinely undermines our work of building and buttressing character in the lives of our students. If we fail to grasp that power for what it is, we may very well do our work from the confines of a White-washed bubble. If we fail to grasp that power for what it is, we may well indulge ourselves in the illusion that we are working at character formation when, in reality, we merely reinforce in the hearts and minds of our students the very same notions of White supremacy that have shaped us, their teachers. If we fail to grasp that power for what it is, we risk raising up students whose goodness and morality chiefly serve the interests of people who look like them. And if we fail to grasp that power for what it is, we inevitably insulate ourselves and our students from the ethical concerns that stood at the heart of Jesus's life and ministry.

James Noel's comment drove me, in time, to thoroughly revise the first edition of *Myths America Lives By* and to place the myth of White supremacy at the very heart of the American experience, for I finally grasped the truth that Black people have understood for years on end—that the Myth of White Supremacy is, indeed, the primal American myth that informs all the others and, second, that one of the chief functions of the other five myths is to protect and obscure the Myth of White Supremacy, to hide it from our awareness, and to assure us that we remain innocent after all.

When I had finished writing the revised edition, I sent the manuscript out to readers, both Black and White, for comments and suggestions. A White scholar—a friend who resists racism with all his might and whose work I hold in the highest esteem—responded with this comment: "I fear that you may . . . undercut yourself by reaching too much [and] depicting this myth [of White supremacy] as the root problematic myth. . . . It seems somewhat arbitrary to me to give . . . White supremacy a sort of logical priority among the myths." He therefore suggested that I eliminate the contention that White supremacy is the primal myth and argue instead that it merely overlaps and connects with the other American myths.

When I asked several Black scholars to assess my friend's critique, they responded viscerally. They argued with passion that James Noel was right—that the Myth of White Supremacy *is indeed the primal myth* that drives American life and history and that to tell this story in any other way would be to speak untruth.

The radically different responses from the White reader, on the one hand, and the Black readers, on the other, was an epiphany for me and helped me see the other truth that underpins this book: that Blacks and Whites in this country live in two very different worlds—so different, in fact, that most Whites (indeed, most White, Christian scholars) have a difficult time even hearing the Black lament, much less understanding it.

How many White Americans in the mid-nineteenth century, including White Christians, could grasp the truth that Frederick Douglass spoke when in 1852 he asked that searing question: "What, to the American slave, is your Fourth of July?" "I answer," he said, "a day that reveals to him, more than all other days in the year, the gross injustice and cruelty to which he is the constant victim. To him, your celebration is sham; your boasted liberty an unholy license; your national greatness swelling vanity; . . . your shouts of liberty and equality hollow mockery." And how many White Americans in the mid-twentieth century, including White Christians, could even begin to grasp the truth that Malcolm X spoke when he said in 1964, "I don't see any American dream; I see an American nightmare."

If we listen to people of color, we will hear a very different story from the one we typically hear, for people of color know from painful experience that White supremacy is not the exclusive property of marginal groups like the Ku Klux Klan. They know from experience that White supremacy is part of the American DNA.

They know this because they have lived it; but most of us resist their voices because we fear they will tell us truths about ourselves that we do not wish to hear. And so we push back. We mute their voices, we distort them, and we malign them. We have done that to every Black prophet who has arisen in the United States. We did it to Dr. Martin Luther King Jr., whom FBI director J. Edgar Hoover labeled a Communist with the strong support of many White American Christians. We did it to Malcolm X, whom we dismissed as a radical subversive. We did it to Muhammed Ali when he refused to fight in Vietnam. And today we accuse sports figures like Colin Kaepernick of betraying the American flag.

There is perhaps no more powerful example of our failure to hear Black voices than the story of Jeremiah Wright, pastor of Trinity United Church of Christ in Chicago from 1971 to 2008.

In 2008, exactly forty-four years after Malcolm affirmed that he saw only an American nightmare, Wright preached a sermon in which he told the truth about the Black experience in the United States:

> When it came to treating her citizens of African descent fairly,
> America failed. She put them in chains. [She] put them in slave
> quarters, put them on auction blocks, put them in cotton fields,
> put them in inferior schools, put them in substandard hous-
> ing, put them in scientific experiments, put them in the lowest
> paying jobs, put them outside the equal protection of the law,

kept them out of their racist bastions of higher education and locked them into positions of hopelessness and helplessness . . . , and then wants us to sing, "God bless America."

And then Wright said the only words that any White person remembered from that sermon—the only words, in fact, that most media outlets reported. "No, no, no," Wright said. "Not 'God Bless America'; God Damn America!"

The media didn't report on the historical context Wright had developed up to that point. And it didn't present Wright's complete statement, for he went on to say, "God Damn America for treating her citizens as less than human. God Damn America as long as she keeps trying to act like she is God and she is supreme."

That single line—"God damn America as long as she keeps trying to act like she is God and she is supreme"—was the lynchpin for Wright's sermon that morning. His text for that sermon might well have been the very first of the Ten Commandments: "You shall have no other Gods before me." But precious few American Whites—including White Christians—could even begin to grasp that point.

The reaction to Wright's statement among Whites was swift and overwhelming. The issue was not the fact that Wright said "damn" from his pulpit, for the majority of Americans had no problem with the judicious use of that word. The issue was the fact that Jeremiah Wright, a Black man, had summoned divine judgment on White America. And Wright made his reason for that judgment crystal clear—"as long," he said, "as [the nation] keeps trying to act like she is God and she is supreme." The issue was that Wright had spoken words very much like the words we read in the biblical book of *Revelation*, condemning ancient Rome, disguised there as Babylon, for trading in slaves and building its empire on the backs of the poor.

"Fallen, fallen is Babylon the Great," John wrote, for she has sold not only gold and silver and sheep and horses, but also "slaves, that is, human souls" (18:2, 11–13 ESV). "Fallen, fallen is Babylon the Great," John wrote, for "the merchants of the earth have grown rich with the wealth of her wantonness" (18:3 RSV).

Then John made the crucial point, that God—not Rome—is Lord. "For the Lord our God the Almighty reigns," John wrote. And unlike Rome, this great God Almighty "will wipe away every tear . . . and there shall be neither mourning nor crying nor pain anymore."

This was precisely the point Jeremiah Wright sought to make, for when he reached the end of his sermon, he said this:

> The United States government has failed the vast majority of her citizens of African descent. [But] where governments fail, God never fails. . . . I want you to know that you are more than a conqueror; through Christ you can do all things. . . . God never fails. You can't put down what God raises up. God never fails. You can't keep down what God wants up. God never fails. He'll abide with you, he'll reside in you, and he'll preside over your problems. . . . God never fails.

But White America, including large numbers of Christians, condemned Wright so completely that Barack Obama—a member of that church since 1988—had to break ties with his pastor or risk losing the election. But we can be sure that not a single person in that congregation of more than 8,500 African American members—and precious few Blacks who lived in Chicago's South Side or elsewhere in the nation, for that matter—criticized Jeremiah Wright for what he said that day.

The nub of the matter is this: if we are serious about the work of character formation, then we must hear what Blacks have been trying to say to us for hundreds of years. If we are serious about character formation, then we must listen to people like Frederick Douglass and Malcolm X and Angela Davis and Ta-Nehisi Coates. If we are serious about character formation, then we cannot afford to marginalize the Black Lives Matter movement, or scholars like Kelly Brown Douglas and Carol Anderson, or sports figures like Colin Kaepernick, or preachers like Jeremiah Wright.

In the speech that likely got him killed—his 1967 speech at the Riverside Church in New York City, where he spoke out against America's war in Vietnam—Martin Luther King Jr. thundered words that captured the heart of Jesus and, for that very reason, stand as a beacon for the work we do with our students in the field of character formation:

Because I believe that the Father is deeply concerned especially for his suffering and outcast children, I come tonight to speak for them. This I believe to be the privilege and the burden of all of us who deem ourselves bound by allegiances and loyalties which are broader and deeper than nationalism and which go beyond our nation's self-defined goals and positions. We are called to speak for the weak, for the voiceless, for victims of our nation and for those it calls enemy, for no document from human hands can make these humans any less our brothers.

I grasped virtually nothing of this vision when I was a college student some fifty-eight years ago. I grasped nothing of this vision because my professors grasped nothing of this vision, even though they imagined themselves seriously engaged in the work of character formation.

Until we, today, begin to grasp the power of White supremacy in our nation, its schools, its churches, and even in ourselves; until we see the world through the eyes of the weak; until we can hear the voices of the voiceless resonating in our hearts; until we can grasp and appreciate what Martin Luther King meant when he said we must stand "with the victims of our nation and those it calls enemy"; and until we, too, can affirm that "no document from human hands can make these humans any less our brothers"—until we can grasp these truths not only with our minds but also with our hearts, our work of character formation will fall miserably short of the ethical vision of Jesus. And we will deceive ourselves, for though we may imagine that we are turning out better people, better Christians, and better citizens, we will turn out instead one-dimensional people—good and moral people in many ways, but people so thoroughly blinded by the bright light of their Whiteness that they are numb to the lament of the oppressed.

THE SUMMONS FROM
THE BIBLICAL TEXT

Over the years, I have been asked time and again what enabled me to respond in such a positive manner to Professor James Noel's pointed criticism of my book on the great American myths. "You completely left out," he said, "the most important myth of all."

I do not view myself as particularly courageous or any less defensive than anyone else. But there were two factors that primed me to hear Noel's criticism with an open mind.

The first is a principle that stands at the very heart of the religious tradition in which I have spent my life—the importance of an unbiased and open search for truth. In the early nineteenth century, when Churches of Christ were forming on the American frontier, virtually all its leaders insisted that Christians are people who embrace a radical search for truth. That principle lived in the heart of my mother and shaped the counsel she offered me when I was sixteen years old and zealous to convert my friends to what I regarded as the one true church. "If you discover that they are right and you are wrong," she said, "you are the one who must be willing to make the change."

The second factor is the image of the upside-down kingdom of God that pervades the teachings of Jesus. I first encountered that vision when I discovered the sixteenth-century Anabaptists as a graduate student at Abilene Christian University. Since that time, that vision has dramatically transformed my understanding of the Christian faith. How could I possibly embrace Jesus's teachings on the upside-down kingdom of God and reject Professor Noel's criticism of my work?

Some years after the University of Illinois Press published the first edition of *Myths America Lives By*, the Press asked if I would be willing to write a book that would focus on only one of those myths. When I asked which of the myths they had in mind, they responded, "the myth of Christian America."

I approached that assignment by contrasting Christian America, with its zeal for power, dominance, and control, with the upside-down values so central to Jesus's vision of the kingdom of God. What follows are excerpts from that text, exploring the notion of the kingdom of God in both the Hebrew Bible and the New Testament.

We begin our discussion of the kingdom of God with a brief definition of that concept offered by the New Testament scholar John Dominic Crossan who contends that, according to the Bible, "The kingdom of God was what this world would look like if and when God sat on Caesar's throne. . . . This is very clear in these parallel phrases of the Lord's Prayer in Matthew 6:10: 'Your kingdom come. Your will be done, *on earth* as it is in heaven.'"[1]

The Kingdom of God in the Hebrew Bible

The actual phrase "kingdom of God" never appears in the Hebrew Bible, but the concept of the kingdom of God—that is, the rule of God—appears often. One of the earliest and most important statements in the Hebrew Bible on the kingdom of God appears in 1 Samuel 8:4–22, where the elders of Israel pled with the prophet Samuel, "Appoint for us, then, a king to govern us, like other nations" (v. 5). When Samuel told the Lord about this request, the Lord told Samuel that the Israelites "have not rejected you,

---

[1] John Dominic Crossan, *God and Empire: Jesus against Rome, Then and Now* (San Francisco: Harper, 2007), 116–17.

but they have rejected me from being king over them." God's statement in this text is terribly important, for it clearly indicates God's intention that the Hebrew nation would be, in fact, a "kingdom of God," ruled directly by God himself.

But what would that mean? How would a "kingdom of God" look different from the "other nations" upon whom Israel sought to pattern itself?

We get a clear indication of the contours of that kingdom when God had Samuel argue with Israel's elders by pointing out the inevitable outcomes of human rule: war, violence, and slavery. Thus Samuel said:

> These will be the ways of the king who will reign over you: he
> will take your sons and appoint them to his chariots and to be
> his horsemen, and to run before his chariots; and he will appoint
> for himself commanders of thousands and commanders of fif-
> ties, and some to plow his ground and to reap his harvest, and
> to make his implements of war and the equipment of his chari-
> ots. (vv. 11–12)

According to the text, "The people refused to listen to the voice of Samuel; they said, 'No! but we are determined to have a king over us, so that we also may be like other nations, and that our king may govern us and go out before us and fight our battles.'" At that, God gave in and said to Samuel, "Listen to their voice and set a king over them" (vv. 19–20, 22).

In the context of the biblical vision of the kingdom of God, this story is a crucially important metaphor, suggesting that the kingdom of God would be both nonviolent and just, while human governments would inevitably practice both violence and oppression.

Under Solomon, Israel's third king, the truth of Samuel's words became apparent, for Solomon controlled an empire that depended on violence and oppression for its very existence. The text of 1 Kings makes this clear:

> Solomon was sovereign over all the kingdoms from the
> Euphrates to the land of the Philistines, even to the border of
> Egypt; they brought tribute and served Solomon all the days
> of his life. Solomon's provision for one day was thirty cors of
> choice flour, and sixty cors of meal, ten fat oxen, and twenty

pasture-fed cattle, one hundred sheep, besides deer, gazelles, roebucks, and fatted fowl. (4:21–23)

Of this stunning level of luxury that characterized the royal court, Walter Brueggemann comments: "Then or now, eating that well means food is being taken off the table of another."[2]

Further, "Solomon also had forty thousand stalls of horses for his chariots, and conscripted twelve thousand horsemen" to drive his chariots of war (1 Kings 4:26). And in order to build the temple in Jerusalem, he "conscripted forced labor out of all Israel; the levy numbered thirty thousand men," whom Solomon put to work in Lebanon (1 Kings 5:13–14). But there was more:

> Solomon also had seventy thousand laborers and eighty thousand stonecutters in the hill country, besides Solomon's three thousand three hundred supervisors . . . . At the king's command, they quarried out great, costly stones in order to lay the foundation of the house with dressed stones. (1 Kings 5:15–17)

Once again, Walter Brueggemann observes: "While the shift had no doubt begun and been encouraged by David, . . . the entire program of Solomon now appears to have been a self-serving achievement with its sole purpose the self-securing of king and dynasty."[3]

After Solomon, much of the history of Israel (the northern kingdom) and Judah (the southern kingdom)—according to the biblical text—is the history of wars those nations fought to maintain their imperial power, the oppression they levied against the poor to maintain the lifestyle of the ruling classes, and their misguided alliances with stronger kingdoms (e.g., Egypt and Assyria) as the Hebrew children slowly lost their dominance and vainly sought to defend themselves from slavery, death, and destruction.

In the eighth century BCE, a most remarkable development began to unfold. The Hebrew prophets from that time on increasingly returned to Samuel's vision of a kingdom ruled by God. These prophets raised serious questions about the viability, even the legitimacy, of waging war. They

---

[2] Walter Brueggemann, *The Prophetic Imagination* (Minneapolis: Fortress Press, 1978), 33.
[3] Brueggemann, *Prophetic Imagination*, 30.

argued that neither violent warfare, nor military alliances, nor fortified cities had the power to save Israel and Judah from their enemies. They argued that only one path would save Israel from destruction, and that was the path of economic justice, especially for the poor who so often had been objects of abuse and exploitation.

When American Christians attempt to defend the United States as a latter-day chosen people, they typically ignore this prophetic literature and appeal instead to those sections of the Hebrew Bible that depict war, violence, and injustice—the very behavior the Hebrew prophets condemned. Because Israel and Judah waged war and killed and subjugated their enemies, they often argue, the Bible justifies this "Christian nation"—the United States—in doing the same.

But how would one know which of these two storylines should be taken as normative—the story of Israel the violent or the vision of Israel the just? This question can be especially acute for Christians who view the Bible as one-dimensional, flat, and entirely consistent with itself. But the Old Testament scholar Gordon Brubacher reminds us that "there is no such thing as *the* OT [Old Testament] witness." Brubacher elaborates as follows: "The OT does not present a single, flat, monolithic 'witness' to be extrapolated by balancing or synthesizing its various elements as found throughout. Instead, the OT presents an extended narrative journey, in which the destination is more important—more authoritative and normative—than the beginning or the middle of that experience."[4]

And what particular books in the Hebrew Bible depict that destination? Again, Brubacher explains that the "new land, that destination for the journey, is proclaimed especially in a group of passages in Second Isaiah and in other, related, prophetic witness[es]." In other words, those sections of the Hebrew Bible that should carry especially normative weight for Christians are the Hebrew prophets, beginning in the eighth century BCE—for example, Isaiah, Jeremiah, Amos, Hosea, and Micah.

At this point, one more question begs for an answer: On what possible basis could we make the judgment that this late prophetic material should be more normative for Christians than, say, Leviticus or Deuteronomy?

---

[4] Gordon Brubacher, "Just War and the New Community: The Witness of the Old Testament for Christians Today," *Princeton Theological Review* 12 (Fall 2006): 19.

Once again, we turn to Brubacher, who makes the logical assumption that the first and highest allegiance of Christians should be to Jesus. After all, Christians claim to be followers of Jesus and have signified that allegiance by wearing his name. They call themselves *Christ*-ians.

The question, then, must be, to which sections of the Hebrew Bible did Jesus appeal as he sought to define his own ministry, identity, and sense of vocation? The answer, quite simply, is that Jesus appealed to those radical Hebrew prophets who rejected war and oppression and proclaimed, instead, nonviolence, peace, and justice. Not only did Jesus appeal to those prophets; he embodied their teachings in his own life and ministry. Brubacher thus concludes that Christians should "take Jesus as [their] guide for deciding *which* stage of the OT journey constitutes the OT witness for the church today."[5]

John Dominic Crossan makes essentially the same point, though in a somewhat different way. Crossan vividly contrasts *human civilization*—which inevitably advocates peace through *victory*, on the one hand—with the *kingdom of God*, which always advocates peace through *justice*, on the other. He also points to the age-old struggle between the two.

It is striking, however, that Crossan wants us to see that this struggle between human civilization and the kingdom of God "is depicted *inside the Bible* itself." We witnessed that struggle, for example, when the Hebrews begged Samuel, "Appoint for us, then, a king to govern us, like other nations," and when God resisted but finally gave in to that request. Later in this chapter, we will witness that struggle again in the biblical texts that juxtapose just and peaceful Israel, on the one hand, with violent and oppressive Israel, on the other.

Crossan concludes, "The Christian Bible forces us to witness the struggle of these two transcendental visions *within its own pages* and to ask ourselves as Christians how we decide between them." Crossan's answer is essentially the same as Brubacher's: "My answer is that *we are bound to whichever of these visions was incarnated by and in the historical Jesus.*"[6]

---

5 Brubacher, "Just War," 19.
6 Crossan, *God and Empire*, 94.

The fact is, when Jesus defined his own mission, identity, and vocation, he never appealed to texts like the one in Deuteronomy 7 that commissioned Israel to "utterly destroy" the nations that lived in the land of Canaan. Nor did he appeal to texts like Joshua 6 that record how Israel "devoted to destruction by the edge of the sword all in the city [of Jericho], both men and women, young and old, oxen, sheep, and donkeys" (Josh. 6:21).

Instead, when Jesus sought to define his ministry, identity, and vocation, he used a text from Isaiah that reads as follows:

> The spirit of the Lord God is upon me,
>   because the Lord has anointed me;
> he has sent me to bring good news to the oppressed,
>   to bind up the brokenhearted,
> to proclaim liberty to the captives,
>   and release to the prisoners;
> to proclaim the year of the Lord's favor,
>   and the day of vengeance of our God;
>   to comfort all who mourn. (Isa. 61:1–2)

Exactly how did Jesus use that passage? The Gospel of Luke records the following:

> When he [Jesus] came to Nazareth, where he had been brought up, he went to the synagogue on the sabbath day, as was his custom. He stood up to read, and the scroll of the prophet Isaiah was given to him. He unrolled the scroll and found the place where it was written:
>
> > "The Spirit of the Lord is upon me,
> >   because he has anointed me
> >   to bring good news to the poor.
> > He has sent me to proclaim release to the captives
> >   and recovery of sight to the blind,
> >   to let the oppressed go free,
> > to proclaim the year of the Lord's favor."

And he rolled up the scroll, gave it back to the attendant, and sat down. The eyes of all in the synagogue were fixed on him. Then he began to say to them, "Today this scripture has been fulfilled in your hearing." (Luke 4:16–21)

It is interesting that while Jesus used Isaiah 61:1–2 as the basis for the proclamation of his vocation, he evidently declined to use one key phrase of that passage: "He has sent me . . . to proclaim . . . the day of vengeance of our God." Whatever else one might say about this omission, it is clear that Jesus focused this proclamation on issues of justice, not issues of vengeance.

The Gospels record only one other instance when Jesus defined the concerns that would characterize his mission, ministry, and vocation. Matthew reports that John the Baptist, languishing in prison, heard of the work Jesus was doing and "sent word by his disciples and said to him, 'Are you the one who is to come, or are we to wait for another?'" Matthew further reports that Jesus replied, "Go and tell John what you hear and see: the blind receive their sight, the lame walk, the lepers are cleansed, the deaf hear, the dead are raised, and the poor have good news brought to them" (Matt. 11:2–5). In using these words, Jesus summarized another passage from Isaiah: "On that day the deaf shall hear the words of a scroll, and out of their gloom and darkness the eyes of the blind shall see. The meek shall obtain fresh joy in the LORD, and the neediest people shall exult in the Holy One of Israel" (29:18–19).

In proclaiming his mission, identity, and vocation in these ways, Jesus was lining out the contours of what he often called "the kingdom of God" or "the rule of God." But the Hebrew prophets who proclaimed the prophetic word beginning in the eighth century BCE had established the basic contours for that kingdom long before Jesus. Jesus's vision for the kingdom of God, therefore, was rooted and grounded in the prophetic imagination and stood squarely in the tradition of the Hebrew prophets.

We must now ask, How did the prophets understand the meaning of the kingdom of God? We mentioned earlier that two primary themes consistently define the kingdom of God in the biblical text, regardless of whether the kingdom vision appears in the Hebrew Bible, the Gospels of the New Testament, or the writings of the apostle Paul. Those two themes are peace and justice. And in the prophetic imagination, they often went hand in hand.

Justice as a Mark of the Kingdom of God

The Hebrew prophets who admonished Israel (the northern kingdom) and Judah (the southern kingdom) in the eighth and subsequent centuries BCE provide a graphic picture of the kingdom of God through their vigorous demands for justice, especially for the poor, the widow, and the orphan.

In the entire Hebrew Bible, there is perhaps no more definitive statement on social justice than that of Amos who prophesied against Israel—the northern kingdom—during the eighth century BCE, most likely during the decade 760–750 BCE. His message was clear: because the ruling elites of Israel oppressed the poor and crushed the needy, the Assyrians would take Israel into captivity. That, of course, is exactly what happened in 721 BCE.

What follows are several passages I have pulled together from chapters 3, 4, 5, and 6 of the book of Amos—passages that unambiguously demonstrate the depth of God's concern for the poor in any society. The combined text that follows is lengthy, but well worth reading in its entirety.

- They do not know how to do right, says the LORD, those who store up violence and robbery in their strongholds. Therefore thus says the Lord GOD: An adversary shall surround the land, and strip you of your defense; and your strongholds shall be plundered. (3:10–11)
- Hear this word, you cows of Bashan who are on Mount Samaria, who oppress the poor, who crush the needy, who say to their husbands, "Bring something to drink!" The Lord GOD has sworn by his holiness: The time is surely coming upon you, when they shall take you away with hooks, even the last of you with fish-hooks. (4:1–2)
- Therefore because you trample on the poor and take from them levies of grain, you have built houses of hewn stone, but you shall not live in them; you have planted pleasant vineyards, but you shall not drink their wine. For I know how many are your

transgressions, and how great are your sins—you who afflict the righteous, who take a bribe, and push aside the needy in the gate. (5:11–12)

- Alas for those who lie on beds of ivory, and lounge on their couches, and eat lambs from the flock, and calves from the stall; who sing idle songs to the sound of the harp, and like David improvise on instruments of music; who drink wine from bowls, and anoint themselves with the finest oils, but are not grieved over the ruin of Joseph! Therefore they shall now be the first to go into exile, and the revelry of the loungers shall pass away. (6:4–7)

Amos also argued that when people practice social injustice, their worship is an abomination to God. Thus in Amos 5:21–24, Amos records God speaking directly to Israel in these harsh and uncompromising words:

I hate, I despise your festivals,
     and I take no delight in your solemn assemblies.
Even though you offer me your burnt offerings and grain offerings,
     I will not accept them;
and the offerings of well-being of your fatted animals
     I will not look upon.
Take away from me the noise of your songs;
     I will not listen to the melody of your harps.
But let justice roll down like waters,
     and righteousness like an ever-flowing stream.

Oracles from the book of Isaiah, reflecting the late sixth century BCE, picked up on this very same theme. Here, however, the prophet directed his critique not against the northern kingdom of Israel but against the southern kingdom of Judah. Like Amos, who claimed that fairness and equity were more important to God than worship and sacrifice, this text critiqued Judah's religious fasts, claiming that the fast God really desired was the fast of justice.

Especially pertinent for our purposes is the clear connection this text from Isaiah makes between social justice and national well-being. Judah had by then returned from Babylonian captivity, and Isaiah argued that if

Judah would feed the hungry, care for the homeless, and clothe the naked, "Your ancient ruins shall be rebuilt; you shall raise up the foundations of many generations; you shall be called the repairer of the breach, the restorer of streets to live in." This passage, like the earlier text from Amos, is lengthy, but bears so directly on our topic that it deserves to be quoted in full:

> Is not this the fast that I choose;
>> to loose the bonds of injustice,
>> to undo the thongs of the yoke,
> to let the oppressed go free,
>> and to break every yoke?
> Is it not to share your bread with the hungry,
>> and bring the homeless poor into your house;
> when you see the naked, to cover them,
>> and not to hide yourself from your own kin?
> Then your light shall break forth like the dawn,
>> and your healing shall spring up quickly;
> your vindicator shall go before you,
>> the glory of the LORD shall be your rear guard. . . .
> If you offer your food to the hungry
>> and satisfy the needs of the afflicted,
> then your light shall rise in the darkness
>> and your gloom be like the noonday.
> The LORD will guide you continually,
>> and satisfy your needs in parched places,
>> and make your bones strong;
> and you shall be like a watered garden,
>> like a spring of water,
>> whose waters never fail.
> Your ancient ruins shall be rebuilt;
>> you shall raise up the foundations of many generations;
> you shall be called the repairer of the breach,
>> the restorer of streets to live in. (Isa. 58:6–8, 10–12)

Another classic prophetic passage demanding social justice comes from Micah, who prophesied against the southern kingdom of Judah during the eighth century BCE when Judah faced the very real possibility of invasion by the Assyrian army and subsequent exile. Like Amos, Micah used strong and graphic words to condemn the way Judah's rulers and elites enriched themselves on the backs of the poor. In fact, he depicted Judah's rulers as cannibals who boiled the poor in cauldrons and then ate their flesh.

> And I said:
> Listen, you heads of Jacob
>   and rulers of the house of Israel!
> Should you not know justice?—
>   you who hate the good and love the evil,
> who tear the skin off my people,
>   and flesh off their bones;
> who eat the flesh of my people,
>   flay their skin off them,
> break their bones in pieces,
>   and chop them up like meat in a kettle,
>   like flesh in a cauldron. (3:1–3)

Precisely because Judah's rulers rejected justice for the sake of personal gain, Micah envisioned the day when the Assyrians would swarm over the land and destroy the nation.

> Hear this, you rulers of the house of Jacob
>   and chiefs of the house of Israel,
> who abhor justice
>   and pervert all equity,
> who build Zion with blood
>   and Jerusalem with wrong! . . .
> Therefore, because of you
>   Zion shall be plowed as a field;
> Jerusalem shall become a heap of ruins. (3:9–10, 12)

These oracles typify the message preached by virtually all the Hebrew prophets who proclaimed God's will to the Hebrew people beginning in the eighth century BCE.

We now must ask, what do all these passages have to do with the kingdom of God? Two prophetic passages make that connection especially clear—one from Micah and one from Isaiah.

Though Micah railed against the injustices entrenched in Judah, he was not without hope, for he envisioned a whole new kingdom that he described as "the mountain of the Lord," clearly a synonym for the kingdom of God.

> In the days to come
>> the mountain of the LORD's house
> shall be established as the highest of the mountains,
>> and shall be raised up above the hills.
> Peoples shall stream to it,
>> and many nations shall come and say:
> "Come, let us go up to the mountain of the LORD,
>> to the house of the God of Jacob;
> that he may teach us his ways
>> and that we may walk in his paths." (4:1–2)

According to Micah, two qualities would define the essence of that kingdom: peace and justice. Thus he proclaimed:

> For out of Zion shall go forth instruction,
>> and the word of the LORD from Jerusalem.
> He shall judge between many peoples,
>> and shall arbitrate between strong nations far away;
> they shall beat their swords into plowshares,
>> and their spears into pruning hooks;
> nation shall not lift up sword against nation,
>> neither shall they learn war any more. (4:2–3)

Isaiah, too, made explicit the connection between social justice and the kingdom of God, for he envisioned a time when Judah would, in fact, become that kingdom—a kingdom defined not by ritual, but by justice, and a kingdom whose ruler would judge the poor and meek with equity and compassion. Further, Isaiah argued that justice embraced by that kingdom would bring peace to the earth. In the entire Bible, there is no more compelling description of the kingdom of God than this:

> A shoot shall come out from the stump of Jesse,
>> and a branch shall grow out of his roots.
> The spirit of the LORD shall rest on him,
>> the spirit of wisdom and understanding,
>> the spirit of counsel and might,
>> the spirit of knowledge and the fear of the LORD.
> His delight shall be in the fear of the LORD.
>
> He shall not judge by what his eyes see,
>> or decide by what his ears hear;
> but with righteousness he shall judge the poor,
>> and decide with equity for the meek of the earth;
> he shall strike the earth with the rod of his mouth,
>> and with the breath of his lips he shall kill the wicked.
> Righteousness shall be the belt around his waist,
>> and faithfulness the belt around his loins.
>
> The wolf shall live with the lamb,
>> the leopard shall lie down with the kid,
> the calf and the lion and the fatling together,
>> and a little child shall lead them.
> The cow and the bear shall graze,
>> their young shall lie down together;
>> and the lion shall eat straw like the ox.
> The nursing child shall play over the hole of the asp,
>> and the weaned child shall put its hand on the adder's den.
> They will not hurt or destroy
>> on all my holy mountain;
> for the earth will be full of the knowledge of the LORD
>> as the waters cover the sea. (11:1–9)

Many Christians take this powerful description of the coming kingdom of God as a prediction of the Messiah—the one they call Jesus the Christ. Whether they are correct in that claim is another question for another place and another time. But one thing is clear: if Christians believe this passage predicts their Messiah, then one would think they would read the entire Hebrew Bible through the lens of texts like this rather than texts that advocate violence, war, and the destruction of the enemies of the chosen people of God. In truth, the prophets portrayed a nonviolent kingdom, devoted to peace throughout all the earth, as we shall now discover.

Peace as a Mark of the Kingdom of God

When one moves from the Pentateuch to the prophetic literature of the eighth century BCE and later, one has come a very long way on the issue of war and peace. While the Pentateuch sanctioned violence, war, and death against Israel's enemies, the prophets proclaimed the way of peace. Already we have seen strong hints of this transition in Micah—"They shall beat their swords into plowshares, and their spears into pruning hooks; nation shall not lift up sword against nation, neither shall they learn war any more" (4:3)—and in Isaiah—"The wolf shall live with the lamb, the leopard shall lie down with the kid, the calf and the lion and the fatling together, and a little child shall lead them" (11:6).

The reason for this transition is not difficult to find: violence and war simply did not work. As Gordon Brubacher notes, "The military defense option . . . rarely worked despite the massive resources invested. A determined army usually succeeded in the end. The fact that even the powerfully fortified cities of the Northern and Southern Kingdoms fell to attack and thus failed in their purpose is a matter of record in the archaeological remains."[7]

Among the eighth-century prophets, none was more insistent that the way of war did not work than Hosea. But Hosea placed that argument in a much larger context. Hosea harked back to Samuel's dispute with the elders of Israel who demanded a human king and rejected the rule of God. As we recall, the elders told Samuel, "We are determined to have a king over us,

---

[7] Brubacher, "Just War," 23.

so that we also may be like other nations, and that our king may govern us and go out before us and fight our battles" (1 Sam. 8:19–20).

Now in the eighth century BCE, with the Assyrian threat looming large over the northern kingdom, Hosea tweaked the Israelites with these biting words: "I will destroy you, O Israel; who can help you? Where now is your king, that he may save you? Where in all your cities are your rulers, of whom you said, 'Give me a king and rulers'?" (13:9–10). Hosea, therefore, based his claim that war did not work on the supporting claim that long, long ago, Israel had exchanged the rule of God—that is, the kingdom of God—for a human kingdom and human rulers who placed their trust in war, violence, and military might. But, Hosea warned, naming an earthly king was counterproductive.

> Because you have trusted in your power
>   and in the multitude of your warriors,
> therefore the tumult of war shall rise against your people,
>   and all your fortresses shall be destroyed,
> as Shalman destroyed Beth-arbel on the day of battle
>   when mothers were dashed in pieces with their children.
>   (10:13–14)

Based on the premise that war does not work and that human kingdoms are deeply flawed, virtually all the later Hebrew prophets became proponents of peace, and they did so in the context of their vision of the coming kingdom of God.

Perhaps the best-known text that makes this point is Isaiah 9:6–7, another passage Christians like to claim as a prophecy of the coming Christ and the passage that inspired George Frideric Handel to compose the classic musical score "The Messiah" in 1741.

> For a child has been born for us,
>   a son given to us;
> authority rests upon his shoulders;
>   and he is named
> Wonderful Counselor, Mighty God,
>   Everlasting Father, Prince of Peace.

His authority shall grow continually,
    and there shall be endless peace
for the throne of David and his kingdom.
    He will establish and uphold it
with justice and with righteousness
    from this time onward and forevermore.

This passage is profoundly a rejection of war and an affirmation of peace and peacemaking in the context of a radically new kingdom with a new and different kind of ruler—a "Prince of Peace." Indeed, if we pick up the verse that immediately precedes the phrase, "For a child has been born to us," the passage reads:

For all the boots of the tramping warriors
    and all the garments rolled in blood
    shall be burned as fuel for the fire.
For a child has been born for us,
    a son given to us;
authority rests upon his shoulders;
    and he is named
Wonderful Counselor, Mighty God,
    Everlasting Father, Prince of Peace. (9:5–6)

Zechariah picked up this very same theme of a radically new kind of ruler but did so with fresh and fascinating imagery. This king would make his appearance not in a chariot of steel but on a donkey, and his power would lie not in military might but in humility. Indeed, this ruler would abolish war throughout the earth. Here is the actual text:

Rejoice greatly, O daughter Zion!
    Shout aloud, O daughter Jerusalem!
Lo, your king comes to you;
    triumphant and victorious is he,
humble and riding on a donkey,
    on a colt, the foal of a donkey.
He will cut off the chariot from Ephraim
    and the war-horse from Jerusalem;

and the battle bow shall be cut off,
and he shall command peace to the nations;
his dominion shall be from sea to sea,
and from the River to the ends of the earth. (9:9–10)

Regarding this text, John Dominic Crossan has observed:

Like any city of the ancient world, Jerusalem knew that a con-
queror entered it at best through opened gates and at worst
through shattered walls. In either case, he came on a battle
chariot or warhorse. But [here] . . . the prophet imagines this
anti-triumphal future entrance of the Messiah on a donkey.[8]

In the New Testament, Matthew made much of this passage, interpreting Jesus as the radically new ruler who exchanged chariots of war for
a donkey. Thus,

Jesus sent two disciples, saying to them, "Go into the village
ahead of you, and immediately you will find a donkey tied, and
a colt with her; untie them and bring them to me. . . ." This took
place to fulfill what had been spoken through the prophet, saying,

"Tell the daughter of Zion,
Look, your king is coming to you,
humble, and mounted on a donkey,
and on a colt, the foal of a donkey."

The disciples went and did as Jesus had directed them; they
brought the donkey and the colt, and put their cloaks on them,
and he sat on them. A very large crowd spread their cloaks on
the road, and others cut branches from the trees and spread
them on the road. The crowds that went ahead of him and that
followed were shouting,

"Hosanna to the Son of David!
Blessed is the one who comes in the name of the Lord!
Hosanna in the highest heaven!" (21:1–9)

---

[8] Crossan, *God and Empire*, 132.

When one compares Zechariah's description of this new kind of ruler—the coming "Prince of Peace"—with Samuel's description of human rulers, we get an extraordinary glimpse into the radical difference between human kingdoms and the kingdom of God. We have already seen that when Israel pled for a king in order to be like other nations, Samuel warned,

> These will be the ways of the king who will reign over you: he
> will take your sons and appoint them to his chariots and to
> be his horsemen, and to run before his chariots; and he will
> appoint for himself commanders of thousands and commanders
> of fifties, and some . . . to make his implements of war and the
> equipment of his chariots. (1 Sam. 8:11–12)

But the ruler whom Zechariah described would "cut off the chariot from Ephraim and the war-horse from Jerusalem; and the battle bow shall be cut off, and he shall command peace to the nations; his dominion shall be from sea to sea, and from the River to the ends of the earth" (9:10).

Not only did the prophets of the eighth and subsequent centuries proclaim peace; they also proclaimed *peacemaking,* and they expected God's people—those who belonged to the kingdom of God—to serve as peacemakers. We find in the prophetic literature three ways in which peace should be pursued.

Over and again the prophets insisted that the first and most important tool for peacemaking was the pursuit of justice. Jeremiah, for example, wrote:

> Thus says the Lord: Act with justice and righteousness, and
> deliver from the hand of the oppressor anyone who has been
> robbed. And do no wrong or violence to the alien, the orphan,
> and the widow, or shed innocent blood in this place. For if you
> will indeed obey this word, then through the gates of this house
> shall enter kings who sit on the throne of David, riding in char-
> iots and on horses, they, and their servants, and their people.
> (Jer. 22:3–4)

On the other hand, Jeremiah warned, "If you will not heed these words, I swear by myself, says the LORD, that this house shall become a desolation" (22:5).

No single prophet made the point that the path of justice was the path of peace more clearly and succinctly than Isaiah: "The effect of righteousness [justice] will be peace, and the result of righteousness [justice], quietness and trust forever. My people will abide in a peaceful habitation, in secure dwellings, and in quiet resting places" (32:17–18).

Isaiah offered an extended commentary on this point in a passage we have already cited.

> Is not this the fast that I choose:
>   to loose the bonds of injustice,
>   to undo the thongs of the yoke,
>   to let the oppressed go free,
>   and to break every yoke?
> Is it not to share your bread with the hungry,
>   and bring the homeless poor into your house;
> when you see the naked, to cover them,
>   and not to hide yourself from your own kin?
> Then . . . your ancient ruins shall be rebuilt;
>   you shall raise up the foundations of many generations;
>   you shall be called the repairer of the breach,
>   the restorer of streets to live in. (Isa. 58:6–7, 12)

The second path to peace is the most obvious path imaginable, though it is one that was seldom tried in ancient Israel and one that is seldom tried today: refuse to fight. Jeremiah made that option central to the message he proclaimed to the southern kingdom on the eve of the Babylonian invasion of Judah and subsequent exile of its people—developments that occurred in 586 BCE. Jeremiah claimed he was setting before the Hebrews "the way of life and the way of death." The way of death was military resistance; the way of life was surrender.

> Thus says the LORD: See, I am setting before you the way of life
>   and the way of death. Those who stay in this city shall die by the

sword, by famine, and by pestilence; but those who go out and surrender to the Chaldeans [Babylonians] who are besieging you shall live and shall have their lives as a prize of war. (21:8–9)

Jeremiah repeated the same message in a later chapter:

Bring your necks under the yoke of the king of Babylon, and serve him and his people, and live. Why should you and your people die by the sword, by famine, and by pestilence, as the LORD has spoken concerning any nation that will not serve the king of Babylon? (27:12–13)

In the midst of that calamity, some self-styled prophets urged Judah to resist, but Jeremiah argued that Judah should reject those preachers as false prophets and preachers of death.

Do not listen to the words of the prophets who are telling you not to serve the king of Babylon, for they are prophesying a lie to you. I have not sent them, says the LORD, but they are prophesying falsely in my name, with the result that I will drive you out and you will perish, you and the prophets who are prophesying to you. (27:14–15)

The context makes it clear that resisting Babylon was resisting God, since God had already decreed that Babylon would take Judah captive as a punishment for its sins against the powerless and the poor. But Gordon Brubacher notes that something else was at work here as well.

The value here was on human life rather than on ego, or on some ephemeral appeal to "freedom." Also, by implication, the value was on reallocating massive defense budgets and human resources from military use to the well-being of the general population. However, this option did not come naturally to people in power, for it had a certain cost in treasure, humility, and loss of face. Moreover, this response took no little faith or trust in God, no small commitment to obedience despite the cost. So it was easier said than done and rarely tried at all, whether in the biblical world or in any other place or time.[9]

Finally, the prophets encouraged God's people to work for peace by praying for their enemies. Thus, Jeremiah encouraged the Jews to "seek the welfare of the [enemy] city where I have sent you into exile, and pray to the LORD on its behalf, for in its welfare you will find your welfare" (29:7)—a recommendation that points us in the direction of Jesus's advice, recorded in the Gospel of Matthew: "Love your enemies and pray for those who persecute you" (5:44).

The Hebrew prophets consistently portrayed the kingdom of God as a radical alternative to politics as usual—to peace and prosperity maintained through war, violence, and oppression. For the most part, they portrayed the kingdom of God as an alternative to conventional politics *within their own nation.*

By the second century BCE, the notion of the kingdom of God took on even more profoundly political overtones. Some in Israel now began to argue that the kingdom of God would transform not only the Jewish nation but would defeat all the empires of the earth and would nurture both peace and justice until the end of time.

The immediate context for this new understanding of the kingdom of God was the reign of Antiochus Epiphanes, a Syrian who ruled over Israel from 175 to 164 BCE. Antiochus Epiphanes sought to force Greek culture on the Jews, a move that stood squarely in the Hellenizing tradition of Alexander the Great. This man whose name, "Epiphanes," meant "God made manifest," forbade Jewish religious practice, dedicated the temple in Jerusalem to Zeus, erected in the temple an altar to Zeus, and defiled the temple in a variety of ways.

Against that backdrop, the book of Daniel appeared sometime between 167 and 164 BCE and used the metaphor of the kingdom of God to stand in judgment on the imperial politics of Antiochus Epiphanes. An example of apocalyptic literature—the only example in the Hebrew Bible—the book of Daniel employed human history not to report on facts, but to interpret current events.

<hr/>

[9] Brubacher, "Just War," 24.

In that context, it told a story about King Nebuchadnezzar, who ruled Babylon some four hundred years before. In this story, the king dreamed of a great statue whose head was of gold, its chest and arms of silver, its middle and thighs of bronze, its legs of iron, and its feet partly of iron and partly of clay. Then, as the dream continued,

> A stone was cut out, not by human hands, and it struck the statue on its feet of iron and clay and broke them in pieces. Then the iron, the clay, the bronze, the silver, and the gold, were all broken in pieces and became like the chaff of the summer threshing floors; and the wind carried them away, so that not a trace of them could be found. But the stone that struck the statue became a great mountain and filled the whole earth. (2:34–35)

Puzzled by this dream, Nebuchadnezzar sought an interpretation from Daniel, who told the king that "you [and by extension, the Babylonian empire] are the head of gold," but that his kingdom would be followed by three others—one of silver, one of bronze, and one of iron. Finally, Daniel offered this interpretation:

> The God of heaven will set up a kingdom that shall never be destroyed, nor shall this kingdom be left to another people. It shall crush all these kingdoms and bring them to an end, and it shall stand forever; just as you saw that a stone was cut from the mountain not by hands, and that it crushed the iron, the bronze, the clay, the silver, and the gold. (2:44–45)

If we keep in mind what we have learned about the kingdom of God to this point, we will be in a better position to understand Daniel's interpretation. As we have worked our way through the prophetic literature of the Hebrew Bible, we have learned that the kingdom of God is a kingdom of justice, especially for the powerless and the poor, and a kingdom that always trumps the violence of this earth with the peace of God. Daniel takes that vision to a new level and suggests that the kingdom of God will finally subvert the violent and oppressive empires of this earth and stand forever.

That understanding of the kingdom of God is precisely the vision at work in the Christian New Testament, for author after author and book after book employ the just and peaceful kingdom of God as a radical alternative to the violent and oppressive Roman Empire—a theme that will become apparent as we turn our attention first to the Gospels, then to the letters of the apostle Paul, and finally to the Apocalypse of John, otherwise known as the book of Revelation.

The Kingdom of God in the New Testament

The kingdom of God is one of the central themes in the New Testament text, and the phrases "kingdom of God" and "kingdom of heaven"—phrases that have the very same meaning—appear there some one hundred times. The mere frequency of those phrases suggests that it may well be impossible to grasp the overall message of the New Testament text unless one first comes to terms with the meaning of the kingdom of God.

The same two ideas that stood at the heart of the kingdom of God motif in the Hebrew Bible also stand at the heart of the kingdom of God ideal in the New Testament. Those two ideas, as we know by now, are the themes of peace and justice. The vision of peace looms large in the New Testament text, as when Jesus—for example—counsels his followers, "Blessed are the peacemakers, for they will be called children of God" (Matt. 5:9), or when he tells them, "Love your enemies and pray for those who persecute you" (Matt. 5:44), or when the apostle Paul writes, "Do not repay anyone evil for evil, but . . . live peaceably with all" (Rom. 12:17–18).

What must be said about the theme of social and economic justice in the New Testament's presentation of the kingdom of God is this: In almost every instance where the phrase "kingdom of God" appears in the New Testament, it is closely linked to concern for the poor, the dispossessed, those in prison, the maimed, the lame, the blind, and all those who suffer at the hands of the world's elites. In other words, the kingdom of God is where the powerless are empowered, where the hungry are fed, where the sick are healed, where the poor are sustained, and where those who find themselves marginalized by the rulers of this world are finally offered both equality and justice.

There is therefore great continuity between the vision of the kingdom of God in the Hebrew prophets and the vision of the kingdom of God in the New Testament. And Jesus—the founder of the Christian religion and the centerpiece of the New Testament text—stood squarely in that prophetic tradition.

But two additional ideas characterize the meaning of the kingdom of God in the New Testament text. Donald Kraybill put his finger on the first of those ideas—the paradoxical dimensions of the kingdom of God—in a book he titled *The Upside-Down Kingdom*.[10] Simply put, the kingdom of God is that kingdom where the poor and the weak are exalted while the rich and the powerful are brought low; where one achieves greatness not by pursuing success, ambition, and self-interest but by emptying one's self on behalf of others; where the wise are foolish and the foolish are wise; and where one preserves and enhances one's life not by pursuing health, wealth, and success but by dying to self so that others might live.

Put another way, the kingdom of God requires what most human beings would never anticipate, what most would view as nonsense, and what most, therefore, would tend to resist. Thus, when we think success lies straight ahead, the kingdom of God takes us backward. When we think we need to go up, the kingdom of God takes us down. And when we think we can meet our goals by going in one direction, the kingdom of God takes us in quite another. This is why the kingdom of God is so fundamentally paradoxical.

In our analysis of the Hebrew Bible, we saw hints of this paradoxical dimension of the kingdom of God when, for example, Zechariah told of the king who would ride on the donkey. But in the New Testament, especially in the teachings of Jesus, the theme of paradox emerges full-blown.

Luke's Understanding of the Kingdom of God

As the Gospel of Luke opens, four messengers—Mary, the mother of Jesus, an angel, John the Baptist, and Jesus himself—announce the emergence of the kingdom of God. Each announcement reinforces the conviction that the kingdom of God will lift up the poor, the downtrodden, and the

---

[10] Donald Kraybill, *The Upside-Down Kingdom*, 25th anniv. ed. (Scottsdale, PA: Herald Press, 2003).

dispossessed, turning the tables on the empire that exploits these people for imperial gain.

The first of these messengers, Mary made her announcement in chapter 1. When she learned she would give birth to Jesus, she burst out in song (Luke 1:46–55). Christians commonly refer to her song as "the Magnificat." While Mary nowhere mentioned the phrase "kingdom of God" in the Magnificat, she unmistakably spoke of the way this radically new order would reverse traditional social roles. After all, had not God selected her, a poor, humble Jewish woman from Galilee, to give birth to the long-expected Messiah? That realization prompted Mary to sing praises to God, "for he has regarded the low estate of his handmaiden." When Mary expanded on her vision, she described what this new social order would look like.

> He has shown strength with his arm;
>> he has scattered the proud in the thoughts of their hearts.
> He has brought down the powerful from their thrones,
>> and lifted up the lowly;
> he has filled the hungry with good things,
>> and sent the rich away empty. (vv. 51–53)

In the second chapter of Luke, an angel announced this new social order. Appearing to shepherds in the field, the angel told them, "Do not be afraid; for see—I am bringing you good news of great joy for all the people: to you is born this day in the city of David a Savior, who is the Messiah, *the Lord*" (Luke 2:10–11). I have italicized the phrase "the Lord" since, in making this announcement, the angel clearly proclaimed a ruler. But in this upside-down kingdom, this ruler would be neither conventional royalty nor someone born to privilege. Rather, the angel said, "You will find a child wrapped in bands of cloth and lying in a manger." In the ancient world, a manger was nothing more than a feeding trough for farm animals—hardly a fitting place for the birth of a king.

Moreover, in the context of imperial Rome, the angel's announcement was both revolutionary and seditious, for its two key words—Savior and Lord—were titles routinely applied to the emperor Caesar Augustus. Indeed, Caesar's titles included "Divine," "Son of God," "God," "God from

God," "Redeemer," "Liberator," "Lord," and "Savior of the World." "[Early] Christians must have understood," John Dominic Crossan concludes, "that to proclaim Jesus as Son of God was deliberately denying Caesar his highest title and that to announce Jesus as Lord and Savior was calculated treason."[11] If Rome could have found the angel and put him or her to death, it surely would have done so.

In the third chapter of Luke, John the Baptist offered the third announcement of the kingdom of God and contrasted that kingdom with the empire's all-pervasive power and splendor. Luke set up the contrast beautifully, referring first to the ruling elites of his day.

> In the fifteenth year of the reign of Emperor Tiberius, when Pontius Pilate was governor of Judea, and Herod was ruler of Galilee, and his brother Philip ruler of the region of Ituraea and Trachonitis, and Lysanias ruler of Abilene, during the high priesthood of Annas and Caiaphas, the word of God came . . . . (3:1–2)

Came to whom? It came, Luke tells us, "to John son of Zechariah in the wilderness." Here, Luke subtly contrasted the wilderness where John resided with the imperial courts of Tiberius Caesar, Herod, Philip, and Lysanias. Later in his Gospel, Luke was not so subtle, since he reports that Jesus himself contrasted John's poverty with the luxury of imperial power. "What then did you go out to see?" Jesus asked the people. "Someone dressed in soft robes? Look, those who put on fine clothing and live in luxury are in royal palaces. What then did you go out to see? A prophet? Yes, I tell you, and more than a prophet" (7:25–26).

Finally, what message did John preach? Did he preach the American gospel that "God helps those who help themselves"? Hardly. According to Luke, John preached a message of radical compassion for those in need. "And the crowds asked him, 'What then should we do?' In reply he said to them, 'Whoever has two coats must share with anyone who has none; and whoever has food must do likewise'" (3:10–11). According to Matthew, John's message of compassion for those in need was nothing more and

---

[11] Crossan, *God and Empire*, 107–8, 141; and Crossan and Jonathan L. Reed, *In Search of Paul: How Jesus's Apostle Opposed Rome's Empire with God's Kingdom* (San Francisco: Harper, 2004), 11.

nothing less than the proclamation of the kingdom of God or, in Matthew's words, the kingdom of heaven (3:2).

Moreover, John apparently used that message to stand in judgment on the empire, for Luke also wrote that John rebuked Herod "because of all the evil things that Herod had done." Little wonder that Herod "shut up John in prison" (3:20). For a while, Herod protected John from those who sought to kill him, "knowing that he was a righteous and holy man" (Mark 6:20). But this preacher of the kingdom of God finally fell victim to imperial decadence and imperial politics.

Indeed, it was Herod's birthday, and the king gave a banquet for the elites of the realm—"for his courtiers and officers and for the leaders of Galilee." When Herod's daughter Herodias danced for the imperial guests, her dance pleased the king and his guests so well that he told the girl, "Ask me for whatever you wish, and I will give it." Herodias's mother, who had a grudge against John the Baptist, advised the girl to ask for John's head on a platter (Mark 6:17-26). Mark reported the rest of the story: "Immediately the king sent a soldier of the guard with orders to bring John's head. He went and beheaded him in the prison, brought his head on a platter, and gave it to the girl. Then the girl gave it to her mother" (Mark 6:27-28). The biblical text could hardly be more graphic in the way it contrasts John's message of compassion for the dispossessed—his proclamation of the kingdom of God—with the brutality of an oppressive empire.

Jesus himself offered the fourth announcement of the kingdom or rule of God—an announcement that appears in Luke chapter 4. We considered this passage earlier in this book in another context but shall do so again here in an effort to complete our catalog of the four Lukan messengers who announced the kingdom of God. As we noted earlier, Jesus in this instance—quoting from Isaiah 61:1-2—defined the scope of his ministry and the nature of his ministry and vocation.

> When he came to Nazareth, where he had been brought up, he
> went to the synagogue on the Sabbath day, as was his custom.
> He stood up to read, and the scroll of the prophet Isaiah was
> given to him. He unrolled the scroll and found the place where
> it was written:

> "The Spirit of the Lord is upon me,
>> because he has anointed me
>>> to bring good news to the poor.
> He has sent me to proclaim release to the captives
>> and recovery of sight to the blind,
>>> to let the oppressed go free,
>> to proclaim the year of the Lord's favor."

And he rolled up the scroll, gave it back to the attendant, and sat down. The eyes of all in the synagogue were fixed on him. Then he began to say to them, "Today this scripture has been fulfilled in your hearing." (Luke 4:16–21)

In its remaining chapters, the Gospel of Luke continues to elaborate on the meaning of the kingdom of God. In that kingdom, those who are first (the rich and the powerful) will be last, while those who are last (the poor and the dispossessed) will be first (13:29–30). Only those who are humble like little children can enter the kingdom of God (18:16–17). And Luke reports Jesus's comment: "How hard it is for those who have wealth to enter the kingdom of God!" (18:24).

In other words, at every step of the way, Luke takes pains to contrast the reign of God with the empires of the world whose values stand opposed to the values of the kingdom of God.

Matthew's Understanding of the Kingdom of God

Like Luke, Matthew's Gospel goes out of its way to set up the contrast between the empires of the world and the kingdom or reign of God. His first four chapters provide both prelude and context for the Sermon on the Mount, and in those chapters, Matthew tells four stories that illustrate this point.

First, Matthew explains in chapter 2 that Herod—technically the "king of the Jews," but in reality a puppet of the Roman Empire—"was frightened" when he learned of the birth of Jesus, since Jesus also had been announced as king of the Jews. And well he should have been, for as John Dominic Crossan points out, "A new and therefore a replacement King of the Jews had been appointed by God and not by Rome. . . . [We should] recognize

THE GRACE OF TROUBLESOME QUESTIONS

that Matthew's first-century counter-story is [therefore] high treason, not just a cute Christmas carol whose historicity we can discuss once a year in our media."[12]

Herod, of course, got this point and made every attempt to have Jesus killed. To make certain he left no stone unturned, Herod even ordered the murder of every child two years old and younger in the entire region of Bethlehem. In reporting this story, Matthew embraces a purpose identical to that of Luke: to highlight the radical difference between empire—a regime that seeks to maintain its power by intimidation, violence, and murder—and the upside-down kingdom of God.

Following on the heels of this story, Matthew juxtaposes the empire and the kingdom of God a second time. Mary and Joseph foiled Herod's attempt to murder their child, Matthew tells us, by fleeing to Egypt. Only when the parents learned that Herod had died did they consider returning to Israel. But when Joseph "heard that Archelaus was ruling over Judea in place of his father Herod, he was afraid to go there. And after being warned in a dream, he went away to the district of Galilee" (2:22).

Immediately after reporting that Archelaus bore all the imperial traits of his father Herod, Matthew tells us that "in those days John the Baptist appeared proclaiming," not in an imperial palace, but "in the wilderness of Judea." And what was John's message? "Repent, for the kingdom of heaven has come near." In keeping with the values of the kingdom of heaven—or the kingdom of God—Matthew wants us to know that John the Baptist was not clad in imperial regalia, but rather "wore clothing of camel's hair with a leather belt around his waist, and his food was locusts and wild honey" (3:4). The contrast between John, on the one hand, and Herod and Archelaus on the other—and therefore between the kingdom of God and empire—could hardly be greater.

In chapter 4, verses 8–10, Matthew sets up the third contrast between empire and the kingdom of God. In that text, Matthew reports that "the devil took him [Jesus] to a very high mountain and showed him all the kingdoms of the world and their splendor; and he said to him, 'All these I will give you, if you will fall down and worship me.'" Here Matthew makes

---

[12] Crossan, *God and Empire*, 107.

a point that is crucial for grasping the New Testament understanding of empire: in the present age, Satan rules all the empires and kingdoms of this world. For this reason, Jesus responds, "Away with you, Satan! For it is written, 'Worship the Lord your God, and serve only him.'" And then, in an effort to contrast empire and the kingdom of God once again, Matthew tells us, "From that time Jesus began to proclaim, 'Repent, for the kingdom of heaven has come near'" (v. 17).

What should we make of these stories? And why would Matthew report that Jesus said, "Repent, for the kingdom of heaven has come near"? Matthew's point is simply this: Empires inevitably embrace greed, self-interest, and violence in order to maintain their power and privilege. But the kingdom of God lifts up those who suffer at the empire's hands. Jesus wants his hearers to know that a radically new kingdom—one that turns the empire's values upside down—has become a reality for them. For this reason, Jesus tells his audience, "Repent, for the kingdom of heaven has come near."

Matthew concludes chapter 4 by relating his fourth vignette, namely that Jesus preached "the good news of the kingdom." Tellingly, Matthew links the phrase "the good news of the kingdom" with Jesus's concern for those whom the Roman Empire had brushed aside. Central to the "good news of the kingdom," therefore, is Matthew's report that Jesus healed "every disease and every sickness among the people. . . . And they brought to him all the sick, those who were afflicted with various diseases and pains, demoniacs, epileptics, and paralytics, and he cured them" (4:23–24). The gospel—the good news—of the kingdom, therefore, proclaims that while empires exalt the rich, the privileged, and the elite, the kingdom of God exalts the poor, the suffering, the sick, and those society has rejected.

A story that illustrates Matthew's message is one told by Eldridge Cleaver, one-time minister of information for the Black Panther Party, in his book *Soul on Ice*. There Cleaver tells of Chris Lovdjieff, an extraordinary teacher who cared so deeply for the prisoners—those outcasts from American life—that he voluntarily taught at San Quentin federal penitentiary every day, from 8:00 a.m. until 10:00 p.m., except Sunday, when the prison officials deliberately kept him away. "Had they given him a cell," Cleaver reports, "he would have taken it." At 10:00 p.m., when the guards made him leave, "he'd go home to suffer in exile until school opened the next day."

Not only did Lovdjieff care more for prisoners than for those outside the prison's walls; within the prison he cared especially for those who were slow to learn. "He was drawn," Cleaver reports, "to those students who seemed impossible to teach—old men who had been illiterate all their lives and set in their ways." Then Cleaver adds: "Lovdjieff didn't believe that anyone or anything in the universe was 'set in its ways.' Those students who were intelligent and quickest to learn he seemed reluctant to bother with, almost as if to say, pointing at the illiterates and speaking to the bright ones: 'Go away. Leave me. You don't need me. These others do.'"[13] This story of Lovdjieff—a man who committed himself to the poorest of the poor and those who were marginal even among the marginalized—illustrates almost perfectly Matthew's understanding of the kingdom of God as he presents that kingdom in chapters 1 through 4.

By the time Matthew relates Jesus's Sermon on the Mount, beginning in chapter 5, he has already set up the context in which the sermon should be understood: the struggle between the empire, with its concern for wealth, power, and privilege, and the kingdom of God, with its concern for the poor, the downtrodden, and the dispossessed.

Warren Carter, whose superb scholarship on the book of Matthew has inspired my own understanding of that text, explains that Matthew's Sermon on the Mount is a "work of imagination" that enables "disciples to envision life shaped by God's reign/empire."[14] In other words, the Sermon on the Mount, and especially the Beatitudes with which that sermon begins, invites the dispossessed to *imagine* a life that is rich and abundant—a life that conforms to the reign of God as opposed to the reign of Caesar.

Matthew's invitation to the imagination was itself a subversive act, for imagination is precisely what all imperial regimes seek to suppress. As Walter Brueggemann explains in his aptly titled book *The Prophetic Imagination*, "The same royal consciousness that makes it possible to implement anything and everything is the one that shrinks imagination

---

[13] Eldridge Cleaver, *Soul on Ice* (New York: Dell, 1968), 31–39.

[14] Warren Carter, "Power and Identities: The Contexts of Matthew's Sermon on the Mount," in *Preaching the Sermon on the Mount: The World It Imagines*, ed. David Fleer and Dave Bland (St. Louis: Chalice Press, 2007), 14.

because imagination is a danger."[15] Indeed, Brueggemann notes that imperial regimes seek to thwart not only imagination but passion as well: "Passion as the capacity and readiness to care, to suffer, to die, and to feel is the enemy of imperial reality. Imperial economics is designed to keep people satiated so that they do not notice. Its politics is intended to block out the cries of the denied ones. Its religion is to be an opiate so that no one discerns misery alive in the heart of God."[16] This is why "the vocation of the prophet [is] to keep alive the ministry of imagination, to keep on conjuring and proposing alternative futures to the single one the king wants to urge as the only thinkable one."[17]

As we know, Jesus stood squarely in the prophetic tradition, and it should therefore come as no surprise to discover that the Beatitudes are, at heart, an invitation to imagine—to imagine a richer, fuller, more abundant life, though a life independent of the values of the empire. And for Jesus, abundant life is life defined by the kingdom of God.

As we begin to explore the Beatitudes, we should recognize that, like the kingdom of God to which they point, they too are concerned with two primary virtues: justice and peace. The first four Beatitudes address the subject of social justice, while the last five address the subject of peace and peacemaking.

The First Four Beatitudes: Justice for the Poor and the Dispossessed

According to Matthew, Jesus begins his comments on social justice in the opening words of the Sermon on the Mount: "Blessed are the poor in spirit," Jesus says, "for theirs is the kingdom of heaven." As we noted earlier, Matthew is the only Gospel writer to use the phrase "kingdom of heaven," and he means for that phrase to signify the kingdom of God. Further, the "poor in spirit" are the poor. I base this interpretation on the Gospel of Luke whose rendition of the Sermon on the Plain has Jesus saying, "Blessed are you who are poor, for yours is the kingdom of God" (6:20).

---

[15] Brueggemann, *Prophetic Imagination*, 45.

[16] Brueggemann, *Prophetic Imagination*, 41.

[17] Brueggemann, *Prophetic Imagination*, 45.

I am aware that some scholars understand the phrase "poor in spirit" to signify humility. But I find very compelling Warren Carter's view that these "are the literal, physical poor, the destitute, those who live in social and economic hardship, lacking adequate resources, exploited and oppressed by the powerful and despised by the elite." The notion that "poor in spirit" means "humility" runs counter, Carter argues, to the overarching theme in Scripture that "God will save the poor."[18]

But why would Matthew have Jesus describe these people as "the poor in spirit" instead of simply "the poor"? He does this because he knows that empire inevitably grinds the faces of the poor, crushes the human spirit, and leaves its victims with little hope, virtually no sense of worth, and minimal self-esteem. In this Beatitude, therefore, Jesus brings good news: Though the empire has rejected these people as completely worthless, the kingdom of God restores their dignity and views them as blessed and highly esteemed. In this way, the first Beatitude—"Blessed are the poor in spirit, for theirs is the kingdom of heaven"—challenged the empire's values with the values of the kingdom of God.

Each of the other Beatitudes picked up on this very same theme. For example, Jesus told those who mourned that they, too, would be blessed. "Blessed are those who mourn, for they will be comforted," Matthew reports that Jesus said (5:4). In the empire they will find no comfort, but in the kingdom of God they will.

In the third Beatitude, Jesus told his hearers, "Blessed are the meek, for they will inherit the earth" (Matt. 5:5). In this Beatitude, Jesus picked up on Psalm 37:11—a passage that assured the meek that they "shall possess the land"—another way of saying that the meek would inherit the earth. Psalm 37 fit Jesus's concern precisely, for it turned the tables on those who aligned themselves with imperial values at the expense of the poor and the dispossessed:

The meek shall inherit the land,
  and delight themselves in abundant prosperity.

The wicked plot against the righteous,
  and gnash their teeth at them;

---

[18] Carter, *Matthew and the Margins: A Sociopolitical and Religious Reading* (Maryknoll, NY: Orbis, 2000), 131.

but the Lᴏʀᴅ laughs at the wicked,
>   for he sees that their day is coming.

The wicked draw the sword and bend their bows
>   to bring down the poor and needy,
>   to kill those who walk uprightly;
their sword shall enter their own heart,
>   and their bows shall be broken. (11–15)

The fourth Beatitude pronounced a blessing on those "who hunger and thirst for righteousness, for they will be filled" (v. 6). Since the Greek language uses the very same word for "justice" as for "righteousness," it is safe to conclude that those who hunger and thirst for righteousness are those who hunger and thirst for justice. But the empire offered precious little justice for the poor and the dispossessed. Indeed, Richard Horsley and Neil Silberman report that early Christians "were rounded up, beaten up, and condemned to execution for atheism and treason—that is, failing to participate in the state-controlled cults of the gods of the Greco-Roman pantheon and abandoning honored family values of pagan society."[19] But Matthew's Sermon on the Mount assured the oppressed that the day would come when their longing for justice would be satisfied.

If the kingdom of God was that place or circumstance in which the poor and the disenfranchised would find justice, compassion, and mercy, Jesus also made it clear that no one could enter the kingdom of God without reaching out to the poor and the dispossessed in precisely those ways. For example, Luke reports that a ruler asked Jesus what he must do to inherit eternal life. Jesus told him to keep the commandments. That response obviously pleased the ruler who quickly replied, "I have kept all these since my youth." Then Luke adds:

> When Jesus heard this, he said to him, "There is still one thing lacking. Sell all that you own and distribute the money to the poor, and you will have treasure in heaven; then come, follow me." But when he heard this, he became sad; for he was very

---

[19] Richard A. Horsley and Neil Asher Silberman, *The Message and the Kingdom: How Jesus and Paul Ignited a Revolution and Transformed the Ancient World* (Minneapolis: Fortress Press, 1997), 9.

rich. Jesus looked at him and said, "How hard it is for those who have wealth to enter the kingdom of God!" (18:22–24)

Luke also reports that Jesus gave this advice to his followers:

> When you give a luncheon or a dinner, do not invite your
> friends or your brothers or your relatives or rich neighbors, in
> case they may invite you in return, and you would be repaid. But
> when you give a banquet, invite the poor, the crippled, the lame,
> and the blind. And you will be blessed, because they cannot
> repay you, for you will be repaid at the resurrection of the righ-
> teous. (14:12–14)

But there is no passage in the entirety of the New Testament that sets the terms for entry into the kingdom of God in such stark relief as does the description of the last judgment that appears in Matthew's Gospel. That passage makes it clear that compassion for the dispossessed is the funda- mental criterion for entry into the kingdom of God. This passage is lengthy, but it is so important for grasping the meaning of the phrase "kingdom of God" that it deserves to be quoted in its entirety:

> When the Son of Man comes in his glory, and all the angels with
> him, then he will sit on the throne of his glory. All the nations
> will be gathered before him, and he will separate people one
> from another as a shepherd separates the sheep from the goats,
> and he will put the sheep at his right hand and the goats at the
> left. Then the king will say to those at his right hand, "Come,
> you that are blessed by my Father, inherit the kingdom prepared
> for you from the foundation of the world; for I was hungry and
> you gave me food, I was thirsty and you gave me something to
> drink, I was a stranger and you welcomed me, I was naked and
> you gave me clothing, I was sick and you took care of me, I was
> in prison and you visited me." Then the righteous will answer
> him, "Lord, when was it that we saw you hungry and gave you
> food, or thirsty and gave you something to drink? And when

was it that we saw you a stranger and welcomed you, or naked
and gave you clothing? And when was it that we saw you sick
or in prison and visited you?" And the king will answer them,
"Truly I tell you, just as you did it to one of the least of these who
are members of my family, you did it to me." Then he will say to
those at his left hand, "You that are accursed, depart from me
into the eternal fire prepared for the devil and his angels; for I
was hungry and you gave me no food, I was thirsty and you gave
me nothing to drink, I was a stranger and you did not welcome
me, naked and you did not give me clothing, sick and in prison
and you did not visit me." Then they also will answer, "Lord,
when was it that we saw you hungry or thirsty or a stranger or
naked or sick or in prison, and did not take care of you?" Then
he will answer them, "Truly I tell you, just as you did not do it to
one of the least of these, you did not do it to me." And these will
go away into eternal punishment, but the righteous into eternal
life. (25:31–46)

To make certain we understand this passage, it will be helpful to cite
Michael Himes, who offers the following comments on this text from
Matthew 25:

> To the best of my knowledge, this is the only passage in the
> whole of the collection of documents which we call the New
> Testament which describes the last judgment. . . . And notice
> what the only criterion of the last judgment is. There is not a
> word about whether you belonged to the church, not a word
> about whether you were baptized, not a syllable about whether
> you ever celebrated the Eucharist, not a question about whether
> you prayed, nothing at all about what creed you professed or
> what you knew about doctrine or theology. Indeed, there is
> nothing specifically religious at all. Not one doctrine, not one
> specifically religious act of worship or ritual turns out to be rele-
> vant to the criterion for the last judgment. The only criterion for

that final judgment according to Matthew 25, is how you treated your brothers and sisters.[20]

As a Roman Catholic priest, Himes was not willing to suggest that prayer, sacraments, and liturgy were unimportant. But he did want to suggest that without compassion for one's brothers and sisters—and especially for those Jesus called "the least of these"—religious ritual becomes essentially meaningless. That, of course, is the witness of the biblical text from start to finish. Some of the passages we have cited—and many we have not—make precisely that point. Recall, for example, these words from Amos that we considered earlier in this book:

> Take away from me the noise of your songs;
> I will not listen to the melody of your harps.
> But let justice roll down like waters,
> and righteousness like an ever-flowing stream! (5:23–24)

Or these words from Isaiah:

> Is not this the fast that I choose:
> to loose the bonds of injustice . . . ?
> Is it not to share your bread with the hungry . . .
> when you see the naked, to cover them . . . ? (58:6–7)

Or these words from Hosea:

> I desire mercy, not sacrifice. (6:6 NIV)

Jesus himself quoted this passage from Hosea—"I desire mercy, not sacrifice"—when he sought to explain that justice and mercy always trump religious ritual (Matt. 12:7). And he told numerous stories that made this very same point. Especially well known is the story about the "good Samaritan" who helped a traveler whom robbers had beaten and left on the side of the road to die. But the Samaritan did so only after religious professionals, eager to tend to their ceremonial duties in the temple, ignored the

---

[20] Michael Himes, *Doing the Truth in Love: Conversations about God, Relationships and Service* (New York: Paulist Press, 1995), 51.

traveler and passed him by on the far side of the road. Then Jesus asked:

> "Which of these three, do you think, was a neighbor to the man
> who fell into the hands of the robbers?" [The lawyer] said, "The
> one who showed him mercy." Jesus said to him, "Go and do like-
> wise." (Luke 10:36–37)

In his book *A Man without a Country*, Kurt Vonnegut told a story that
captures the compelling power of Jesus's teachings—especially his teachings in the Sermon on the Mount—about the vulnerable and the poor.
Vonnegut's story also explains why those who have embraced the values
of empire find Jesus's teachings so puzzling.

Reflecting on the fact that so many socialists aided the poor in the early
years of the twentieth century, Vonnegut told of one of those socialists with
whom he was personally acquainted—Powers Hapgood, a Hoosier from
Indianapolis. Hapgood was reared in a middle-class home and earned a
degree from Harvard but decided to devote his life to tireless labor on
behalf of the poor. After graduating from Harvard, he took a job as a coal
miner and, as Vonnegut put it, urged "his working-class brothers to organize in order to get better pay and safer working conditions." When the
state of Massachusetts executed anarchists Nicola Sacco and Bartolomeo
Vanzetti in 1927, Hapgood was there, protesting their execution. Having
sketched out this background, Vonnegut then recalled:

> We met in Indianapolis after the end of the Second World War.
> He had become an official in the CIO. There had been some
> sort of dust-up on a picket line, and he was testifying about
> it in court, and the judge stops everything and asks him, "Mr.
> Hapgood, here you are, you're a graduate of Harvard. Why
> would anyone with your advantages choose to live as you have?"
> Hapgood answered the judge: "Why, because of the Sermon on
> the Mount, sir."[21]

What more can one say?

---

[21] Kurt Vonnegut, *A Man without a Country* (New York: Random House, 2007), 13–14.

The Last Five Beatitudes: Jesus's Teachings on Peacemaking, Suffering, and Nonviolence

The fifth through ninth Beatitudes are all closely related, since they counsel mercy, peacemaking, and nonviolence. "Blessed are the merciful," Jesus says in the fifth of these statements, "for they will receive mercy." And then in the seventh, "Blessed are the peacemakers, for they will be called children of God."

When Jesus says that peacemakers will be called "children of God," he rejected the values of the empire in two respects. First, as we have seen, "Son of God" was one of the titles the emperor ascribed to himself. And second, the word used here for "peacemaker" (*eirenepoios* in Greek) was inscribed on imperial coins during Jesus's own time, thereby suggesting that the emperor—that imperial "son of God"—was himself a peacemaker.[22] And indeed he was. But the emperor made peace by force of arms, thereby sustaining the *Pax Romana* (the peace of Rome), while the peacemakers Jesus commends made peace through kindness, forgiveness, and patience. Indeed, they made peace by showing mercy. In this way, they resisted the empire's values and embraced instead the values of the kingdom of God. Jesus's blessing on these peacemakers—and his affirmation that they would be called the "children of God"—was itself an act of subversion.

Both mercy and peacemaking are essentially foreign to the imperial vision and those who support it, both then and now. This truth helps explain why so many Americans were shocked in October 2006 when the Amish near Nickel Mines, Pennsylvania, refused to take vengeance against the killer of their children—or against the killer's family—but forgave instead. It explains why most Americans were shocked once again in June 2015 when members of Mother Bethel AME Church in Charleston, South Carolina, rejected vengeance against the man who murdered church members during an evening prayer service but forgave instead. It also explains why the United States responded to the tragedy of September 11, 2001, with vengeance and retribution. In other words, the American response to 9/11 reflected the way empires inevitably behave. But in these two Beatitudes,

---

[22] Roland Bainton, *Christian Attitudes toward War and Peace: A Historical Survey and Critical Re-Evaluation* (Nashville: Abingdon, 1960), 64.

Jesus counsels values that are foreign to any empire but central to the kingdom of God: mercy and peacemaking.

The sixth, eighth, and ninth Beatitudes continue the themes of peacemaking and nonviolence, since they pronounce blessings both on the pure in heart and on those who suffer persecution for righteousness' sake. Here is the way those Beatitudes read:

> Blessed are the pure in heart, for they will see God. (Matt. 5:8)

> Blessed are those who are persecuted for righteousness' sake, for theirs is the kingdom of heaven. (5:10)

> Blessed are you when people revile you and persecute you and utter all kinds of evil against you falsely on my account. Rejoice and be glad, for your reward is great in heaven, for in the same way they persecuted the prophets who were before you. (5:11–12)

Why do I suggest that these three Beatitudes go together? Because those who are pure in heart are those who reject the impulse to hate when faced with oppression and persecution. And in the context of the Roman Empire, the poor were faced with oppression every day.

Later in the Sermon on the Mount, in his most explicit and radical teaching on peacemaking and nonviolence, Jesus expounded on the Beatitudes that focused on these themes when he counseled love for one's enemies. Here is the way Matthew reports that teaching:

> You have heard that it was said, "An eye for an eye and a tooth for a tooth." But I say to you, Do not resist an evildoer. But if anyone strikes you on the right cheek, turn the other also; and if anyone wants to sue you and take your coat, give your cloak as well; and if anyone forces you to go one mile, go also the second mile. Give to everyone who begs from you, and do not refuse anyone who wants to borrow from you.
>
> You have heard that it was said, "You shall love your neighbor and hate your enemy." But I say to you, Love your enemies and pray for those who persecute you, so that you may be children of your Father in heaven. (5:38–45)

It is difficult for Americans, so accustomed to violence and retribution, to imagine that Jesus could possibly have meant these teachings in any literal sense. Yet the emphasis on peacemaking and nonviolence is constant throughout the New Testament. In fact, there is no theme more central to what Christians call their "gospel" (good news), since the gospel focuses on the Christian claim that Jesus refused to resist those who sought to kill him but instead gave his life for the sake of others.

According to Matthew, just hours before he was crucified, one of his disciples, in an obvious attempt to defend Jesus, drew a sword and "struck the slave of the high priest, cutting off his ear." But Matthew reports that Jesus said to his disciples: "Put your sword back into its place; for all who take the sword will perish by the sword. Do you think that I cannot appeal to my Father, and he will at once send me more than twelve legions of angels?" (26:51–53).

John's Gospel reports that during the course of his trial, Jesus said to Pilate, "My kingdom is not from this world. If my kingdom were from this world, my followers would be fighting to keep me from being handed over to the Jews. But as it is, my kingdom is not from here" (18:36). Indeed, it was not, for Jesus consistently claimed that he represented an altogether different kingdom that he called "the kingdom of God." And this kingdom was one of peacemaking and nonviolence.

Paul's Understanding of the Kingdom of God

Second only to Jesus, the apostle Paul stands at the heart of the New Testament text. Scholars have credited Paul with writing between seven and thirteen of the twenty-two New Testament epistles. And Luke's history of the earliest Christians—a book called the Acts of the Apostles—devotes an extraordinary amount of time, space, and attention to Paul's work as a missionary to the Gentile world. Because Paul plays such an integral role in the New Testament, it is important to ask how he understood the meaning of the kingdom of God.

Before addressing that question, we need to address two preliminary issues. First, we must acknowledge that many Christians over the past five hundred years, at least in Protestant circles, have been slow to discern Paul's theology of the kingdom of God. This theological blind spot is largely due to Martin Luther. In 1517 Luther discovered the theme of justification by grace through faith—surely one of the central themes in Paul's thought—and built the Reformation around it.

In elaborating the notion of justification by grace through faith, Paul argues that the human condition is so compromised that no person can possibly win God's favor—that is, God's love and forgiveness—by performing good works. Rather, God bestows his favor freely, by *grace.* That is such an incredible proposition, Paul argues, that it makes no sense to human reason. The gospel therefore asks men and women to accept God's grace through *faith.* Ever since Luther, Christians have used a shorthand description for this rather elaborate theology, and that shorthand is this simple phrase: *justification by grace through faith.*

There is no question that justification by grace through faith is a central theme in Paul's theology. The passage that first alerted Luther to the prominence of that motif is Romans 1:16–17: "For I am not ashamed of the gospel [good news]; it is the power of God for salvation to everyone who has faith, to the Jew first and also to the Greek. For . . . 'The one who is righteous will live by faith.'" In time, Luther found that theme throughout Paul's writings. For example, Paul writes in Galatians, "We ourselves are Jews by birth and not Gentile sinners; yet we know that a person is justified not by the works of the law but through faith in Jesus Christ" (2:15–16). The most pointed statement on justification by grace through faith appears in Ephesians 2:8–9: "For by grace you have been saved through faith, and this is not your own doing; it is the gift of God—not the result of works, so that no one may boast."

Many Christians have supposed that justification by grace through faith precludes a robust theology of the kingdom of God, simply because kingdom theology entails ethics and behavior—what some Christians regard as *works.* As we have seen, Paul clearly warned that no good works of any kind, whether moral or ceremonial, can possibly secure one's salvation. But in Paul's theology, justification by grace through faith by no means precludes the theme of the kingdom of God, as we shall shortly see. In fact, these two themes are closely related to each other, tied together by the centerpiece of Paul's theology—namely, Jesus the Christ.

The second preliminary issue concerns the extent to which Paul may have built his understanding of the kingdom of God on the Hebrew prophets and on the teachings of Jesus. In the context of that question, the fact that Paul was martyred in Rome sometime between 62 and 67 BCE is a crucial consideration. Since all the Gospels—Matthew, Mark, Luke, and John—appeared during the last third of the first century BCE, Paul's epistles obviously precede the Gospel accounts of the life and teachings of Jesus. At the same time, Paul must have known the oral tradition of Jesus's understanding of the kingdom of God. And as a learned Jew who studied at the rabbinical school of Gamaliel, he clearly was familiar with the Hebrew prophets who preached to Israel and Judah during the eighth century BCE and afterward.

Paul seldom uses the actual phrase, "kingdom of God." If, however, we allow Jesus and the prophets to define the meaning of the kingdom of God, then it is clear that Paul employs the *concept* of the kingdom of God with great regularity. In fact, it is safe to say that the notion of the kingdom of God—that is, God's rule, dominion, and authority over all the earth—is among the most important motifs in Pauline thought, for Paul returns time and again to the two principal characteristics of that kingdom: peace and justice.

What sets Paul apart from the prophets, on the one hand, and Jesus, on the other, is the way he grounds his vision of the kingdom of God in his conviction that Jesus Christ is Lord. Of course, one finds the claim that Jesus is Lord in the Gospels as well—a point we emphasized in a previous discussion. The angel, for example, announced to the shepherds, "To you is born this day . . . a Savior, who is the Messiah, the Lord" (Luke 2:11). But Paul turns that confession into an elaborate theological framework that undergirds everything he says about peace and justice in the kingdom of God.

Paul's starting point for understanding the kingdom of God is a notion we encountered in the Gospels and the notion Donald Kraybill has described as "the upside-down kingdom." In other words, Paul begins with a paradox, and the heart of that paradox is this: because Jesus emptied himself, took on the form of common humanity, and finally succumbed to the most disgraceful form of death in the ancient world—death by

crucifixion—he has become Lord of the universe. It would be difficult to
find a more striking paradox than this, for by the standards of the Roman
Empire, this assertion was simply absurd.

Paul makes this argument often, but he never makes it more forcefully
than he does in Philippians 2:5–11:

> Let the same mind be in you that was in Christ Jesus,
>> who, though he was in the form of God,
>>> did not regard equality with God
>>> as something to be exploited,
>> but emptied himself,
>>> taking the form of a slave,
>>> being born in human likeness.
>> And being found in human form,
>>> he humbled himself
>>> and became obedient to the point of death—
>>> even death on a cross.
> Therefore God also highly exalted him
>> and gave him the name
>> that is above every name,
> so that at the name of Jesus
>> every knee should bend,
>> in heaven and on earth and under the earth,
> and every tongue should confess
>> that Jesus Christ is Lord,
>> to the glory of God the Father.

Three features of this passage deserve special comment, and these
three features are, in fact, the defining elements of Paul's understanding of
the kingdom of God. First, in this text Paul clearly—and no doubt deliberately and self-consciously—rejects the Roman Empire's claim of supremacy
and the emperor's claim of divinity. In fact, since the proclamation that
"Jesus is Lord" was treason against the empire, one would be hard-pressed
to find a more treasonous statement than this in the entire New Testament.
For Paul here not only claims that Jesus is Lord. He also claims that the
day will come when, at the name of Jesus, *every* knee will bend and *every*

tongue will confess that Jesus is Lord. Further, one would be hard-pressed to find anywhere in the biblical text a more definitive description of the kingdom of God—the rule of Christ over all the earth.

We begin to grasp how radical Paul's assertions in this text really are when we realize that he wrote these words from an imperial prison, and that from that prison he could claim that "our citizenship is in heaven [i.e., in God's kingdom], and it is from there [and not from the empire] that we are expecting a Savior, the Lord Jesus Christ" (Phil. 3:20). Both here and in his other letters, Paul hammers on this anti-imperial theme time and again. For example, in 1 Corinthians 15:24–25, he writes that when the end finally comes, Christ will "hand over the kingdom to God the Father, after he has destroyed every ruler and every authority and power. For he must reign until he has put all his enemies under his feet." It is important to note that Paul in this text classifies "*every* ruler and *every* authority and power" as among God's "enemies" whom Christ will place "under his feet."

Second, Paul portrays Jesus as one who "emptied himself," "humbled himself," and "became obedient to the point of death." In other words, by accepting persecution and death on behalf of others, Jesus modeled self-giving and self-abasing love. That kind of love, Paul writes, is essentially unknown: "Rarely will anyone die for a righteous person—though perhaps for a good person someone might actually dare to die. But God proves his love for us in that while we still were sinners Christ died for us" (Rom. 5:7–8).

In Paul's judgment, that sort of radical, self-giving love is utterly foreign to the empires and rulers of this world and beyond their comprehension. For them, therefore, the story of Jesus is utter foolishness. "For the message about the cross is foolishness to those who are perishing," he writes in 1 Corinthians 1:18. And that assertion becomes the basis for an extended contrast Paul makes between the "wisdom of God" that is foolishness to this world, and the "wisdom of this world" that, in the grand scheme of things, is utter foolishness, at least if judged by what we know about God (1 Cor. 1:18–2:8). In drawing that contrast, Paul once again revels in paradox—this time the paradox of the upside-down-ness of the kingdom of God.

Indeed, Paul uses the term *God's wisdom* to describe radical, self-giving love, and the term *human wisdom* to describe the depths of self-interest, violence, and greed that always characterize the imperial powers. The "wisdom" that characterized his preaching, he claims, was "not a wisdom of this age or of the rulers of this age, who are doomed to perish. But we speak God's wisdom" (1 Cor. 2:6–7). Further, "none of the rulers of this age understood this; for if they had, they would not have crucified the Lord of glory" (1 Cor. 2:8). John Dominic Crossan and Jonathan Reed are exactly right when they note that "the rulers of this age are, proximately, the Roman authorities who executed Jesus, but they are, ultimately, the cosmic powers that make imperial violence and human injustice the normalcy of human history and the permanent patina of civilization."[23] This means that Paul's judgment on the Roman Empire is equally a judgment on the American empire, for both are rooted in what Paul calls the "wisdom of this age."

Third, based on this Christ who "empties" and "humbles" himself, Paul develops his understanding of social ethics—the way those who belong to the kingdom of God must behave. And the heart of Paul's social ethic appears in the very first line of our paradigmatic passage: "Let the same mind be in you that was in Christ Jesus" (Phil. 2:5). And as we have seen, the mind that was in Christ Jesus was a mind of humility, compassion, and self-giving love.

Based on that "mind of Christ" and that "wisdom of God," Paul places two themes at the heart of his social ethic—an ethic that reflected his view of the kingdom of God. Those two themes are justice, on the one hand, and peace and peacemaking, on the other. As we have seen, these are the same two themes that defined the kingdom of God in both the preaching of the Hebrew prophets and the teachings of Jesus.

The Kingdom of God in the Book of Revelation

We turn now to the last book of the New Testament—the Apocalypse of John, otherwise known as the book of Revelation. Scholars debate whether this book was written by John the apostle or by another John, sometimes known as John of Patmos. They also debate whether the book was written

[23] Crossan and Reed, *In Search of Paul*, 336.

near the end of the reign of the Roman Emperor Nero, in the late 60s CE, or near the end of the reign of Emperor Domitian in 95 or 96 CE.

Either way, we can be confident of at least one of the book's central themes: the conviction that the kingdom of God will finally triumph over the oppressive, imperial power that was the Roman Empire. And we can be confident that the backdrop to this book was imperial persecution of the Christian movement. Revelation reflects these persecutions in several passages, but especially chapter 20, verse 4:

> I also saw the souls of those who had been beheaded for their testimony to Jesus and for the word of God. They had not worshiped the beast [read: empire or emperor] or its image and had not received its mark on their foreheads or their hands.

In the face of harassment and persecution, therefore, John counsels Christians to refuse allegiance to the empire but to remain faithful to the values of the kingdom of God, even unto death. In this way, the book of Revelation simply continues a theme that is prominent throughout the New Testament: the struggle between empire and the kingdom of God. One verse in Revelation captures this message nicely:

> Do not fear what you are about to suffer. Beware, the devil is about to throw some of you into prison so that you may be tested, and for ten days you will have affliction. Be faithful unto death, and I will give you the crown of life. (2:10)

The metaphor for empire in this particular text is Babylon. Since Babylon had long since vanished from the earth, it seems clear that Babylon is a symbol for Rome and its dominance over the ancient world. Indeed, John presents Rome as a violent and licentious empire that has corrupted the earth with its lust for power and wealth, defiled the nations with its greed, built its empire by oppressing the poor, and persecuted those who pledged allegiance to Jesus and refused allegiance to the state. John therefore writes to assure the Christian community that, even though Babylon seems all-powerful now, the day will come when Babylon will fall and the kingdom of God will emerge victorious. Thus, he writes:

Fallen, fallen is Babylon the great!
It has become a dwelling place of demons . . . .
For all the nations have drunk
of the wine of the wrath of her fornication,
and the kings of the earth have committed fornication with her,
and the merchants of the earth have grown rich from the
power of her luxury. (18:2–3)

Further, the merchants of Babylon (read Rome)—the elites of the earth—had built their fortunes on the blood of the marginalized and the dispossessed. Reflecting on that fact, John continues:

For your merchants were the magnates of the earth,
and all nations were deceived by your sorcery.
And in you was found the blood of prophets and of saints,
and of all who have been slaughtered on earth. (18:23–24)

When Babylon falls—and fall she will—the kings and merchants of the earth will find themselves in despair, since the source of their own ill-gotten gain will be no more. John therefore offers this vision:

The kings of the earth, who committed fornication and lived
in luxury with her, will weep and wail over her when they see
the smoke of her burning; they will stand far off, in fear of her
torment, and say,
"Alas, alas, the great city,
Babylon, the mighty city!
For in one hour your judgment has come." (18:9–10)

[And] the merchants . . . who gained wealth from her, will stand
far off, in fear of her torment, weeping and mourning aloud,
"Alas, alas, the great city
clothed in fine linen,
in purple and scarlet,
adorned with gold,
with jewels, and with pearls!
For in one hour all this wealth has been laid waste!" (18:15–17)

Even the sailors from neighboring nations will weep and mourn, for they understood all too well that Babylon's destruction would put an end to their profit-taking.

> And all shipmasters and seafarers, sailors and all whose trade is
> on the sea, stood far off and cried out as they saw the smoke of
> her burning,
>> "What city was like the great city?"
> And they threw dust on their heads, as they wept and mourned,
> crying out,
>> "Alas, alas, the great city,
>>> where all who had ships at sea
>>> grew rich by her wealth!
>> For in one hour she has been laid waste." (18:17–19)

According to Revelation, what allowed Babylon to commit such extraordinary crimes was the fact that Babylon arrogated to itself qualities that belong only to God. Indeed, the text says that Babylon "glorified herself" (18:7). Through her extraordinary wealth and power, she sought to determine the course of human history. She denied she committed evil deeds and claimed for herself a radical sense of innocence. Though she herself was demonic, she confused herself with the holy city, Jerusalem. For all these reasons, she imagined that she was eternal and would have no end. Thus she said, "I rule as a queen; I am no widow, and I will never see grief" (18:7).

What an extraordinary description of the Roman Empire this was! Domitian, who may have ruled when John wrote this book, required his subjects to address him as "*dominus et deus*," that is, "Lord and God," and worship his image. In truth, Rome imagined that she was the very "kingdom of God," though in point of fact, she opposed the kingdom of God at every step along the way.

The book of Revelation insists that glory and honor belong not to Babylon but to God. John therefore exults over the destruction of Babylon in the following words:

After this I heard what seemed to be the loud voice of a great
multitude in heaven, saying,
> "Hallelujah!
> Salvation and glory and power to our God,
>> for his judgments are true and just;
> he has judged the great whore
>> who corrupted the earth with her fornication,
> and he has avenged on her the blood of his servants." (19:1–2)

Finally, John draws the contrast between Babylon, filled with brutality
and debauchery, and the gentle kingdom of God:

And I saw the holy city, the new Jerusalem, coming down out of
heaven from God, prepared as a bride adorned for her husband.
And I heard a loud voice from the throne saying,
> "See, the home of God is among mortals.
> He will dwell with them;
> they will be his peoples,
> and God himself will be with them;
> he will wipe every tear from their eyes.
> Death will be no more;
> mourning and crying and pain will be no more,
> for the first things have passed away." (21:2–4)

Upon reading this passage, one can hardly help but recall the Beatitudes in Matthew's rendition of the Sermon on the Mount. In both texts,
the kingdom of God will bring peace, mercy, justice, and comfort to those
who have suffered and endured the twisted values of a brutal empire.
Throughout the New Testament, this is the fundamental meaning—and
the fundamental promise—of the kingdom of God.

Still, we must admit that in its portrayal of the kingdom of God,
Revelation is a highly ambiguous text. It clearly depicts the triumph of
the kingdom of God over the brutal, self-serving nations of the earth. But
unlike other New Testament texts that argue that the kingdom of God will
triumph not by might nor by power but, instead, by humility, patience, and
love—even love for one's enemies—Revelation argues that the kingdom of

God will triumph over the imperial powers through violent destruction. Put another way, while other New Testament texts present the paradoxical dimension of the kingdom of God—one lives by dying to self, one wins by losing, one becomes first by putting one's self last, and so on—one finds in Revelation no hint of paradox at all.

Indeed, Revelation 18:6–7 has an angel from heaven passing judgment on the Roman Empire, metaphorically depicted here as Babylon:

Render to her as she herself has rendered,
  and repay her double for her deeds;
    mix a double draught for her in the cup she mixed.
As she glorified herself and lived luxuriously,
  so give her a like measure of torment and grief.

This judgment can only be described as "an eye for an eye and a tooth for a tooth" carried to an extreme, for the admonition is clear: "repay her double," an ethic utterly foreign to the vision of the kingdom of God depicted in the rest of the New Testament text. After this portrayal of Babylon's utter destruction, this book offers a picture of the heavenly host rejoicing that God "has avenged on her [Babylon] the blood of his servants" (19:2).

After working one's way through the entire New Testament and growing accustomed to the standard picture of the kingdom of God—that is, "Blessed are those who are persecuted for righteousness' sake, for theirs is the kingdom of heaven"—one can only be startled by Revelation's portrayal of divine vengeance. But one is startled even further when one discovers that the purveyor of this violence is none other than Jesus, the Prince of Peace! Thus, according to Revelation 19:11–16:

I saw heaven opened, and there was a white horse! Its rider is called Faithful and True, and in righteousness he judges and makes war. His eyes are like a flame of fire, and on his head are many diadems; and he has a name inscribed that no one knows but himself. He is clothed in a robe dipped in blood, and his name is called The Word of God. And the armies of heaven, wearing fine linen, white and pure, were following him on white horses. From his mouth comes a sharp sword with which to strike down the nations, and he will rule them with a rod of iron; he will tread the wine press of the fury of the wrath of God the Almighty. On his robe and on his thigh he has a name inscribed, "King of kings and Lord of lords."

On the other hand, some have argued that the violent aspects of this book are metaphorical, not literal, since by its very nature, apocalyptic literature is highly symbolic. Certain aspects of this text seem to confirm that interpretation. Thus, the sword Jesus wields is not held in his hand but comes from his mouth, suggesting "the sword of the Spirit, which is the word of God" (Eph. 6:17). Likewise, some have argued that the "robe dipped in blood" is dipped in the blood of Jesus himself, not in the blood of his enemies.[24]

Be that as it may, this single text has encouraged endless appeals to violence and retribution on the part of Christians who support the imperial powers. Julia Ward Howe, who celebrated the victories of the Union Army in her "Battle Hymn of the Republic," offers a case in point. When Howe wrote the line that is so familiar to virtually every American—"Mine eyes have seen the glory of the coming of the Lord, He is trampling out the vintage where the grapes of wrath are stored"—she clearly found her source in Revelation 19:15: "He will tread the wine press of the fury of the wrath of God the Almighty."

Revelation's picture of Jesus, whose robe is "dipped in blood" and who will "strike down the nations" and "rule them with a rod of iron," also inspires many contemporary fundamentalists who see the United States as God's chosen agent in the final Battle of Armageddon and who sanction nuclear weapons as the means by which God will finally destroy his opponents.

When one considers that Revelation's portrayal of divinely sponsored vengeance, violence, and retribution is so out of line with the dominant picture of the kingdom of God that we find elsewhere in the New Testament, one is forced to return again to John Dominic Crossan's observation that the struggle between human civilization, on the one hand, and

---

[24] John Yeatts, *Believers Church Bible Commentary: Revelation* (Scottdale, PA: Herald Press, 2003), 357.

the kingdom of God, on the other, "is depicted *inside the Bible* itself. . . . The Christian Bible forces us to witness the struggle of these two transcendental visions *within its own pages* and to ask ourselves as Christians how *we* decide between them." Crossan's conclusion bears repeating: "*We are bound to whichever of these visions was incarnated by and in the historical Jesus.*"[25]

On that basis, Crossan rejects the picture of violence presented in Revelation as completely out of keeping with the picture of the kingdom of God incarnate in the historical Jesus. He writes:

> In the last century alone we humans have done worse things to one another on this earth and to the earth itself than anything imagined even in that terrible vision of the Warrior Christ or in any of the other visions of the Great Apocalypse. And we may yet destroy our species or our earth. But how do we dare say that God plans and wants it or that Jesus leads and effects it? For me as a Christian, that seems to be *the* crime against divinity, *the* sin against the Holy Spirit.[26]

And yet the overall message of Revelation remains enormously instructive, namely, that the kingdom of God will finally triumph over the oppressive nations and empires of the earth.

[25] Crossan, *God and Empire*, 94–95.
[26] Crossan, *God and Empire*, 227.

WHY I AM NOT AN EVANGELICAL CHRISTIAN

I have spent fifty years teaching religion to mostly White evangelical students at Christian colleges and universities from California to Pennsylvania and points in between. Most of those students came from evangelical homes and grew up in evangelical churches, and most were—and are—abysmally ignorant of the biblical text.

For years I have asked my students what they know about the book of Amos in the Hebrew Bible. This tiny book has inspired virtually every Christian advocate for social and racial justice for centuries on end. It inspired Ida B. Wells and Frederick Douglass in the nineteenth century, Dr. Martin Luther King Jr. and Fannie Lou Hamer in the twentieth century, and in our time the honorable John Lewis, Reverend William Barber, and scholar-activist Catherine Meeks, to name just a few.

But when I ask my students about Amos, no hands go up. Instead, their eyes register goose eggs. They have no idea. They've never read it and know nothing about it.

That simple fact tells us much about the biblical illiteracy that reigns in the churches from which these students come. It also helps solve the riddle of why 82 percent of White evangelical Christians supported Donald

J. Trump in spite of his sexism and sexual affairs, in spite of his lies, in spite of the insurrection he inspired, in spite of his racism, and in spite of his self-serving narcissism. Indeed, Donald Trump is a man whose life, values, and policies stand in stunning contrast to the teachings of Jesus.

Yet the vast majority of White, evangelical Christians supported Donald Trump because Trump had sworn to defend them, exalt them, and restore their cultural power.

The question that begs for an answer is this: What happened to the guardrails that might have kept them true to their own prophetic faith?

There are three of those guardrails—a serious engagement with the biblical text, a knowledge of Christian history, and critical thinking—all of which White evangelicals have, for the most part, abandoned.

Of the three, the most important by far is the biblical text, and especially the teachings of Jesus.

White evangelicals seem not to know—and perhaps not to care—that Jesus's favorite topic was "the kingdom of God," a kingdom that turns conventional values upside down. If you want to save your life, Jesus said, you must lose it, and if you want to be first, you must be last.

They seem not to know—and perhaps not to care—that in the kingdom of God, Yahweh always stands with the oppressed against the oppressor.

They seem not to know—and perhaps not to care—that in the kingdom of God, there is no room for a world where children are caged, systemic poverty goes unaddressed, and Black and Brown bodies are always at risk.

They seem not to know—and perhaps not to care—that the Bible paints only one panoramic picture of the final judgment. It appears in Matthew 25, where only one criterion determines who enters the kingdom of God and who does not. That criterion is how we treat the hungry, the naked, the homeless, those in prison, and the stranger—those Jesus called "the least of these."

And they seem not to know—and perhaps not to care—that in the realm of power politics, the kingdom of God is always upside down. "The rulers of the Gentiles lord it over them, and their great men exercise authority over them. It shall not be so among you," Jesus said, "but whoever would be great among you must be your servant."

When they do read the Bible, most White evangelicals read it through a lens that completely obscures Jesus's emphasis on the kingdom of God.

The lens of American nationalism helps conflate the kingdom of God with the United States of America, robbing it of its countercultural power.

The lens of American individualism helps them imagine the gospel in exclusively private terms, robbing the kingdom of God of its focus on the common good.

The lens of Whiteness obscures people of color, enabling White evangelicals to whitewash the kingdom of God.

And their exclusive fixation on the world to come obscures the kingdom's focus on poverty, injustice, and oppression in the here and now.

Once White evangelicals have squeezed the kingdom of God out of the biblical text, they are left with little more than a cartoonish caricature of Jesus and the ethic he taught, a caricature that routinely shows up on signs in front of their churches—signs like "Warning: Exposure to the SON May Prevent Burning" (Indiana), "Ketchup with Jesus & Relish His Love" (Idaho), or "God Bless America—Land That He Loves" (Tennessee).

The biblical ignorance that reigns in the White, evangelical world is matched only by ignorance of Christian history. If they knew their history, they would know that when Christians have welcomed secular rulers as defenders of their religion, they have always surrendered the integrity of the Christian faith.

When Constantine the Great became the protector and defender of the Christian religion in the early fourth century, a countercultural movement devoted to a radical Jesus became an imperial church—a church that chiefly served the interests of Rome. And as White evangelical Christians embrace secular rulers as defenders of the faith, they turn their backs on the countercultural kingdom of God.

Finally, a book published a quarter-century ago pointed to another guardrail that White evangelicals would abandon over time. That book was Mark Noll's *The Scandal of the Evangelical Mind*, whose opening sentence says it all: "The scandal of the evangelical mind is that there is not much of an evangelical mind." Noll lamented then that evangelicals have "largely abandoned the universities, the arts, and other realms of 'high' culture."

Today, the "scandal of the evangelical mind" includes not only their failure to seriously engage the biblical text or know their history; it also includes their failure to engage in critical thinking. That failure helps explain why they so often mistake blatant and demonstrable falsehoods for objective truth, why they fall prey to conspiracy theories, and why they so readily imagine that demonstrable good is really evil and demonstrable evil is really good.

Having lost their cultural dominance, White evangelical Christians in the United States now live in a perfect storm—a storm defined by their ignorance of the biblical text, their ignorance of Christian history, and their loss of any significant measure of critical thinking.

And having abandoned all those constraints, it is little wonder that 82 percent of those Christians paid homage (and, as I write these words, still pay homage) to a man who promised to defend and exalt them, even as that man promoted policies that exalted the rich, that undermined impoverished and marginalized people, and that stood opposed to Jesus's teachings on the kingdom of God.

And that is why I am not an evangelical Christian.

CALLED TO QUESTION—THE RESTORATION VISION, INNOCENCE, AND RACE

Today, the "scandal of the evangelical mind" includes not only their failure to seriously engage the biblical text or know their history; it also includes their failure to engage in critical thinking. That failure helps explain why they so often mistake blatant and demonstrable falsehoods for objective truth, why they fall prey to conspiracy theories, and why they so readily imagine that demonstrable good is really evil and demonstrable evil is really good.

Having lost their cultural dominance, White evangelical Christians in the United States now live in a perfect storm—a storm defined by their ignorance of the biblical text, their ignorance of Christian history, and their loss of any significant measure of critical thinking.

And having abandoned all those commitments, it is little wonder that 81 percent of those Christians paid homage—and, as I write these words, still paid homage—to a man who promised to defend and exalt them, even as that man promoted policies that exalted the rich, that undermined impoverished and marginalized people, and that stood opposed to Jesus's teachings on the kingdom of God.

And that is why I am not an evangelical Christian.

How a Naïve and Innocent Student Slowly Discerned the Umbilical Cord That Tied His Church to His Nation—and the Nation to His Church

I'm not sure when it dawned on me that my church—the Church of Christ—is in certain important respects a microcosm of the American nation and that, in many of the very same ways, my nation is my church writ large. That discovery was a long time coming but reached its fruition at Pepperdine University where I took up my very first teaching position in 1971.

Pepperdine required that all its students take three religion courses, including a junior-level course on "Religion and Culture"—a variable content course that allowed each professor to teach the course as he or she saw fit, so long as students learned that religion invariably shapes culture even as culture inevitably shapes religion.

I made the decision early on to focus my course on the way certain religious myths have shaped the United States even as the national experience has shaped and reshaped those myths. That theme was a natural for me, given my conservative upbringing first in Lubbock, then in Dallas, and finally in San Angelo, Texas. But Texas was Texas, regardless of the cities where we lived, and that meant a conservative approach to religion (in my case, the one true church), politics (Barry Goldwater conservatism), and economics (people who didn't work shouldn't eat). Moreover, I absorbed from an early age the idea that the Christian religion had shaped the political and economic principles to which most adults in my world—and I as well—paid homage. As a result, my conservative convictions regarding both politics and economics took on a sacred quality.

When I was eighteen years of age, I matriculated at Harding College, a Church of Christ-related institution in Searcy, Arkansas. I should have known when I enrolled that Harding—an excellent institution in many respects—was nonetheless home to the National Education Program, an anti-Communist propaganda mill run by Harding's president. Had I been aware of that reality, it likely would have made no difference since my decision to enroll there had nothing to do with academic quality, in any event, but everything to do with the lush beauty of the campus. I had spent the better part of my life in West Texas where, for the most part, the largest trees were mesquites, where prickly pears dotted the rural landscape, and where cow patties seemed to grow right out of the ground. No wonder the majestic trees on Harding's campus seductively drew me in.

The religious, political, and economic values I had absorbed in Texas were only accentuated at Harding, where the success of the president's anti-Communist campaign convinced me that Harding loomed large on the Kremlin's radar screen. Surely, I thought, someone on the faculty was a Communist spy. That idea drove me to scrutinize all my professors until, finally, I identified a mild-mannered—and mildly liberal—professor of political science as the most likely suspect.

Still and all, it was at Harding that I began to question the validity of at least some of my beliefs about the one true church and what I took as the sacred, God-inspired qualities of conservative politics and laissez-faire capitalism.

Those doubts were heightened during my graduate studies at Abilene Christian College in 1966–67, for there I discovered a truth that, for me at least, was both radical and disconcerting. I understood already that religion could shape culture, confident as I was that the Christian religion had created both American democracy and American capitalism. But I had not understood the extent to which culture can shape religion. After all, if the one true church was really the one true church, then it had passed through the ages in a hermetically sealed capsule, immune to the impact of wars, famines, diseases, scientific discoveries, artistic and musical achievements, intellectual awakenings, and anything else that helped create the contours of human culture.

Then I discovered the sixteenth-century Anabaptists who, like my Churches of Christ, were as committed to the restoration vision as we were, but who framed it in ways that were radically different from the highly rational grid to which we conformed that task. Soon I began to suspect that the difference between sixteenth-century Swiss culture, shaped as it was by the Reformation and the Renaissance, and the nineteenth-century American frontier, shaped by Enlightenment ideals and the birth of a brand-new nation, helped explain the difference between these two traditions.

Just flirting with that suspicion was, for me, both revolutionary and exciting, and exploring such a seemingly forbidden path made me feel giddy beyond words. I almost felt naughty, entertaining the staggering notion that perhaps my church was not the one true church I had always thought it to be, but was perhaps a reflection—even a creation—of the culture in which it emerged. I shared these views with one of my closest friends in graduate school who, like me, reveled in this scintillating thesis. But his wife found these thoughts so threatening, so heretical even, that she counseled him to dampen down our friendship.

Still, I had not even begun to discern all the ways in which the Church of Christ was a microcosm of the American nation. It was a home-grown, born-in-the-USA religious tradition in any event. But my gradual discovery of the theological dynamics that shaped both my church and my nation came through the writings of Sidney Mead, one of my professors at the University of Iowa and the widely acknowledged "dean" of historians of American religion. Mead helped me see the extent to which the United States, from its founding, imagined itself rooted in the golden age of pure beginnings and launching a final golden age of freedom, peace, and democracy for all humankind.

Even more important, since I studied at Iowa from 1967 to 1971, I began to make those connections during the years of the Freedom Movement and the Vietnam War. I saw on the one hand the power of the student protests against racial oppression and injustice, and I saw on the other the widespread resistance against those protests and the claim of American innocence in the face of what so many took as American atrocities, both at home and abroad.

It slowly became clear to me that the deeply held sense of American innocence was rooted in the same effort to transcend and escape the guilt of history that had defined my church; that the racism that defined the nation was closely akin to the exclusivism that defined my religion; and that both were rooted in the same complex of history-denying convictions that were part and parcel of the restoration vision as it has emerged so often in the United States.

So when I arrived at Pepperdine as a first-year teacher, my choice to teach a course exploring the connections between the Christian religion and American culture was almost axiomatic. My book—*Myths America Lives By: White Supremacy and the Stories That Give Us Meaning*—grew directly from that course, and themes from that book—and one of its chapters—have shaped this section of *The Grace of Troublesome Questions*.

THE RESTORATION VISION AND THE MYTH OF THE INNOCENT NATION

I n his wonderful memoir that describes what it meant to grow up in the 1960s and 1970s, Lawrence Wright reflects on the innocence that characterized America during the period of World War II:

> When my father went off to war, I understood that he was going to make the world safe for democracy and that that was what the world wanted. . . . [He had] matured in a magic age, the 1940s, when great evil and great good faced each other. In that splendid moment he knew which side he was on. He was an American farm boy doing what God and his country had designed for him. . . . Here he was, saving the world. I grew up expecting to inherit his certainty.[1]

The fact is, a profound sense of innocence characterized the American experience for much of the twentieth century and especially between

---

[1]Lawrence Wright, *In the New World: Growing Up with America, 1960–1984* (New York: Alfred A. Knopf, 1988), 109–10.

THE GRACE OF TROUBLESOME QUESTIONS

World War I and the 1960s. Some periods were exceptions to that generalization, of course. The Great Depression, for example, generated enormous doubt and despair among both Blacks and Whites. Still, in the mainstream of American life, most had no doubt about the ultimate meaning of their nation: America stood for good against evil, right against wrong, democracy against tyranny, and virtue against vice. What can account for this extraordinary sense of innocence that many in later years would view as profoundly naïve?

The Ahistorical Dimensions of American Innocence

By the twentieth century, America was heir to all the myths I discussed in *Myths America Lives By: White Supremacy and the Stories that Give Us Meaning*. The myth of America as a Christian Nation is a case in point. That perception alone was enough to sustain a powerful sense of innocence.

In addition, the myth of the Chosen Nation was still a vibrant, dynamic theme in American life and culture. As Lawrence Wright noted in his memoir, "America had a mission—we thought it was a divine mission—to spread freedom, and freedom meant democracy, and democracy meant capitalism, and all that meant the American way of life."[2] Would God choose America for such a mission if America lacked the qualities of goodness, virtue, and innocence?

In my judgment, however, the two most important myths sustaining America's sense of innocence were the myths of Nature's Nation and the Millennial Nation. Important in this context is the way those myths converged to preclude any meaningful sense of history in the United States. And since the honest telling of history is the only way we can know the truth about tragedy, suffering, injustice, and oppression, the best way to obscure those realities is to obscure history itself. And that is precisely what happened when the myths of Nature's Nation and the Millennial Nation came to define the American nation.

The notion of "Nature's Nation" emerged when the framers grounded the American experiment in "Nature and Nature's God," to borrow a phrase from the Declaration of Independence. It was easy to imagine that the

---

[2] Wright, *In the New World*, 109.

United States simply reflected the way God himself intended things to be from the beginning of the world. In other words, the American system was not spun out of someone's imagination or contrived by human wit. Instead, it was based on a natural order, built into the world by God himself.

Jefferson said as much when he spoke of "self-evident truths." John Adams concurred when he affirmed that "the United States of America have exhibited, perhaps, the first example of governments erected on the simple principles of nature." The fullest expression of this conviction came from Jefferson's friend and confidant, Thomas Paine, who announced that "the case and circumstance of America present themselves as in the beginning of the world." Indeed, Paine wrote, "We are brought at once to the point of seeing government begin, as if we had lived in the beginning of time. The real volume, not of history, but of facts, is directly before us, unmutilated by contrivance, or the errors of tradition."[3] Here one finds the Myth of Nature's Nation full-blown.

The myth of the Millennial Nation was simply the belief, widespread in the early national period, that this new nation, with liberties grounded in "Nature and Nature's God," would in time extend those liberties around the globe until the world was free. This conviction even found its way onto the Great Seal of the United States. There, an unfinished pyramid grows from arid desert sands. Inscribed on the pyramid's base is that notable date, 1776. Clearly, the pyramid represents the new nation. The barren desert terrain, above which the pyramid towers and from which it seems to grow, signifies all human history prior to 1776. For all their glories and achievements, past civilizations were essentially barren compared to the glories that would mark the new American state. The pyramid is unfinished since the American experiment

---

[3] John Adams, *A Defense of the Constitutions of the Government of the United States of America*, abridged in *The Political Writings of John Adams: Representative Selections*, ed. George A. Peek (New York: Liberal Arts Press, 1954), 117; and Thomas Paine, *Rights of Man* [1791-1792], in *The Complete Writings of Thomas Paine*, ed. Philip S. Foner (New York: Citadel Press, 1945), 1:376.

THE GRACE OF TROUBLESOME QUESTIONS

remained incomplete. Above this scene, the eye of God looks down with obvious pleasure, and the Latin inscription records his response: "annuit cœptis," or "he [God] has favored our undertakings." Beneath this picture stands the most relevant phrase of all: "novus ordo seclorum," or "a new order of the ages."

Many Americans living in the late eighteenth and early nineteenth centuries believed this new republic was exactly that. For them, America was no ordinary nation, corrupted by time and tradition. Instead, it had restored the golden age of pure beginnings and would therefore bless all the nations of the world with the glories of the long-anticipated millennial age.

One finds stirrings of this vision even before the Revolution. John Adams, for example, confided to his diary in 1765: "I always consider the settlement of America with reverence and wonder, as the opening of a grand scene and design in Providence for the illumination of the ignorant, and the emancipation of the slavish part of mankind all over the earth."[4]

What is crucial to grasp is the way these two myths stood outside of human history. The myth of Nature's Nation pointed to the time of creation before human history began, while the myth of the Millennial Nation pointed to the end of history when the perfections of creation would be restored.

By identifying itself so completely with these mythic periods of perfection, America lifted itself above the plane of ordinary human history where evil, suffering, and death dominated the drama of human existence. America became, as the Great Seal of the United States so clearly declares, a *novus ordo seclorum*, a new order of the ages. Other nations were mired in the bog of human history, but not the United States. Other nations had inherited the taint of human history, but not the United States. Other nations had been compromised by human history, but not the United States. In effect, then, America had removed itself from the power of human history with all the ambiguity that history inevitably bears. In this way, America emerged as an innocent child among the nations of the world, without spot or wrinkle, unmarred and unblemished by the finite dimensions of human history.

---

[4]Quoted in Ernest Lee Tuveson, *Redeemer Nation: The Idea of America's Millennial Role* (Chicago: University of Chicago Press, 1968), 25.

President Ronald Reagan perhaps put it best when he said in his State of the Union address of 1987: "The calendar can't measure America because we were meant to be an endless experiment in freedom, with no limit to our reaches, no boundaries to what we can do, no end point to our hopes."[5]

Having rejected the bounds of finite human history, it is little wonder that when America launched a war against Islamic terrorists in retaliation for the September 11, 2001, attacks, US military strategists initially called the war "Operation Infinite Justice." They finally scuttled that phrase when people of religious faith—Muslims, Christians, and Jews—pointed out that only God can dispense "infinite justice."

Indeed, the starting point for the American illusion of innocence lies in the way Americans typically deal with history and its contents. Henry Ford perhaps put it best when he said flatly, "History is bunk." If Americans wish to say someone is irrelevant to a particular situation, we often say to that person, "You're history." American students typically avoid history, believing that history itself is irrelevant. We bulldoze buildings of any age at all to create something bright, shiny, and new. These are just some of the ways Americans routinely reject the reality of history. The truth is that many Americans live their lives in the eternal present, a present informed and shaped not by history but by those two golden epochs that bracket human time.

Because many Americans so often reject history, they also reject the most fundamental contents of history, especially finitude, suffering, and death. In 1963, Jessica Mitford published an important book called *The American Way of Death*. While many cultures cope with death by embracing it—by handling the corpse, for example—Americans, Mitford noted, have adopted funeral practices that effectively mask the reality of death so that it never intrudes on the perfect world they seek to create.[6]

Americans often deal with suffering in the very same way, as the patterns of our neighborhoods abundantly attest. Indeed, one could argue that racial segregation has always had more to do with poverty, suffering, and death than with color. In this scenario, Whites despised Blacks because

---

[5] Ronald Reagan, "Address before a Joint Session of Congress on the State of the Union," January 27, 1987, in *Public Papers of the Presidents of the United States: Ronald Reagan: 1987*, vol. 1: *January 1 to July 3, 1987* (Washington, DC: Government Printing Office, 1989), 59–60.

[6] Jessica Mitford, *The American Way of Death* (New York: Simon and Schuster, 1963), 13–17.

black skin became in the United States a powerful symbol of the suffering and death that no one wanted and with which no one wished to come into contact. And so for many years, White America has segregated Blacks into neighborhoods far removed from the manicured lawns and the beautiful homes of the privileged. This is the truth to which James Baldwin pointed when he wrote, "White Americans do not believe in death, and this is why the darkness of my skin so intimidates them."[7]

Our prison system performs much the same function, effectively removing from the daily lives of privileged Americans the Black, the Brown, and the poor. Society's concern to remove them from the perfect world we seek to create is particularly evident in its resistance to prevention and its commitment to punishment. By and large, Americans would far prefer to lock people up than to provide the kinds of programs that might prevent crime in the first place or that might rehabilitate offenders. When one couples that reality with a privatized prison system that encourages incarceration, we find we cannot build prisons quickly enough to cope with the vast population we seek to place behind bars.

The point I seek to make through all these examples should be clear: privileged Americans are committed to creating for themselves a perfect world in a golden age that has little to do with the tragic contents of human history with which so many people, both in the United States and in so many other parts of the world, must deal every day. In this context, historian Edward T. Linenthal, describing the April 19, 1995, bombing of the Alfred P. Murrah Federal Building in Oklahoma City, wrote, "There was, seemingly, nowhere in the storehouse of American meaning to place the bombing, to make sense of it. It was, quite literally, 'out of place.'" It was out of place, Linenthal wrote, because it "activated enduring convictions that Americans were peaceable citizens of an innocent and vulnerable nation in a largely wicked world. Thus the evocative power of headlines: 'Myth of Midwest safety shattered'. . . [and] 'American innocence buried in Oklahoma.'"[8]

---

[7] James Baldwin, "The Fire Next Time," in *Baldwin: Collected Essays*, ed. Toni Morrison (New York: Library Classics of the United States, 1998), 339.

[8] Edward T. Linenthal, *The Unfinished Bombing: Oklahoma City in American Memory* (Oxford: Oxford University Press, 2001), 16.

Similarly, Mark Slouka suggested that Americans found the September 11, 2001, attack on the Pentagon and the World Trade Center particularly traumatic because

> it simultaneously exposed and challenged the myth of our own uniqueness. A myth most visible, perhaps, in our age-old denial of death.
>
> Consider it. Here in the New Canaan, in the land of perpetual beginnings and second chances, where identity could be sloughed and sloughed again and history was someone else's problem, death had never been welcome. Death was a foreigner—radical, disturbing, smelling of musty books and brimstone. We wanted no part of him.
>
> And now death had come calling. That troubled brother, so long forgotten, so successfully erased, was standing on our porch in his steel-toed boots, grinning. He'd made it across the ocean, passed like a ghost through the gates of our chosen community. We had denied him his due. . . . Yet here he was.

Slouka concluded, "This was not just a terrorist attack. This was an act of metaphysical trespass."[9]

Since September 11, 2011, the United States has grown far more familiar with wholesale death from terror attacks. Still and all, the American predisposition to cling to an image of the nation as fundamentally innocent remains firmly embedded in the American psyche and has its deepest roots in the two great myths that gripped the imagination of the American people when the nation was young—the myth of Nature's Nation and the myth of the Millennial Nation.[10]

---

[9] Mark Slouka, "A Year Later: Notes on America's Intimations of Mortality," *Harper's Magazine* 305 (Sep. 2002): 36.

[10] For a far more expanded discussion of the illusions of innocence in American life and the way those illusions grow from the attempt to sidestep human history, see Richard T. Hughes and C. Leonard Allen, *Illusions of Innocence: Protestant Primitivism in America, 1630–1875* (Chicago: University of Chicago Press, 1988). In addition, Robert Jewett and John Shelton Lawrence have written perceptively on the myth of American innocence in a variety of texts, though their focus is somewhat different from my own. See, for example, Jewett's *The Captain America Complex* (1973; rev., Santa Fe: Bear & Company, 1984); Jewett and Lawrence, *The American Monomyth* (Garden City: Doubleday, 1977); and Jewett and Lawrence, *The Myth of the American Superhero* (Grand Rapids: Eerdmans, 2002). For a more recent treatment of American innocence, see Suzy Hansen, "Unlearning the Myth

The Paradox of the Myth of Innocence

Any exploration of the history of the myth of innocence almost invariably reveals that it finally transforms itself into its opposite. Indeed, it typically encourages those who march under its banner to repress those they regard as corrupted or defiled. Paradoxically, then, the innocent become guilty along with the rest of the human race, though the myths they have embraced prevent them from discerning their guilt.

The dynamics of this paradox are illumined by two Christian traditions that first emerged on the nineteenth-century American frontier—the Latter-day Saints (Mormons) and the Disciples/Churches of Christ. These two traditions take us to the heart of America's mythic self-understanding, for both embraced the recovery of pure beginnings (primitive church) as the means to usher in the golden age at the end of time (millennium). Like the larger nation, therefore, they stood with one foot in the dawn of time—or at least the only time that mattered for them—and the other in the world's evening shadows, and both, like the larger nation, regarded the intervening history as essentially irrelevant. And because they had leap-frogged over human history, both traditions imagined they had achieved a level of purity and innocence denied to those earthlings still rooted in the messy ambiguities of ordinary time and space.[11]

Though defending their innocence all the while, it was therefore not uncommon for early adherents to these two traditions to threaten other Christians with divine retribution, rooted in the innocence both presumed about themselves. A single example from each tradition will suffice.

With respect to the Disciples/Churches of Christ, one of their preachers, John R. Howard, warned in 1843 that "the coming of the Lord, in vengeance to destroy his enemies, cannot . . . be very far off. . . . And should *you* not be found among his true people—his genuine disciples—but arrayed in opposition against them, he will 'destroy' you 'with the *breath* of his *mouth*, and with the *brightness* of his *coming*.'"[12]

---

of American Innocence," *The Guardian*, August 8, 2017, at https://www.theguardian.com/us-news/2017/aug/08/unlearning-the-myth-of-american-innocence, accessed October 1, 2017.

[11] On this point, see Richard T. Hughes, "Soaring with the Gods: Early Mormons and the Eclipse of Religious Pluralism," in *Mormons and Mormonism: An Introduction to an American World Religion*, ed. Eric A. Eliason (Urbana: University of Illinois Press, 2001), 23–46.

[12] John R. Howard, "A Warning to the Religious Sects and Parties in Christendom," *Bible Advocate* 1 (Jan. 1843): 82.

On the Mormon side of the ledger, Parley Pratt, an early Mormon missionary, published in 1837 *A Voice of Warning*, a book that Mormon scholars have regarded as "the most important of all non-canonical Mormon books" and "the most important missionary pamphlet in the early history of the church."[13] In that book, Pratt argued that the Mormon faith "is the gospel which God has commanded us to preach. . . . And no other system of religion . . . is of any use; every thing different from this, is a perverted gospel, bringing a curse upon them that preach it, and upon them that hear it." In fact, all who resisted the Mormon message "shall alike feel the hand of the almighty, by pestilence, famine, earthquake, and the sword: yea, ye shall be drunken with your own blood . . . until your cities are desolate . . . until all lyings, priestcrafts, and all manner of abomination, shall be done away."[14]

Both of these traditions asserted their innocence on the grounds that they had fully replicated the perfections of the first age. As it turned out, however, they fell into the guilt of history in spite of themselves. The innocence they presumed prompted an arrogance they could not admit, for the myth of innocence shielded them from their sins. So they persisted in their claims to perfection, even as they broke community and ruptured relations with their brothers and sisters in other communities of the Christian faith.

These two traditions provide a microcosmic window onto the myth of innocence that played itself out in the early years of the larger Republic, for both emerged and grew up when the nation was young and borrowed from the larger culture the mythic themes that defined them. For this reason, when we explore the mythic dimensions of these two traditions, we can learn much about the mythic dimensions of the nation at large.

Like the Mormons and Disciples/Churches of Christ, the larger nation grounded its sense of innocence in the way it identified with the golden age of the past (the time of creation) and the golden age of the future (the millennium). Since America refused to admit its debt to human history

---

[13] Peter Crawley, "The Passage of Mormon Primitivism," *Dialogue* 13 (Winter 1980): 33; and "Introduction," to *Key to the Science of Theology/A Voice of Warning* (Salt Lake City: Deseret Book Co., 1978), i–ii.

[14] Parley P. Pratt, *A Voice of Warning and Instruction to All People, Containing a Declaration of the Faith and Doctrine of the Church of the Latter Day Saints, Commonly Called Mormons* (New York: W. Sanford, 1837), 140–42. This chapter, which is the pivotal "warning" section of *Voice of Warning*, has been deleted from the modern 1978 edition.

and imagined itself a "new order of the ages," it also imagined it could lead the world into a golden age of "liberty and justice for all."

The problems emerged when other nations resisted the American version of "liberty and justice for all"; or when America failed—as it often did—to separate its vision of "liberty and justice for all" from its own political, economic, and military interests; or when, on the domestic front, it confused "liberty and justice for all" with liberty and justice for Whites. In this way, while proclaiming its innocence and the purity of its motives, America—like all other nations of the world—also fell into the guilt of history. This is the point, however, that White Americans often failed to see, since the myth of the Innocent Nation shielded them from the realities that were so apparent to minorities at home and to so many others around the world.

America: The Innocent Nation

While the myth of innocence was implicit in American culture at the time of the Founding, it became especially prominent in American life from World War I to the Vietnam War.

World War I

The way America defined its role in World War I established the essential pattern to which the myth of innocence would conform itself for the rest of the twentieth century. No one did more to define that pattern than President Woodrow Wilson, who viewed the enemy as implacably evil. In a message to Congress on April 2, 1917, Wilson described the Imperial German government as one "which has thrown aside all considerations of humanity and of right and is running amuck."[15] When the war was over and Wilson presented the treaty for ratification, he reflected once again on what he regarded as the demonic character of the Imperial German government. America entered this war, he said,

> because we saw the supremacy, and even the validity, of right
> everywhere put in jeopardy and free government likely to be

---

[15] Woodrow Wilson, "We Must Accept War," Message to Congress, April 2, 1917, in *Why We Are at War: Messages to the Congress, January to April, 1917* (New York: Harper & Brothers, 1917), 57.

everywhere imperiled by the intolerable aggression of a power which respected neither right nor obligation and whose every system of government flouted the rights of the citizen as against the autocratic authority of his governors.[16]

At the same time, Wilson presented the American cause as righteous, innocent, and free of self-interest. Shortly after America entered the war in 1917, Wilson explained to the American people that "there is not a single selfish element so far as I can see, in the cause we are fighting for. We are fighting for what we believe and wish to be the rights of mankind and for the future peace and security of the world."[17]

Two weeks earlier, he presented a similar case to the US Congress: "We have no selfish ends to serve. We desire no conquest, no dominion. We seek no indemnities for ourselves, no material compensation for the sacrifices we shall freely make. We are but one of the champions of the rights of mankind."[18]

When the war was over, he confirmed that judgment. "The United States entered the war upon a different footing from every other nation except our associates on this side of the sea," he said. "We entered it, not because our material interests were directly threatened or because any special treaty obligations to which we were parties had been violated." Rather, America entered the war "only as the champion of rights which she was glad to share with free men and lovers of justice everywhere. . . . We were welcomed as disinterested friends. . . . We were generously accepted as the unaffected champions of what was right."[19]

Wilson could make these claims because he so completely grounded the American mission in what he imagined were the principles built into the natural order from the time of creation. Accordingly, in a speech to

[16] Wilson, "Presenting the Treaty for Ratification," in *God's New Israel: Religious Interpretations of American Destiny*, ed. Conrad Cherry (Chapel Hill: University of North Carolina Press, 1998), 280.

[17] Wilson, "Speak, Act and Serve Together," Message to the American people, April 15, 1917, in Wilson, *Why We Are at War*, 71.

[18] Wilson, "We Must Accept War," Message to Congress, April 2, 1917, in Wilson, *Why We Are at War*, 55.

[19] Wilson, "Presenting the Treaty for Ratification," in *God's New Israel*, 280, 287.

the Senate on January 22, 1917, he stated flatly, "American principles [and] American policies . . . are the principles of mankind, and must prevail."[20]

Wilson also believed that American principles and policies would usher in a final golden age for all humanity. American soldiers fought, he said, not for a penultimate or short-term peace, but "for the ultimate peace of the world." He hoped, like the British politician David Lloyd George, that this conflict would be the war to end all war. Further, through the implementation of American principles and policies, he hoped to make the world "safe for democracy."[21] Clearly, Wilson aimed for nothing less than a golden age of liberty, democracy, and justice for all humankind, a goal that allowed him to imagine that American involvement in the war was innocent of self-serving motivations.

One fact belied that conviction, however—the widely held ambition so baldly stated by Senator Albert Beveridge only twenty years before: "we are enlisted in the cause of American supremacy, which will never end until American commerce has made the conquest of the world." When one combines that objective with the fact that American commercial investments abroad quadrupled between 1897 and 1914, it becomes apparent that American entry into World War I was hardly free of self-serving motivations. Wilson described how German attacks on American vessels had produced a "very serious congestion of our commerce . . . which is growing rapidly more and more serious every day." Indeed, he noted, American commerce suffered not only from direct attack, but from the many commercial vessels that sat idly in port "because of the unwillingness of our ship-owners to risk their vessels at sea without insurance or adequate protection."[22]

When the war was over, Edward N. Hurley, head of the US Shipping Board, confirmed the way Americans at that time often confused the dream of universal peace and justice with the dream of the economic conquest of the world. In a memo to Bernard Baruch, head of the War Industries Board, Hurley wrote,

---

[20] Wilson, "A World League for Peace," Message to the Senate, January 22, 1917, in Wilson, *Why We Are at War*, 16.

[21] Wilson, "We Must Accept War," Message to Congress, April 2, 1917, in Wilson, *Why We Are at War*, 55.

[22] Wilson, "Request for a Grant of Power," Message to Congress, February 26, 1917, in Wilson, *Why We Are at War*, 31.

If America would invest substantially in the essential raw materials of all foreign countries . . . America would then be in a position to say to the rest of the world, that these commodities would be sold at a fair price. . . . In what better way could we be of real service than by the use of our financial strength to control the raw materials for the benefit of humanity?[23]

Nonetheless, Wilson obscured the commercial motivation for American involvement in the war when he told Congress:

I have spoken of our commerce and of the legitimate errands of our people on the seas, but you will not be misled as to my main thought. . . . I am thinking not only of the rights of Americans to go and come about their proper business by way of the sea, but also of something much deeper, much more fundamental than that. I am thinking of those rights of humanity without which there is no civilization.[24]

There is no reason to doubt Wilson's sincerity when he claimed that his foremost consideration was the "rights of humanity without which there is no civilization," but why did he obscure the commercial motivation for American involvement in the war? It is safe to say Wilson—along with many other Americans—might not have discerned the dimensions of self-interest inherent in American commerce. After all, they had for many years believed that capitalism and commercial activity simply reflected the universal "principles of mankind."

One other event belied American claims during World War I that it was an innocent participant, altogether free of self-interested motivation. When the government took extraordinary steps to punish dissenters and to convince the American people to support the war, one can only conclude that the official rationale—to secure the rights of all mankind—was

---

[23] Cited in Emily Rosenberg, *Spreading the American Dream: American Economic and Cultural Expansion, 1890–1945* (New York: Hill and Wang, 1982), 74.

[24] Wilson, "Request for a Grant of Power," Message to Congress, February 26, 1917, in Wilson, *Why We Are at War*, 36–37.

not all that self-evident, and that many Americans detected a dimension of self-interest that the government refused to admit.

Indeed, the Committee on Public Information (CPI), directed by Denver newsman George Creel, aimed a vigorous propaganda campaign directly at the American people. Employing artists, musicians, journalists, historians, and a host of other creative professionals, the CPI produced patriotic posters, books like *German War Practices*, and films like *The Beast of Berlin*, all designed to demonize the enemy and portray the American cause as both innocent and righteous. Strikingly, Creel never admitted that CPI productions were propagandistic in any sense at all. Rather, they simply presented "value-free" facts that were self-evident to any reasonable observer—a conclusion completely in harmony with the notion that America was an "innocent nation," standing for "the principles of mankind."[25]

By and large, the American public responded positively to the campaign, demonizing all things German and equating German people, German language, and German culture with disloyalty to American principles and the American mission. Schools throughout the country, for example, dropped the study of the German language, and while Americans continued to eat "sauerkraut," they renamed it "liberty cabbage."

Still, there were dissenters. Consequently, the CPI censored materials that disagreed with its own propaganda and sought to squelch those who dared to question the dominant ideology. The Espionage and Sedition Acts, in fact, essentially made criticism of the government and its war policies illegal. Passed on June 15, 1917, the Espionage Act made it possible to fine dissenters up to $10,000 and imprison them for up to twenty years. Possible offenses included disloyalty, statements that might interfere with the war effort, giving aid to the enemy, refusing duty in the armed services, or inciting insubordination in the armed services. Passed almost a year later, on May 16, 1918, the Sedition Act extended these penalties to anyone who spoke, wrote, or printed anything that might be considered "disloyal, profane, scurrilous, or abusive" about the government, the Constitution, or the armed services.

---

[25] Emily Rosenberg explores the "self-evident" qualities of CPI propaganda in *Spreading the American Dream*, 86.

The irony, of course, lies in the fact that while America sought, through participating in World War I, to secure the rights of all mankind and to make "the world safe for democracy," it abridged the rights of American citizens and undermined the democratic process in the homeland. In this way, the myth of innocence turned in upon itself. When all was said and done, America participated in the guilt that inevitably belongs to participants in human history despite every effort to avoid it. Most Americans, however, could scarcely discern that guilt, so strong was the myth of America as the Innocent Nation.

The notion of national innocence not only blinded President Wilson to the nation's self-serving motivations in World War I—its drive toward "American supremacy" and the economic "conquest of the world"—it also blinded him to the degree of White supremacy that flourished within the borders of the United States.

Wilson served as president of Princeton University between 1902 and 1910—a time when Paul Robeson, an African American destined to achieve great fame as an athlete, an actor, and a singer, was growing up in the shadow of that institution. The Witherspoon Street Presbyterian Church called his father, Reverend W. D. Robeson, to pastor that congregation in 1898, the same year Paul was born.

Robeson later recalled:

> the Princeton of my boyhood . . . was for all the world like
> any small town in the deep South, [a town that routinely prac-
> ticed] the most rigid social and economic patterns of White
> Supremacy. . . . Rich Princeton was white. . . . The people of
> our small Negro community were, for the most part, a servant
> class—domestics in the homes of the wealthy, serving as cooks,
> waiters and caretakers at the university, coachmen for the town
> and laborers at the nearby farms and brickyards. . . . The grade
> school that I attended was segregated and Negroes were not per-
> mitted in any high school.

Princeton, Robeson flatly affirmed, "was Jim Crow."

In that context, his father became a "bridge between the Have-nots and the Haves," and, working in that capacity, he was well known and respected throughout the Princeton community, even by the president of the university. "But though the door of the university president might be open to him, Reverend Robeson could not push open the doors of that school for his son, when Bill was ready for college. The pious president, a fellow Presbyterian, said: No, it is quite impossible. That was Woodrow Wilson . . . advocate of democracy for the world and Jim Crow for America!"[26]

World War II

The American experience in World War I prepared the country to imagine itself an innocent, disinterested participant in the conflicts of the world. Grounded in the laws of "Nature and Nature's God" and defined by Christian virtues, America stood poised to lead the world into a golden age of liberty and justice for all. American involvement in World War II only confirmed the validity of these myths in the minds of the American people. In part, this was because in that particular war, the face of evil seemed so thoroughly apparent.

President Franklin D. Roosevelt framed the issues in his message to Congress on January 6, 1942, only a month after the Japanese attacked Pearl Harbor. Above all else, Roosevelt sought to portray the Axis forces as fundamentally demonic and America as fundamentally good.

> Our enemies are guided by brutal cynicism, by unholy contempt
> for the human race. We are inspired by a faith which goes back
> through all the years to the first chapter of the Book of Genesis:
> "God created man in His own image." We on our side are striving
> to be true to that divine heritage. We are fighting, as our fathers
> have fought, to uphold the doctrine that all men are equal in the
> sight of God. Those on the other side are striving to destroy this
> deep belief and to create a world in their own image—a world
> of tyranny and cruelty and serfdom. . . . There never has been—
> there never can be—successful compromise between good and
> evil. Only total victory can reward the champions of tolerance
> and decency, and freedom, and faith.[27]

---

[26] Paul Robeson, *Here I Stand* (Boston: Beacon Press, 1958), 10–11.

[27] Franklin D. Roosevelt, "Annual Message to Congress," January 6, 1942, in Cherry, *God's New Israel*, 295.

In this way, Roosevelt kept alive the theme of American innocence that had been articulated so well by Woodrow Wilson a quarter of a century earlier.

In addition, Roosevelt grounded the theme of American innocence in the very same myths to which Wilson had appealed. He invoked the myth of Nature's Nation when he declared the American cause a universal cause. Americans were fighting, he said, "not only for ourselves, but for all men, not only for one generation, but for all generations."[28] And he invoked the venerable myth of the Millennial Nation when he declared the American intention "to cleanse the world of ancient evils, ancient ills" and "to make very certain that the world will never suffer again."[29]

Here is the old, familiar pattern: The anticipated golden age of liberty and justice for all is grounded in the golden age of creation. By identifying with these mythic times that bracketed the history of humankind, America emerged as God's agent for good in a sinful world. Perhaps most striking, one of the myths to which Roosevelt appealed was the myth of the Christian Nation. "The world is too small to provide adequate 'living room' for both Hitler and God. In proof of that [the] Nazis have now announced their plan for enforcing their new German, pagan religion throughout the world—the plan by which the Holy Bible and the Cross of Mercy would be displaced by 'Mein Kampf' and the swastika and the naked sword."[30]

Significantly, it was the way this "innocent nation" treated Blacks during and following World War II that became, for James Baldwin, "a turning point in the Negro's relation to America. To put it briefly, and somewhat too simply, a certain hope died, a certain respect for white Americans faded." Then Baldwin explained:

> You must put yourself in the skin of a man who is wearing the
> uniform of his country, is a candidate for death in its defense,
> and who is called a "nigger" by his comrades-in-arms and his
> officers; who is almost always given the hardest, ugliest, most
> menial work to do; who knows that the white G.I. has informed
> the Europeans that he is subhuman . . . ; who does not dance

---

[28] Cherry, *God's New Israel*, 295.
[29] Cherry, *God's New Israel*, 290, 295.
[30] Cherry, *God's New Israel*, 291.

at the U.S.O. the night white soldiers dance there, and does not drink in the same bars white soldiers drink in; and who watches German prisoners of war being treated by Americans with more human dignity than he has ever received at their hands. And who, at the same time, as a human being, is far freer in a strange land than he has ever been at home. *Home!* The very word begins to have a despairing diabolical ring. You must consider what happens to this citizen, after all he has endured, when he returns home: search, in his shoes, for a job, for a place to live; ride, in his skin, on segregated buses; see, with his eyes, the signs saying "White" and "Colored," and especially the signs that say "White Ladies" and "Colored *Women*"; look into the eyes of his wife; look into the eyes of his son; listen, with his ears, to political speeches, North and South; imagine yourself being told to "wait." And all this is happening in the richest and freest country in the world, and in the middle of the twentieth century.[31]

That is the context for the story Toni Morrison relates of Isaac Woodard, a Black veteran of World War II, who in 1946 returned from Europe to his home in North Carolina. "He had spent four years in the army," Morrison writes, "in the Pacific Theater (where he was promoted to sergeant) and in the Asiatic Pacific (where he earned a Campaign Medal, a World War II Victory Medal, and the Good Conduct Medal)." Woodard was on a Greyhound bus on the final leg of his journey.

When the bus reached a rest stop, he asked the bus driver if there was time to use the restroom. They argued, but he was allowed to use the facilities. Later, when the bus stopped in Batesburg, South Carolina, the driver called the police to remove Sergeant Woodard (apparently for going to the bathroom). The chief, Linwood Shull, took Woodard to a nearby alleyway where he and a number of other policemen beat him with their nightsticks. Then they took him to jail and arrested him for disorderly conduct. During his night in jail, the chief of police beat Woodard

---

[31] Baldwin, *The Fire Next Time*, 317–18.

with a billy club and gouged out his eyes. The next morning Woodard was sent before a local judge, who found him guilty and fined him fifty dollars. Woodard asked for medical care and two days later it arrived. Meantime, not knowing where he was and suffering from mild amnesia, he was taken to a hospital in Aiken, South Carolina. Three weeks after he was reported missing by his family, he was located and rushed to an army hospital in Spartanburg. Both eyes remained damaged beyond repair. He lived, though blind, until 1992, when he died at age seventy-three. After thirty minutes of deliberation, Chief Shull was acquitted of all charges, to the wild applause of an all-white jury.[32]

The Communist Threat

I have observed several times that it is far easier to think of oneself as righteous and pure if one confronts an enemy that can be characterized as utterly evil. Germany became that enemy during World War I, and Germany, Japan, and Italy all presented Americans with the face of evil during World War II. By the 1950s, those wars were over and the enemy had disappeared. But communism—symbolized best by the Soviet Union— emerged to fill the void. In that context, one American summoned the nation to "faith in Jesus Christ" as the best and surest defense against "godless" Communism. That American was Billy Graham.

Graham came to national prominence in 1949 when he held a revival in Los Angeles and told the crowd, "Do you know that the Fifth Columnists, called Communists, are more rampant in Los Angeles than any other city in America?" Graham saw a solution, a solution rooted deeply in William Tyndale's notion of the national covenant. "If we repent, if we believe, if we turn to Christ in faith and hope, the judgment of God can be stopped."[33]

Graham's appeal to the nation to turn to Christ as the way to fulfill the requirements of the national covenant and thereby defeat godless communism became a feature of Graham's preaching for many years. In sermon after sermon, he appealed to the covenant theme. On one occasion, he

---

[32] Toni Morrison, *The Origin of Others* (Cambridge, MA: Harvard University Press, 2017), 59–61.
[33] Cited in William G. McLoughlin Jr., *Billy Graham: Revivalist in a Secular Age* (New York: Ronald Press, 1960), 48.

counseled his audience, "Until this nation humbles itself and prays and . . . receives Christ as Savior, there is no hope for preserving the American way of life." On another occasion, he flatly stated, "Only as millions of Americans turn to Jesus Christ at this hour and accept him as their Savior, can this nation possibly be spared the onslaught of a demon-possessed communism."[34] William G. McLoughlin Jr., a historian of American religion at Brown University, observed in 1960 that "scarcely one of his Sunday afternoon sermons over a nine-year period has failed to touch on communism."[35]

Graham perhaps did as much as any other American in the 1950s to divide the world into good versus evil. "Christian America" embodied good while communism and the Soviet Union embodied evil. "America," he said in 1952, "is the last bulwark of Christian civilization." On the other hand, "Communism is . . . master-minded by Satan," and the two were engaged in a life-and-death struggle. In this way, Graham reaffirmed the myth of American innocence.

Little wonder that Graham rejoiced when Dwight Eisenhower was elected president in 1952. After Eisenhower prayed at his own inauguration, Graham exulted, "The overwhelming majority of the American people felt a little more secure realizing that we have a man who believes in prayer at the helm of our government at this critical hour." After he attended a prayer meeting with Eisenhower in 1953, Graham affirmed that "God is giving us a respite, a new chance. . . . We are no longer going to be pushed around [by the Communists]."[36]

By 1955 the innocence that Americans believed was their birthright seemed to have been realized. As William Lee Miller put it, "Ike was in his White House and all was right with the world."[37] By then, Americans had inherited the entire mythic history of the Republic. They understood themselves as an Innocent Nation, standing with one foot in the golden age of the past (Nature's Nation) and the other in the golden age of the future (the Millennial Nation). They had been chosen by Almighty God to enlighten the world with liberty and justice for all. And if America was

---

[34] McLoughlin, *Billy Graham*, 139, 142–43.

[35] McLoughlin, *Billy Graham*, 138–39.

[36] McLoughlin, *Billy Graham*, 117.

[37] William Lee Miller, *Piety on the Potomac* (Boston: Houghton Mifflin, 1964), 28.

not altogether a Christian nation, at least it was infused with the virtues taught by the Christian faith.

An African American Critique of the Myth of American Innocence

Suddenly, almost without warning, a bombshell dropped into the idyllic American garden of the 1950s. We call that bombshell the 1960s. When we use the phrase *the 1960s*, we don't mean a decade that ran from 1960 to 1969. Rather, we mean a period of American history defined by intense social unrest that focused especially on racial discrimination and civil rights, on the one hand, and the Vietnam War, on the other. In a very real sense, that period began in Montgomery, Alabama, in 1955 when Rosa Parks refused to give up her seat on a city bus to a White man. It is difficult to determine precisely when that period ended, but one convenient date is March 29, 1973, when the last American combat troops left Vietnam.

By any measure, the 1960s was a watershed in American history. It shattered the sense of innocence that prevailed in the 1950s and exposed layers of guilt that, in turn, deeply divided the nation. At the beginning of this chapter, we noted how Lawrence Wright envied his father. "He matured in a magic age, the 1940s," Wright recalled, "when great evil and great good faced each other." And Wright "grew up expecting to inherit his [father's] certainty."

Yet, as a child of the 1960s, he found himself part of a disillusioned generation, entertaining the deepest doubts regarding the meaning of the United States. "It is easy to understand my anger, and the anger of my generation when we realized that our country had taken a wrong turn," Wright wrote. "Eisenhower was right: we had forfeited our moral position. We had surrendered our anticolonial past. Now that we were compromised, the world did not divide so neatly between good and evil."[38]

The Black Revolution

Black Americans emerged in the 1960s as some of the nation's most insightful social critics, offering important critiques of the myth of American

---

[38] Wright, *In the New World*, 110–11.

innocence. In this limited space, I will consider five: Dr. Martin Luther King Jr., Angela Davis, James Baldwin, Eldridge Cleaver, and Malcolm X. We will hear their critiques in the context of the two most important events in this period: the Civil Rights Movement and the war in Vietnam.

Dr. Martin Luther King Jr.

On December 1, 1955, Rosa Parks refused to abandon her seat on a Montgomery, Alabama, city bus for a White man. For this infraction of the Southern code, she was arrested. The Black community in Montgomery, under the leadership of Dr. Martin Luther King Jr., a young minister for the Dexter Avenue Baptist Church, responded with a massive nonviolent bus boycott that crippled downtown businesses and eventually won bus desegregation. Similar protests, organized and executed by Blacks, soon erupted in other parts of the South.

Inspired by King's nonviolent philosophy, Blacks protested the segregation of Southern restaurants in a series of lunch-counter sit-ins, staged in numerous Southern cities, beginning in 1960. The following year, they protested the segregation of interstate buses in the South that continued despite a 1946 Supreme Court ruling (*Morgan v. Virginia*) and an Interstate Commerce Commission order in 1955, both of which had made segregation on interstate travel facilities illegal. The Congress of Racial Equality (CORE), led by James Farmer, commissioned "freedom rides": buses that carried Blacks and Whites together through many sections of the American South, testing whether the federal government would enforce its own laws. Though nonviolent themselves, protesters in almost all these efforts met with violence, instigated by Whites.

Because the Montgomery bus boycott catapulted Martin Luther King into national leadership of the Civil Rights Movement, it is important to come to terms with his character and his commitments. First, it is impossible to understand King apart from his allegiance both to the American nation and to the American Creed. At the same time, he was convinced that, through years of segregation and racial discrimination, the nation had sold its soul and abandoned its founding aspirations. In his view, most White Americans had no clear sense of the nation's meaning or, if they did, they paid it no serious heed. He therefore determined to call the nation back to its own noblest ideals.

Perhaps nowhere did King make that case more effectively than in his "I Have a Dream" speech, delivered to the throngs of people who had assembled for a massive March on Washington in 1963—a march that A. Philip Randolph and others had proposed as early as 1941. At one point in that speech he told the crowd, "When the architects of our republic wrote the magnificent words of the Constitution and the Declaration of Independence, they were signing a promissory note to which every American was to fall heir." That note, King believed, promised "that all men, yes, black men as well as white men, would be guaranteed the unalienable rights of life, liberty, and the pursuit of happiness." Nevertheless, he noted,

> it is obvious today that America has defaulted on this promissory note insofar as her citizens of color are concerned. Instead of honoring this sacred obligation, America has given the Negro people a bad check; a check which has come back marked "insufficient funds." We refuse to believe that there are insufficient funds in the great vaults of opportunity of this nation. And so we've come to cash this check, a check that will give us upon demand the riches of freedom and the security of justice.

King explained that this dream was "a dream deeply rooted in the American dream that one day this nation will rise up and live out the true meaning of its creed—we hold these truths to be self-evident, that all men are created equal."[39] For King, the true meaning of the American Creed demanded racial integration at every significant level of American life.

Nor can one understand King apart from his Christian heritage. A Baptist minister himself, and the son and the grandson of Baptist ministers, King understood the message of Jesus on the value of every human being. In addition, the works of Reinhold Niebuhr (especially his book *Moral Man and Immoral Society*) had convinced King that dispossessed people must challenge their oppressors through "direct action"—behavior that would inconvenience the oppressor in some significant way. Finally,

[39] Martin Luther King Jr., "I Have a Dream," August 28, 1963, in *A Testament of Hope: The Essential Writings and Speeches of Martin Luther King, Jr.*, ed. James Melvin Washington (San Francisco: Harper, 1986), 217, 219.

inspired both by Jesus and by India's Mahatma Gandhi, King preached a message of nonviolent resistance against the policies of segregation and discrimination. King argued that only a nonviolent approach to these issues would preserve the integrity of the protesters while revealing the racist dimensions of American life for all to see.

That strategy paid especially rich dividends in 1963 when King led a protest march through the streets of Birmingham, Alabama. Television cameras were rolling when Sheriff Eugene "Bull" Connor's men turned police dogs and high-powered fire hoses on the nonviolent demonstrators, most of them children. The next day, pictures of police hosing demonstrators and clubbing young Black girls appeared in newspapers and magazines throughout the United States and the world. These events captured the imaginations of many young Whites throughout the nation. The issues for them were clear: Blacks were only demanding what the American Creed had promised them, but their parents' generation had refused to make that promise good.

Lawrence Wright was a case in point. He recalled:

> In Dallas we didn't know what to make of the Freedom Riders. When the first busload . . . approached Anniston, Alabama, in 1961, a mob punctured the bus's tires and set it on fire. The next bus made it to Birmingham, where the police stood aside and let the white mob beat the riders nearly to death. . . . I didn't clearly understand that the Freedom Riders were not fighting back. Nonviolence was such a foreign idea to me that I assumed the blacks and several whites on the buses had provoked the mob and got what was coming to them. I didn't grasp the philosophy of nonresistance—but then nothing in my years of churchgoing had prepared me to understand the power of suffering, or redemptive love.

Wright found it "unsettling to hear Martin Luther King . . . talking about Jesus." He recalled King's words at the 1960 lunch-counter sit-ins in Durham, North Carolina: "I am still convinced that Jesus was right. . . . I can hear Him saying, 'He who lives by the sword will perish by the sword.' I can hear him crying out, 'Love thy enemies.'"

King's rhetoric, coupled with Black-led struggles for equal opportunity, caused Larry Wright—as it caused a whole generation of White youth—to raise serious questions about the meaning of the American experiment. King's injunctions to "love thy enemies" were themes, Wright recalled, that "I also heard nearly every Sunday, but didn't we, as a nation, live by the sword? . . . Our doctrine was brotherly love. And yet no one ever proposed that Jesus might return as a Negro."[40]

If Martin Luther King Jr. and the nonviolent, Southern phase of the Civil Rights Movement called on America to "live out the true meaning of its creed," other Blacks wondered whether the American Creed had been so badly betrayed that there was little left to retrieve. As a result, many of these Blacks turned their backs on nonviolence as a workable strategy for change and embraced Black power instead. Some in this group advocated socialism and the overthrow of capitalism. James Forman, for example, wrote, "Our fight is against racism, capitalism and imperialism, and we are dedicated to building a socialist society inside the United States."[41]

Who were these radicals, many of whom had lost faith both in America and the American Creed?

Angela Davis

One was a woman named Angela Davis. Born in 1944, Davis grew up in Birmingham, Alabama, where Whites rigidly maintained segregation by custom and by law, enforced by intimidation, violence, and the threat of violence. She recalled in her autobiography what life was like for her as a child.

> Near my father's service station downtown was a movie house
> called The Alabama. . . . A luxurious red carpet extended all
> the way to the sidewalk. On Saturdays and Sundays, the mar-
> quee always bore the titles of the latest children's movies. . . .
> We weren't allowed in The Alabama—our theaters were the
> Carver and the Eighth Avenue, and the best we could expect
> in their roach-infested auditoriums was reruns of *Tarzan*. . . .

---

[40] Wright, *In the New World*, 137.

[41] James Forman, "The Black Manifesto," in *To Redeem a Nation: A History and Anthology of the Civil Rights Movement*, ed. Thomas R. West and James W. Mooney (St. James, NY: Brandywine Press, 1993), 251.

Downtown . . . , if we were hungry, we had to wait until we
retreated back into a Black neighborhood, because the restaurants
and food stands were reserved for whites only. . . . If we needed
to go to the toilet or wanted a drink of water, we had to seek out a
sign bearing the inscription "Colored." Most Southern Black children of my generation learned how to read the words "Colored"
and "White" long before they learned "Look, Dick, look."[42]

She learned as a child "the prevailing myth . . . that poverty is a punishment for idleness and indolence. If you had nothing to show for yourself,
it meant that you hadn't worked hard enough." Further, at Carrie A. Tuggle
Elementary School, many of her teachers "tended to inculcate in us the
official, racist explanation for our misery" and explained to the children
that if they would only work hard, "[we could] lift ourselves singly and
separately out of the muck and slime of poverty by 'our own bootstraps.'"

These explanations made less and less sense to Davis. She knew how
hard her parents had worked, and "it didn't make sense to me that all those
who had not 'made it' were suffering for their lack of desire and the defec-
tiveness of their will to achieve a better life for themselves. If this were true,
then, great numbers of our people—perhaps the majority—had really been
lazy and shiftless, as white people were always saying."[43]

At the age of fourteen, Davis left Birmingham to participate in a
program in New York City that brought Black students from the South
to integrated schools in the North. There she first read the *Communist
Manifesto*, and there she first encountered a circle of Blacks devoted to
Marxist ideals. She later recalled that "the *Communist Manifesto* hit me
like a bolt of lightning."[44]

In 1963, Angela Davis was studying in France when she read in an
English language newspaper a story about some murders in her own
hometown of Birmingham: "I saw a headline about four girls and a church
bombing. At first I was only vaguely aware of the words. Then it hit me!
It came crashing down all around me. Birmingham. 16th Street Baptist
Church. The names. I closed my eyes, squeezing my lids into wrinkles

[42] Angela Davis, *Angela Davis: An Autobiography* (New York: Random House, 1974), 83.
[43] Davis, *Autobiography*, 89–90, 92–93.
[44] Davis, *Autobiography*, 109.

as if I could squeeze what I had just read out of my head. . . . I kept star-
ing at the names. Carole Robertson. Cynthia Wesley. Addie Mae Collins.
Denise McNair."

Davis had known each of these girls and known them well. "When
the lives of these four girls were so ruthlessly wiped out," she wrote, "my
pain was deeply personal." In time she began to think clearly about the
meaning of these murders. "This act was not an aberration," she wrote.
"On the contrary, it was logical, inevitable. The people who planted the
bomb in the girls' restroom in the basement of 16th Street Baptist Church
were not pathological, but rather the normal products of their surround-
ings." Whoever committed this act, she believed, "wanted to terrorize
Birmingham's Black population," regardless of who might be killed. "The
broken bodies of Cynthia, Carole, Addie Mae and Denise were incidental
to the main thing—which was precisely why the murders were even more
abominable than if they had been deliberately planned."[45]

In 1968, Angela Davis joined the Communist Party.[46] In 1970, Governor
Ronald Reagan fired her from her position as professor of philosophy at
UCLA on the grounds that "the board will not tolerate any Communist
activities at any state institution." In that same year, she found herself on
the FBI's "Ten Most Wanted" list. The bureau charged her with planning
the rescue of three San Quentin prisoners and supplying the gun that
killed four people during the rescue attempt. In 1972, thanks to a massive
international campaign, she was acquitted.

The year before her acquittal, Davis wrote from her cell in the Marin
County, California, jail of the system she had come to reject. She wrote of
"unjust laws, bolstering the oppression of Black people." She wrote of the
"racist oppression [that] invades the lives of Black people on an infinite
variety of levels." And she wrote of the police who, she said, were "the
oppressor's emissaries, charged with the task of containing us within the
boundaries of our oppression."[47] Quite clearly, for Angela Davis, the notion

---

[45] Davis, *Autobiography*, 128–31. One of the suspects in this crime died in 1994 without being charged. Three others were convicted, one in 1977, one in 2001, and one in May of 2002, almost forty years after the bomb exploded and the girls were killed.

[46] Davis, *Autobiography*, 189.

[47] Davis, *If They Come in the Morning: Voices of Resistance* (New York: The Third Press, 1971), 20, 31, 32.

that America was an Innocent Nation was a myth completely lacking in legitimacy or justification.

The story of Angela Davis helps us understand in considerable depth how and why the meaning of America was unraveling in the 1960s and early 1970s, at least within the Black community. Indeed, Davis viewed her story as the story of a much larger cause. "The forces that have made my life what it is are the very same forces that have shaped and misshaped the lives of millions of my people," she wrote.[48] This is why her story demands thoughtful consideration.

James Baldwin

By any measure, James Baldwin provided the literary voice for the Civil Rights Movement. Born in 1924, some thirty years before the rise of that movement, he experienced the brunt of racism and segregation as a youth growing up in Harlem. At only twenty-four years old, he fled the United States and settled in France, where he spent much of his life.

It is safe to say that no one during the 1960s mounted a more devastating critique of White supremacy and the myth of innocence that gave it protection than James Baldwin. For example, in his "Letter to My Nephew," one of the essays of his 1963 classic *The Fire Next Time*, Baldwin spoke forcefully of the myth of American innocence and the terror for which it provided cover. "My country and my countrymen," he said, "have destroyed and are destroying hundreds of thousands of lives and do not know it and do not want to know it." Indeed, most of all "it is the innocence which constitutes the crime."

Baldwin then explained to his nephew what his nephew already knew from experience—the nature of the terror for which the myth of innocence provided cover.

> This innocent country set you down in a ghetto in which, in fact, it intended that you should perish. Let me spell out precisely what I mean by that, for the heart of the matter is here, and the root of my dispute with my country. You were born where you were born and faced the future that you faced because you were

---

[48] Davis, *Autobiography*, ix.

black and *for no other reason.* The limits of your ambition were, thus, expected to be set forever. You were born into a society which spelled out with brutal clarity, and in as many ways as possible, that you were a worthless human being. You were not expected to aspire to excellence: you were expected to make peace with mediocrity. Wherever you have turned, James, in your short time on this earth, you have been told where you could go and what you could do (and *how* you could do it) and where you could live and whom you could marry.

And then, fully anticipating the objections from Whites whose sense of innocence would prompt both denial and disbelief, Baldwin continued, "I know your countrymen do not agree with me about this, and I hear them saying, 'You exaggerate.' [But] they do not know Harlem, and I do. So do you."[49]

Significantly, Baldwin grounded the myth of American innocence in America's failure—perhaps its refusal—to grasp its own history and the guilt its history bears. "These innocent people . . . [are] still trapped in a history which they do not understand; and until they understand it, they cannot be released from it," Baldwin wrote. Typically, however, they could not afford to grapple with their history, and what prevented that grappling was "the danger . . . in the minds of most white Americans [about] the loss of their identity," which was rooted in Black subservience. Indeed, Baldwin wrote, "the black man has functioned in the white man's world as a fixed star, as an immovable pillar: and as he moves out of his place, heaven and earth are shaken to their foundations."[50]

In October 1970, shortly after the FBI placed Angela Davis's name on its Ten Most Wanted Fugitive List and following her capture, *Newsweek* placed a photo of a handcuffed Davis on its cover with the headline, "Angela Davis: Black Revolutionary."[51] In response, Baldwin penned "An Open Letter to My Sister, Miss Angela Davis." In that letter, he returned to the myth of innocence and how it was rooted in White America's refusal to come to terms with the terrors of its history. America was "on the edge

---

[49] Baldwin, *The Fire Next Time*, 292–93.
[50] Baldwin, *The Fire Next Time*, 294.
[51] Kenneth Auchincloss, "The Angela Davis Case," *Newsweek*, October 25, 1970, 218–22, 24.

of absolute chaos," he wrote. The period of the Black revolution "was a day which Americans never expected or desired to see, however piously they may declare their belief in 'progress and democracy.'" They were not prepared because White Americans "never expected to be confronted with the algebra of their history."

Blacks, on the other hand, understood all too well "the algebra of [American] history" and the impact of that history on Black consciousness and Black self-esteem.

> The American triumph—in which the American tragedy has always been implicit—was to make black people despise themselves. When I was little I despised myself, I did not know better. And this meant, albeit unconsciously, or against my will, or in great pain, that I also despised my father. *And* my mother. *And* my brothers. *And* my sisters. Black people were killing each other every Saturday night out on Lenox Avenue, when I was growing up; and no one explained to them, or to me, that it was *intended* that they should; that they were penned where they were, like animals, in order that they should consider themselves no better than animals. Everything supported this sense of reality, nothing denied it: and so one was ready, when it came time to go to work, to be treated as a slave.

While the question of the American future was far from clear in 1970, of one thing Baldwin was certain—that Blacks, unlike Whites, had come to terms with their history and, through that action, had taken decisive steps toward freedom. Baldwin therefore encouraged Davis with this assessment: "What has happened, it seems to me, and to put it far too simply, is that a whole generation of people have assessed and absorbed their history, and, in that tremendous action, have freed themselves of it and will never be victims again." Indeed, Baldwin wrote, "we must fight for your life as though it were our own—which it is—and render impassable with our bodies the corridor to the gas chamber. For, if they take you in the morning, they will be coming for us that night."[52]

---

[52] Baldwin, "An Open Letter to My Sister, Miss Angela Davis," *New York Review of Books*, January 7, 1971, http://www.nybooks.com/articles/1971/01/07/an-open-letter-to-my-sister-miss-angela-davis/, accessed July 19, 2017.

Eldridge Cleaver

Eldridge Cleaver, minister of information of the Black Panther party, offered a striking critique of several American myths in *Soul on Ice*, a book he wrote from his cell at Folsom Prison. He began his critique with the myth of American innocence and the way that myth was rooted in White America's denial of its history. The White youth of America, he wrote,

> must face and admit the moral truth concerning the works of their fathers. That such venerated figures as George Washington and Thomas Jefferson owned hundreds of black slaves, that all of the Presidents up to Lincoln presided over a slave state, and that every President since Lincoln connived politically and cynically with the issues affecting the human rights and general welfare of the broad masses of the American people.

Cleaver rejoiced that at last, in the midst of the revolution of the 1960s, "these facts weigh heavily upon the hearts of these young people."[53]

For Cleaver, however, the problem was not just America. It was the entire White race, "whose heroes have been revealed as villains and its greatest heroes as the arch-villains; . . . heroes whose careers rested on a system of foreign and domestic exploitation, rooted in the myth of white supremacy and the manifest destiny of the white race."[54] For many years, White Americans could not discern these realities, protected as they were by the Great American Myths. As Cleaver noted,

> Even when confronted with overwhelming evidence to the contrary, most White Americans have found it possible, after steadying their rattled nerves, to settle comfortably back into their vaunted belief that America is dedicated to the proposition that all men are created equal and endowed by their Creator with certain inalienable rights—life, liberty and the pursuit of happiness.

---

[53] Eldridge Cleaver, *Soul on Ice* (New York: Dell Publishing, 1968), 70.
[54] Cleaver, *Soul on Ice*, 68.

Indeed, Cleaver observed, "It is remarkable how the system worked for so many years, how the majority of whites remained effectively unaware of any contradiction between their view of the world and that world itself."[55]

However one might regard Eldridge Cleaver, his words can help us understand the dynamics that accompanied the erosion of America's myths in the 1960s and 1970s, especially the myth of America as an Innocent Nation.

Malcolm X

Typically, Blacks who argued as Cleaver did were northern and urban, or perhaps western and urban like Cleaver himself, but generally not Southern or rural. In their view, King's nonviolent strategies might work well in the South but were unsuited to major urban centers outside the South like New York, Boston, Los Angeles, and Chicago. They also disagreed with King's support for racial *integration*. Often more militant than King, these Blacks rejected the ideal of integration, insisting on racial *separation* instead. They increasingly abandoned the banner of civil rights, defined by Martin Luther King, and embraced instead the banner of Black power.

No one typified this more militant tradition better than Malcolm X. Malcolm spent his early years in Michigan, though he experienced there the same intense level of discrimination that so many Americans today associate only with the historic American South. When Malcolm was in the eighth grade in Mason, Michigan, for example, his teacher—Mr. Ostrowski—asked if he had given any thought to a possible career. Malcolm told his teacher that he wanted to become a lawyer, and Mr. Ostrowski responded,

> Malcolm, one of life's first needs is for us to be realistic. Don't misunderstand me, now. We all here like you, you know that. But you've got to be realistic about being a nigger. A lawyer— that's no realistic goal for a nigger. You need to think about something you *can* be. You're good with your hands—making things. Everybody admires your carpentry shop work. Why don't you plan on carpentry? People like you as a person—you'd get all kinds of work.

---

[55] Cleaver, *Soul on Ice*, 76–78.

His teacher's statement, Malcolm later recalled, was a turning point in his life.[56]

Later, in Boston's Roxbury district, Malcolm found that jobs of all kinds were closed to Blacks. After a short career of thieving, hustling, and pimping, he landed in prison where he encountered a new religion, the Nation of Islam, popularly styled the Black Muslim tradition. He embraced that faith and soon became its most prominent spokesperson. His new faith taught him that "the only way the black people caught up in this society can be saved is not to *integrate* into this corrupt society, but to *separate* from it, to a land of our *own*, where we can reform ourselves, lift up our moral standards, and try to be godly."

Malcolm carefully distinguished between *separation* and *segregation*. "We reject *segregation* even more militantly than you say you do," Malcolm told more moderate Black leaders. "Segregation is that which is forced upon inferiors by superiors. But *separation* is that which is done voluntarily, by two equals—for the good of both!" Separation, he said, was important, since "as long as our people here in America are dependent upon the white man, we will always be begging him for jobs, food, clothing, and housing. And he will always control our lives, regulate our lives, and have the power to segregate us."[57]

Especially in his early years, Malcolm strongly criticized Martin Luther King on this issue. "I knew," he wrote, "that the great lack of most of the big-name 'Negro leaders' was their lack of any true rapport with the ghetto Negroes. How could they have rapport when they spent most of their time 'integrating' with white people?"[58] Malcolm therefore argued for a strategy he called "Black nationalism."[59] He meant by this term that Blacks should strive for total independence from Whites. He meant that Blacks should run their own farms, their own businesses, and their own banks. He meant that Blacks should cultivate their own traditions and value their own heritage and culture.

---

[56] Malcolm X with Alex Haley, *The Autobiography of Malcolm X* (New York: Grove Press, 1966), 36.

[57] Malcolm X, *Autobiography*, 246.

[58] Malcolm X, *Autobiography*, 310.

[59] Malcolm X, *Autobiography*, 374.

His embrace of the Nation of Islam symbolized his deepest misgivings both about America and about the Christian faith. In his judgment, Western society in general and America in particular had "become overrun with immorality, and God is going to judge it, and destroy it."[60] For these reasons and more, Malcolm rejected his Anglo and Christian surname, "Little," and adopted instead the name "X." The X, he said, symbolized his African name, long since sacrificed to the racism that dominated Anglo-American culture.

Malcolm differed profoundly from Martin Luther King on the issue of violence. "I'm not for wanton violence," he said. "I'm for justice." This meant for Malcolm, however, that violence might sometimes be appropriate: "I believe it's a crime for anyone who is being brutalized to continue to accept that brutality without doing something to defend himself. If that's how 'Christian' philosophy is interpreted, if that's what Gandhian philosophy teaches, well, then, I will call them criminal philosophies."[61] In 1964, Malcolm made his position unmistakably clear: "We should be peaceful, law-abiding—but the time has come for the American Negro to fight back in self-defense whenever and wherever he is being unjustly and unlawfully attacked."[62]

Malcolm and his message grew immensely popular with American Blacks, especially the younger generation of Blacks who lived in northern cities. Typified by second-wave leaders of the Civil Rights Movement like H. Rap Brown and Stokely Carmichael, those Blacks modeled their protest on Malcolm's strategies and essentially rejected King's nonviolent tactics along with his dream of racial integration.

By the 1990s, Malcolm's vision remained the model for thousands of Blacks throughout America. In 1991, for example, Sam Fulwood explained how "my generation . . . is so disillusioned by the persistent racism that continues to define and limit us that we are abandoning efforts to assimilate into the mainstream of society." Although they were the "sons and daughters of those who faced the dogs, water hoses and brutal cops" for the

---

[60] Malcolm X, *Autobiography*, 246.

[61] Malcolm X, *Autobiography*, 366–67.

[62] Malcolm X, "A Declaration of Independence," March 12, 1964, in *Malcolm X Speaks: Selected Speeches and Statements*, ed. George Breitman (New York: Grove Weidenfeld, 1965), 22.

sake of integration, thousands of Black professionals, Fulwood reported, were "turning away from our parents' great expectations of an integrated America." He told how

> many middle-class black executives are moving out of their
> corporate roles to create fulfilling jobs that serve black cus-
> tomers. Black colleges are experiencing a renaissance. Black
> organizations—churches, fraternities, sororities and professional
> groups—are attracting legions of new members. And, most sur-
> prising to me, upscale blacks are moving to neighborhoods that
> insulate them from the slings and arrows of the larger society.

And why? "Trying to explain my life to white people, who just don't care to understand," Fulwood explained, "is taxing and, ultimately, not worth the trouble. Sort of like singing 'Swing Low, Sweet Chariot' *en fran-cais*. Why bother? Once translated, it's just not the same song."[63]

What, then, should we make of the Black Revolution and these five leaders? Simply put, each articulated what every African American had always known, that powerful American myths had long defined the American Creed, subverted its true meaning, and crippled its ability to fulfill its promise for all human beings. As a result, Blacks formed the van-guard of the counterculture of the 1960s. Some, like Martin Luther King, called on Americans "to live out the true meaning of the American creed." Others, like Malcolm X, argued that if Blacks were to find any meaning in the American experience, they would have to find that meaning in themselves.[64]

The Vietnam War

American involvement in Vietnam grew from small beginnings. In the aftermath of World War II, numerous Asian and African nations, colonized by European powers, declared their independence from European colonial domination. Among these was the Democratic Republic of Vietnam, led by Ho Chi Minh, who in 1945 declared his country's independence in words

---

[63] Sam Fulwood, "The Rage of the Black Middle Class," *Los Angeles Times Magazine*, November 5, 1991. See also "White and Black Lies," *Newsweek*, November 15, 1993, 52-54.

[64] See James H. Cone, *Martin & Malcolm & America: A Dream or a Nightmare* (Maryknoll: Orbis Books, 1991).

borrowed from Thomas Jefferson: "We hold these truths to be self-evident, that all men are created equal."

When the French, dominant in that region since the nineteenth century, refused to abandon Vietnam and sought to establish a new colonial outpost in the southern provinces, the First Indochina War erupted in 1946. Ho Chi Minh increasingly turned to Red China for support, while the French turned to America and Great Britain.

The government of the United States sympathized with Ho Chi Minh and his declarations of independence for his nation. At the same time, America feared the expansion of communism in Southeast Asia and increasingly provided support for French control of that region. That support began under the Harry Truman administration but accelerated under President Dwight Eisenhower. In 1953, the United States paid $1 billion to achieve its objective—two-thirds of the cost of the French occupation. In 1954, President Eisenhower articulated the infamous "domino theory": "You have a row of dominoes set up, you knock over the first one, and what will happen to the last one is the certainty that it will go over very quickly." For years to come, that theory would govern the American response to Vietnam.

When the French first enlisted American support in their ongoing struggle with Ho Chi Minh, the US government sent "advisers" into the region. By 1963, the number of "advisers" had escalated to 16,000. In 1964, President Lyndon Johnson ordered bombings of North Vietnam, and in 1965, America committed combat troops to defend the South against communist aggression from the North.

Public support for American involvement in that war soon began to erode for one fundamental reason. The administration feared that an American commitment to total victory might risk a military engagement with the Chinese and the Soviets. As a result, America settled for a more limited objective: to prevent the Communists from winning.

In the meantime, the number of American ground troops committed to the war escalated dramatically, reaching 385,000 in 1966 and 542,000 in 1969. American casualties escalated as well. Each night, the American public learned the official body count for the day on the evening news, and when the war finally concluded in 1973, 51,000 Americans had died. By the mid-1960s, when it became apparent that the government had no strategy to end the war, the mood of a very large segment of the public turned sour.

While America's failure to win the war fueled a broad, general dissatisfaction with the military venture in Vietnam, moral issues related to the war inflamed the counterculture, including religious progressives and America's minorities. In the first place, the government of South Vietnam, which the United States supported, seemed as brutal and oppressive as the Communist government of the North. Critics therefore wondered how America could possibly support such a regime without betraying its noblest ideals. Beyond that consideration, the broad countercultural coalition placed the war squarely in the context of the struggle for equal rights for Blacks and other minorities in the United States. Inescapably, the war wrought devastation on the homes, lands, and lives of people of color. Many therefore saw the war as yet another manifestation of American racism and Western imperialism.

The boxing champion Muhammad Ali, for example, refused induction into the United States military and gave his reasons for that decision in March of 1967:

> Why should they ask me to put on a uniform and go 10,000 miles from home and drop bombs and bullets on Brown people in Vietnam while so-called Negro people in Louisville are treated like dogs and denied simple human rights? No, I'm not going 10,000 miles from home to help murder and burn another poor nation simply to continue the domination of white slave masters of the darker people the world over.

Ali knew that decision might land him in jail, but he asked, "So what? We've been in jail for 400 years."[65] As it was, he was stripped of his title and barred from the ring.

One month later, on April 4, 1967, Martin Luther King Jr. addressed many of these same issues at a meeting of Clergy and Laity Concerned at the Riverside Church in New York City. Early in that speech, he anticipated the inevitable question, "Why are *you* speaking about war, Dr. King? Why

---

[65] Muhammed Ali, "Muhammed Ali Refuses to Fight in Vietnam (1967)," Alpha History, http://alphahistory.com/vietnamwar/muhammed-ali-refuses-to-fight-1967/, accessed March 22, 2017.

are *you* joining the voices of dissent?" To this question, King affirmed that he was a minister of Jesus Christ, and for that reason, "the path from Dexter Avenue Baptist Church—the church in Montgomery, Alabama, where I began my pastorate—leads clearly to this sanctuary tonight." Because of his Christian convictions, he had to speak.

King argued that the war worked hand in hand with domestic racism to destroy the lives of poor Black people. The war, he pointed out, sent the poor "to fight and to die in extraordinarily high proportions to the rest of the population." It took "black young men who had been crippled by our society" and sent "them eight thousand miles away to guarantee liberties in Southeast Asia which they had not found in southwest Georgia and East Harlem." He also lamented the fact that the war diverted money, energy, and attention from the domestic war for civil rights. He recalled that "a few years ago there was a shining moment in [the] struggle [for equal rights]. . . . Then came the buildup in Vietnam and I watched the program broken and eviscerated as if it were some idle political plaything of a society gone mad on war."

For King, the most fundamental issue by far was the massive level of destruction that America had rained on Vietnam. Because of that destruction, King concurred with a man he called "one of the great Buddhist leaders of Vietnam": "The image of America will never again be the image of revolution, freedom and democracy, but the image of violence and militarism." In that context, King spoke of the violence in America's ghettos. When he tried to counsel young Blacks to embrace nonviolent protest, they inevitably asked, "What about Vietnam?"

> They asked if our own nation wasn't using massive doses of violence to solve its problems, to bring about the changes it wanted. Their questions hit home, and I knew that I could never again raise my voice against the violence of the oppressed in the ghettos without having first spoken clearly to the greatest purveyor of violence in the world today—my own government.

King spoke to these issues, he said, because of his "commitment to the ministry of Jesus Christ." Because of that commitment, he felt "called to speak for the weak, for the voiceless, for victims of our nation and for those it calls enemy, for no document from human hands can make these humans any less our brothers."

The audience at the Riverside Church that night was a sympathetic audience. When King's remarks hit the newspapers the following morning, though, many Americans were puzzled, perplexed, and angry. It was fine to speak on behalf of the weak, the voiceless, and the poor. But to speak on behalf of the nation's enemies? That was going too far. King knew his remarks would prompt that reaction. Perhaps that is why, at one point in his speech, he explained what he called "the true meaning and value of compassion and nonviolence": "It helps us to see the enemy's point of view, to hear his questions, to know his assessment of ourselves. For from his view we may indeed see the basic weaknesses of our own condition, and if we are mature, we may learn and grow and profit from the wisdom of the brothers who are called the opposition."[66]

9/11 and Beyond

The terrorist attacks of September 11, 2001, resurrected the myth of American innocence with a vengeance, and—along with it—the effort to divide the world into a simple grid of right versus wrong, good versus evil. President George W. Bush, for example, wondered out loud why "people would hate us" since "I know how good we are."[67] In his 2002 State of the Union address, he identified three nations—North Korea, Iran, and Iraq—as "an axis of evil, arming to threaten the peace of the world."[68] And in an address to a joint session of Congress on September 20, 2001, he gave the world an ultimatum that rested squarely on the good-versus-evil divide: "Every nation in every region now has a decision to make," the president said. "Either you are with us or you are with the terrorists."

This robust sense of American innocence informed the American sense of self during all the years of the "War on Terror" and provided the backdrop for race relations in the early years of the twenty-first century. With that backdrop in place, nothing did more to define race relations

---

[66] All citations are from King, "A Time to Break Silence," speech delivered at Riverside Church, New York City, April 4, 1967, in *A Testament of Hope*, 231–43.

[67] "This Is a Different Kind of War," *Los Angeles Times*, October 12, 2001, A16.

[68] George W. Bush, "State of the Union Address," January 29, 2002.

during those years than a series of fatal shootings of unarmed Black males by armed security guards or police. While those killings had transpired under the radar on a regular basis for years, cell phone–camera technology finally brought them into the public consciousness. Now the public could see who did the killings, who was killed, and under what circumstances.

When in 2012 a neighborhood watch volunteer killed Trayvon Martin—a teenager carrying candy and soda as he walked through a gated community in Miami Gardens, Florida—the reality of Black lives snuffed out at the hands of police or White vigilantes became national news. The fact that those responsible were seldom convicted became national news as well.

Following Martin's death, scores of other cases emerged. A small sample of those include Eric Garner, suspected of illegally selling cigarettes and choked to death on July 17, 2014, by New York City police; Michael Brown, killed on August 9, 2014, by a White policeman in Ferguson, Missouri, following a petty robbery; Tamir Rice, age twelve, killed on November 22, 2014, in Cleveland, Ohio, for holding a toy gun; Freddie Gray, who died in a police van on April 19, 2015, in Baltimore, Maryland, while handcuffed and shackled to the floor; Walter Scott, shot by police in North Charleston, North Carolina, on April 4, 2015, following a minor traffic violation; and Sandra Bland, found hanged in a Waller County, Texas, jail cell on July 13, 2015, also following a minor traffic violation.

The Black community responded to these and other killings with the affirmation that "Black Lives Matter" and with the creation in 2013 of a national organization that wore that name. On the other hand, many in the White community responded with affirmations of innocence. "I didn't do it, I'm not responsible," and "Don't put that guilt trip on me" became a common refrain among Whites who seemed to have no sense of the meaning of systemic racism—the fundamental inequalities embedded into America's social structures and economic systems.

At the same time, many Whites essentially trivialized the affirmation that "Black lives matter" by making the obvious point that "all lives matter." Former New York City mayor Rudy Giuliani even demonized the affirmation that "Black lives matter." "When you say 'black lives matter," Giuliani said, "that's inherently racist. Black lives matter, white lives matter, Asian lives matter, Hispanic lives matter. That's anti-American and it's racist."[69]

Following the terror attacks of September 11, 2001, and in the context of the racial divide that intensified in subsequent years, three Black writers, all of them public intellectuals, wrote important books designed, at least in part, to help the public understand in depth the realities of White supremacy, systemic racism, and the myth of American innocence: Ta-Nehisi Coates's *Between the World and Me*, Molefi Kete Asante's *Erasing Racism: The Survival of the American Nation*, and Michael Eric Dyson's *Tears We Cannot Stop: A Sermon to White America.*

Ta-Nehisi Coates

Coates wrote his book as an intimate letter to his young son. Born in 1975, Coates grew up in Baltimore, where his experience of systemic racism and police brutality rendered the Freedom Movement of the 1960s all but incomprehensible. He recalled:

> Every February, my classmates and I were herded into assemblies for a ritual review of the civil rights movement. Our teachers urged us toward the example of freedom marchers, Freedom Riders, and Freedom Summers, and it seemed that the month could not pass without a series of films dedicated to the glories of being beaten on camera. The black people in these films seemed to love the worst things in life. . . . I judged them against the country I knew, which had acquired the land through murder and tamed it under slavery, against the country whose armies fanned out across the world to extend their dominion. The world, the real one, was civilization secured and ruled by savage means.[70]

Indeed, Coates judged the Freedom Movement against the backdrop of his own reality—the routine murder of Blacks in America's streets.[71]

---

[69] Jason Silverstein, "Rudy Giuliani Says Black Children Have a '99% Chance' of Killing Each Other, Calls Black Lives Matter 'Inherently Racist,'" *New York Daily News*, July 10, 2016, http://www.nydailynews.com/news/national/rudy-giuliani-black-kids-99-chance-killing-article-1.2706349.

[70] Ta-Nehisi Coates, *Between the World and Me* (New York: Spiegel & Grau, 2015), 30–32.

[71] Coates, *Between the World and Me*, 9.

While lamenting police brutality against Black American citizens, Coates made it clear that he did not blame the police so much as he blamed the nation. Speaking of the killing of Howard University student Prince Carmen Jones in Prince George's County, Virginia, in 2000, Coates wrote that "Prince was not killed by a single officer so much as he was murdered by his country." Indeed, he wrote, "to challenge the police is to challenge the American people."[72]

In the face of these realities, most Whites proclaimed their innocence, prompting Coates to speak of White Americans as "the Dreamers"—people whose American Dream glorifies manicured suburbs and picnics and portrays the United States as "exceptional, the greatest and noblest nation ever to exist, a lone champion standing between the white city of democracy and the terrorists, despots, barbarians, and other enemies of civilization." To challenge that dream, Coates wrote, was difficult precisely because of the myth of American innocence. "There exists, all around us," he observed, "an apparatus urging us to accept American innocence at face value and not to inquire too much. And it is easy to look away, to live with the fruits of our history and to ignore the great evil done in all of our names."[73]

Paradoxically, Coates insisted, the myth of American innocence simply assumed the existence of a brutalized, Black underclass. "The right to break the black body," he told his son, "is the meaning of their sacred equality. . . . There is no them without you, and without the right to break you they must necessarily fall from the mountain, lose their divinity, and tumble out of the Dream."[74]

Coates understood that the American claim to innocence is deeply rooted in the claim the Dreamers make that the United States transcends the constraints of history—the notion voiced by Ronald Reagan, noted earlier in this chapter, that "the calendar can't measure America because we were meant to be an endless experiment in freedom, with no limit to our reaches, no boundaries to what we can do, no end point to our hopes."[75]

---

[72] Coates, *Between the World and Me*, 78.

[73] Coates, *Between the World and Me*, 8–9.

[74] Coates, *Between the World and Me*, 105.

[75] Ronald Reagan, "Address before a Joint Session of Congress on the State of the Union," January 27, 1987, in *Public Papers of the Presidents of the United States: Ronald Reagan: 1987*, vol. 1: *January 1 to July 3, 1987* (Washington, DC: Government Printing Office, 1989), 59–60.

For Coates, Americans who embrace that assumption must inevitably look away from the terrors of their history, not to mention the terrors of their own time. "The mettle that it takes to look away from the horror of our prison system, from police forces transformed into armies, from the long war against the black body," Coates wrote, "is not forged overnight. This is the practiced habit of jabbing out one's eyes and forgetting the work of one's hands."[76]

Coates found this habit of forgetting in virtually every nook and corner of American history. The Civil War is but one example. "American reunion was built on a comfortable narrative that made enslavement into benevolence, white knights of body snatchers, and the mass slaughter of the war into a kind of sport in which one could conclude that both sides conducted their affairs with courage, honor, and élan. The lie of the Civil War is the lie of innocence, is the Dream." For that reason, America's national battlefields "had been retrofitted," Coates believed, "as the staging ground for a great deception"—a deception designed to protect the myth of American innocence. He recalled how he and his son had visited the Petersburg Battlefield where "every visitor seemed most interested in flanking maneuvers, hardtack, smoothbore rifles, grapeshot, and ironclads, but virtually no one was interested in what all of this engineering, invention, and design had been marshaled to achieve," namely, the perpetuation of enslavement in the United States.[77]

With that history in mind, Coates placed upon Ground Zero—that area of Manhattan devastated by the attacks of September 11, 2001—an interpretation altogether different from the one that was generally accepted. "I kept thinking about how southern Manhattan had always been Ground Zero for us. They auctioned our bodies down there, in that same devastated, and rightly named, financial district. And there was once a burial ground for the auctioned there." And then he recalled how America had covered up that history and denied that it ever existed. "They built a department store over part of it and then tried to erect a government building over another part. Only a community of right-thinking black people stopped them. . . ."

---

[76] Coates, *Between the World and Me*, 98.
[77] Coates, *Between the World and Me*, 102–3, 106, 99–100.

Bin Laden was not the first man to bring terror to that section of the city. I never forget that." To his young son, he counseled, "Neither should you."[78]

Having to live among Dreamers who consistently deny their own history has placed an almost unbearable burden on Blacks, Coates contended, for they tell "you that the Dream is just, noble, and real, and you are crazy for seeing the corruption and smelling the sulfur. For their innocence, they nullify your anger, your fear, until you are coming and going, and you find yourself inveighing against . . . your own humanity and raging against the crime in your ghetto, because you are powerless before the great crime of history that brought the ghettos to be."[79]

Molefi Kete Asante

After graduating from several institutions related to Churches of Christ—one of the two restorationist traditions I explored earlier in this chapter—Molefi Kete Asante earned his PhD in communication studies at UCLA and later served as professor and chair in the Department of African American Studies at Temple University. Widely recognized as the father of Afrocentric Studies, Asante authored more than seventy-five books and, with Robert Singleton, cofounded the *Journal of Black Studies*.

In his book *Erasing Racism*, first published in 2003, Asante offered two metaphors for the racial divide in the United States: the Promised Land and the Wilderness, metaphors that extend Coates's appraisal of "the Dreamers" who live in the land of innocence, completely unaware of the Wilderness that is everywhere in the American nation.[80]

From his own childhood in the American South, Asante knew the Wilderness well. He was born Arthur Lee Smith Jr. in Valdosta, Georgia, "a place where in the early twentieth century a black woman named Mary Turner was violently murdered and her unborn fetus ripped from her womb and stomped to death, because Turner protested the lynching of her husband." Asante "never forgot . . . the uncontrolled hatred against black

[78] Coates, *Between the World and Me*, 86–87.
[79] Coates, *Between the World and Me*, 106.
[80] Molefi Kete Asante, *Erasing Racism: The Survival of the American Nation*, 2nd ed. (New York: Prometheus Books, 2009), 10.

people [that] was palpable, real, immediate, and violent in my father's, as well as my own, lifetime."

When he was only twelve, he entered a "whites only" barbershop and "asked permission to shine the shoes of the customers for twenty-five cents." While bent over to prepare his supplies, his very first customer spat on his head. Asante recalled that "other whites, including the owner of the shop, began to laugh. Knowing precisely the disdain and hatred the men in the barbershop had for him, he gathered his shoebox with his waxes, cloths, and brushes and, without saying anything, walked out of the shop."[81]

> Growing up in Georgia and Tennessee, my earliest memories
> are of a society without whites, segregated, self-contained, and
> filled with the Holy Ghost. Nevertheless, we all knew that dis-
> tant whites had created the miserable world in which we lived.
> We knew this because from time to time they entered our world,
> and their entry was vile, oppressive, arrogant, and brutal. They
> were bill collectors, police, night riders, and others looking to
> harass African people.[82]

With no sense of history, Asante wrote, Whites have steadfastly maintained their innocence in matters of race. "Quite frankly," he wrote, "we are basically historically illiterate as a nation about the destructive nature of white supremacy as an ideology of dominance pervading every arena of American life. We have come to accept the abnormality as normal, the distortion of racial supremacy as the only American way of life." Their lack of a sense of history helps explain "the surprise some whites feel hearing of the fury felt by many African Americans. They wonder why African Americans seem never to be satisfied. They act as if all debts have been paid and the scores settled."[83]

Asante told one particularly poignant story that illustrates this:

> A white man from the tree-lined and rock-manicured streets of
> Simi Valley made his way in the late evening toward a section

---

[81] Asante, *Erasing Racism*, 7-8, 227.
[82] Asante, *Erasing Racism*, 48.
[83] Asante, *Erasing Racism*, 88, 92.

of the American Wilderness in South Central Los Angeles soon after the 1992 uprising. Smoke still lingered in the air, broken glass was everywhere, the bombed-out buildings were the skeletal remains of the rage of Los Angeles . . . [and] this Simi Valley Samaritan was struck dumb by the intensity of the collective fury of the people.

"Why?" he asked, half muttering to himself as he walked toward a knot of people who were already helping with the cleanup effort. "Why?" he repeated, almost in disbelief. He walked resolutely, as he mentally prepared himself to assist in the rebuilding of the community and do anything he could to create a climate of goodwill.

The perplexed Samaritan from Simi Valley was genuine in his earnestness, but he did not know very much about the bewildering conditions that caused the fury in the American Wilderness. . . . This man, with his Simi Valley consciousness, was like so many other whites—and some African Americans who exist on the fringes of the American Wilderness. . . . To them, the Wilderness represents strangeness, distance, mystery, and alienation like they have never known. . . . Their daily encounters with Wilderness dwellers . . . yield no real understanding of life in the Wilderness.

As David, the Samaritan from Simi Valley, walked deeper into the burned-out war zone, he encountered Kofi, a man whose store had been destroyed. Perhaps Kofi could answer the question, "Why?" But David's questions revealed his innocence and naïveté and frustrated Kofi, who responded,

"Man, you're taking my time. You want a lesson, I'll give you a lesson in American history. Our ancestors worked in hot fields and . . . wore burlap to protect their scarred and bleeding feet while building up this country for other people. No, it is not the same. We've worked as hard and longer than anyone, but let me try to get $50,000 or $100,000 to start my business from your bank. Racial prejudice and discrimination are ingrained in the way whites respond to African Americans."

"What do you mean?"

"I mean even the police treat us differently: rudely, almost with hatred," Kofi argued.

"This is America; are you serious?" David said in disbelief.

"Let me tell you something. In the most affluent white suburbs, we're the ones the police follow the most, the ones who must always give an accounting of our presence, the ones who are stalked like prey in department stores. . . ."

"Well, I want to help. What should I do?" David exasperatedly asked.

"Damn, David, you've got to start in your own neighborhood by getting your friends and neighbors to discuss their own prejudices against African Americans. . . . Hell, I don't know what kind of therapy whites need. Anyway, I've got to think about rebuilding my store. Have fun." Kofi turned and walked toward a parked car a half a block away.[84]

Innocence? Innocence, indeed!

Michael Eric Dyson

Police brutality against Black lives also prompted Michael Eric Dyson, sociologist at Vanderbilt University, prolific author, and radio host, to address the realities of White supremacy, systemic racism, and American innocence in his *Tears We Cannot Stop: A Sermon to White America*. Dyson wants Whites to understand that "to be black in America is to live in terror"—a terror that intrudes on Black lives in a thousand different ways. "That terror is fast," he wrote. "It is glimpsed in cops giving chase to black men and shooting them in their backs without cause. Or the terror is slow. It chips like lead paint on a tenement wall, or flows like contaminated water through corroded pipes that poison black bodies. [Or] it is slow like genocide inside prison walls where folk who should not be there perish."

---

[84] Asante, *Erasing Racism*, 135–38.

From the perspective of many Blacks, Dyson wrote, the police have been the American equivalent of ISIS.

> At any moment, without warning, a blue-clad monster will swoop down on us to snatch our lives from us and say that it was because we were selling cigarettes, or compact discs, or breathing too much for his comfort, or speaking too abrasively for his taste. Or running, or standing still, or talking back, or being silent, or doing as you say, or not doing as you say fast enough.[85]

Dyson, like Coates and Asante, argued that most Whites do not understand, do not "feel our terror," because the pervasive myth of American innocence blinds their moral vision. And like Coates and Asante, he traced the myth of innocence to the nation's denial of its history or, failing that, to its effort to rewrite history in ways that sustained the myth.

The Civil War was a case in point. "A flood of writing," Dyson lamented, "tells us that the Civil War wasn't really about slavery but about the effort to defend states' rights. . . . The right wing," he noted, promoted the notion that the war "was fought over the ability of individual states to beat back a federal government out to impose its will. From the left wing there's the belief that the Civil War was a conflict between the planter class and the proletariat. In each case, race as the main reason for the war is skillfully rewritten, or, really, written out."[86] Moreover, Dyson wrote, in the normative telling of American history, "black lives were excluded from the start."[87]

Dyson also rooted the myth of innocence in another great American myth—the myth of American individualism, which allows Whites to reject systemic racism, even as they deny personal responsibility for crimes against Blacks. Obviously, no single person is responsible for those crimes. The issue, rather, is complicity in a massive system that no American citizen, Black or White, can escape. But "by sidestepping complicity," Dyson wrote, "you hold fast to innocence. By holding fast to innocence, you

---

[85] Michael Eric Dyson, *Tears We Cannot Stop: A Sermon to White America* (New York: St. Martin's Press, 2017), 177–78.

[86] Dyson, *Tears We Cannot Stop*, 87.

[87] Dyson, *Tears We Cannot Stop*, 92.

maintain power."[88] And that, Dyson wrote, "is why the cry 'Black Lives Matter' angers you so greatly, why it is utterly offensive and effortlessly revolutionary. It takes aim at White innocence and insists on uncovering the lie of its neutrality, its naturalness, its normalcy, its normativity."[89]

Similarly, Dyson argued, that is why so many White Americans were so offended when San Francisco 49ers quarterback Kevin Kaepernick chose to kneel, not stand, during the national anthem. "He did so," Dyson wrote, "to protest injustice against black folk . . . to offer correction rather than abandon the nation. . . . But innocent whiteness recoils at such instruction. It pushes back against the notion that it could possibly learn anything from a black body kneeling on white sacred territory." Dyson, however, hoped the nation might somehow come to view "Kaepernick's criticism as . . . the tough love that America needs."[90]

Conclusion

I began this chapter with Lawrence Wright who discovered, along with millions of other White youth in the 1960s, that the world does not divide as neatly between good and evil as the myth of the Innocent American Nation might suggest. That realization came as a shock to Wright's generation since, in the aftermath of World War II, the nation had raised its children to believe that the United States always stood on the side of right against wrong and good against evil. Had the nation listened to the voices of African Americans, it would have known better. It would have known what Blacks knew all along—that the myth of American innocence is an illusion.

Human innocence is always an illusion in any event. But in the case of the American nation, innocence was grounded in a grand deception—the claim that Whites were superior to Blacks. So powerful was that deception that it sealed the ears of Whites against the truth and their hearts against the massive guilt upon which the nation was founded.

Malcolm X shed abundant light on the myth of American innocence when he claimed that the notion of White supremacy was "deeply rooted . . .

---

[88] Dyson, *Tears We Cannot Stop*, 105.

[89] Dyson, *Tears We Cannot Stop*, 104.

[90] Dyson, *Tears We Cannot Stop*, 112, 114.

in the national white subconsciousness."[91] That phrase—"national white subconsciousness"—helps us understand how it is possible to have "racism without racists," as sociologist Eduardo Bonilla-Silva so memorably put it. During the Obama presidency, for example, many Whites mounted the claim that the United States had entered a "post-racial" period. In point of fact, as Bonilla-Silva reminds us, they had substituted for the older, more blatant racism a series of rationalizations that could allow racism to flourish amid denial. Bonilla-Silva labeled that phenomenon "color-blind racism."[92] Tim Wise extended that analysis when he argued that many Americans, even liberal Americans, "carve out acceptable space for individuals such as Obama who strike them as different, as exceptions who are not like the rest . . . [while continuing] to look down upon the larger mass of black and brown America with suspicion, fear, and contempt."[93]

Whatever mechanisms the nation may employ to assert and protect its myth of innocence, that myth is the nation's Achilles' heel. Frederick Buechner once observed that "reality can be harsh and . . . you shut your eyes to it only at your peril because if you do not face up to the enemy . . . , then the enemy will come up from behind . . . and destroy you while you are facing the other way."[94] The myth of American innocence is the enemy of the nation that may yet destroy us. It is that enemy precisely because it encourages the American people to deny the extent to which White supremacy pervades American culture, to shut their eyes, and to face the other way.

---

[91] Malcolm X, *The Autobiography of Malcolm X*, 369.

[92] Eduardo Bonilla-Silva, *Racism without Racists: Color-Blind Racism and the Persistence of Racial Inequality in America*, 4th ed. (New York: Rowman & Littlefield, 2014), 73–96, 301–9.

[93] Tim Wise, *Between Barack and a Hard Place: Racism and White Denial in the Age of Obama* (San Francisco: City Light Books, 2009), 23.

[94] Frederick Buechner, *The Sacred Journey: A Memoir of Early Days* (New York: HarperOne, 1991), 45.

How Slavery Still Shapes the World of White Evangelical Christians

Henry Louis Gates's two-part series on "The Black Church" dramatically exposed the gaping chasm that divides the way Black Christians and privileged White Christians—especially White evangelicals—understand God, protest, and politics.

For many Blacks who follow Jesus, God is the God of justice who stands with marginalized people and turns the tables on those who carve out their wealth from the backs of the poor. The renowned Black theologian James Cone summed it up in a single phrase. Whatever else God may be, God is always "the God of the oppressed."

From beginning to end, the Hebrew and Christian Scriptures bear them out.

When Austin Channing Brown was only ten years old, she discovered "the God of the oppressed" in a Black Baptist church where "Jesus sounded like a Black person, dealing with familiar hardships of life—injustice, broken relationships, the pain of being called names."

Not until she was an adult did she hear the name James Cone or read about Black Liberation theology. "But by the time I learned of Black Jesus and his liberating power, I knew I had already met him at ten years old, in a Baptist church where the Spirit moved us every week."[1]

Most White evangelicals, especially those who are steeped in privilege, find that language utterly baffling. For them, God has little or nothing to do with economic or racial justice in this world, but everything to do with one's private walk with Jesus and salvation in the world to come.

There are many reasons for the White embrace of this severely truncated gospel, but one factor seems especially clear: the reality of American slavery that still casts its shadow over American religion and politics.

Slave owners, though they may well have professed the Christian faith, could never acknowledge that the deity they worshipped was, in reality, "the God of the oppressed."

While building their wealth on the backs of people they had enslaved, they could never acknowledge God's concern with economic justice.

Nor could they rape, maim, and lynch people with darker skin and acknowledge the biblical truth that God always sides with marginalized people against their oppressors.

As a result, White evangelicals across the South transformed the Christian faith into a religion that was inward, private, and otherworldly. With their focus on private talks with Jesus and salvation in the world to come, they could enslave human beings with consciences free from guilt.

In 1845, Frederick Douglass graphically described the brutal result. "The dealers in the bodies and souls of men erect their stand in the presence of the pulpit. The dealer gives his blood-stained gold to support the pulpit, and the pulpit, in return, covers his infernal business with the garb of Christianity."

In the early to mid-nineteenth century, some evangelical Christians in northern states led a frontal assault on slavery, but evangelicals in the American South, determined to resist that challenge, rooted their defense

---

[1] Austin Channing Brown, *I'm Still Here: Black Dignity in a World Made for Whiteness* (New York: Convergent Books, 2018), 37–38.

of slavery ever more firmly in their privatized, otherworldly version of the Christian religion.

Once slavery was abolished, that truncated version of the Christian faith slowly conquered the nation and helped create what we know today as "Christian America." It legitimated Jim Crow segregation and silenced voices that might have spoken in protest against that system.

One might have thought that White Southern Christians would have heard in the message of the Freedom Movement of the 1950s and 1960s an echo of the biblical text and stood with Blacks in their struggle for justice. But they did not, and their calculated silence led Dr. Martin Luther King Jr. to wonder, "What kind of people worship here? Who is their God?"

The privatized, otherworldly piety of American evangelicalism still inspires silence in the face of injustice.

When the Trump administration, for example, separated children from their parents on the southern border and placed those children in cages, Attorney General Jeff Sessions, a devout evangelical Christian, marshaled the Bible to defend that practice and silence dissent. "I would cite to you," he said, "the Apostle Paul and his clear and wise command in Romans 13 to obey the laws of the government because God has ordained the government for his purposes."

Sessions's words fit a long, historic pattern. In the face of atrocities committed by their government against people of color—the Vietnam War, for example, or Jim Crow segregation, or voter suppression, or the crimes at America's southern border—White evangelicals have typically run to the very passage cited by Attorney General Sessions to support their claim that Christians should obey the government, even if its policies are patently racist, unjust, oppressive, and unfair.

They consistently take that position when government policies sustain their place of privilege in America's social order.

But when their privilege is threatened, all bets are off.

Televangelist Jim Bakker made that point crystal clear in 2017 when he claimed that without Donald Trump, evangelical Christians would "be permanently shut up." If Trump were impeached, he warned, Christians would "come out of the shadows" and "there will be a civil war in the United States of America."

Suddenly, Romans 13 was irrelevant. Protest—even violent insurrection—was legitimate, enabled in part by the Jesus-and-me, otherworldly theology that is now so dominant in the United States of America.

White Christians clearly have much to learn from Black Christians about the meaning of their faith. To some small degree, the fate of the nation hangs on whether they are willing to open their hearts and take that crucial step.

RESISTING WHITE SUPREMACY

I f the heart of Jesus's preaching was his concern and compassion for disenfranchised and oppressed people, then the first step toward becoming
his disciple is to listen carefully and attentively to what those people wish
to tell us about the contours of their lives. In America, oppressed and
marginalized Black people have testified almost unanimously to the twin
realities of White supremacy, on the one hand, and the racial failures of
White Christianity, on the other.[1]

The great abolitionist Frederick Douglass offers a case in point:

> Between the Christianity of this land, and the Christianity of
> Christ, I recognize the widest possible difference—so wide, that
> to receive the one as good, pure, and holy, is of necessity to
> reject the other as bad, corrupt, and wicked. . . . I love the pure,
> peaceable, and impartial Christianity of Christ: I therefore hate
> the corrupt, slaveholding, women-whipping, cradle-plundering,
> partial and hypocritical Christianity of this land. Indeed, I can
> see no reason, but the most deceitful one, for calling the religion
> of this land Christianity.[2]

---

[1] Some of the language in this chapter is taken from Richard T. Hughes, *Christian America and the Kingdom of God* (Urbana: University of Illinois Press, 2009)—especially the section on "the gospel of the kingdom"—so some repeats are present from Chapter Eight in this volume.

[2] Frederick Douglass, *Narrative of the Life of Frederick Douglass* (1845; New York: Signet Books, 1968), 120.

Some one hundred years later, many White churches were still complicit in racial oppression, leading Martin Luther King Jr. to ask regarding those churches, "What kind of people worship here? Who is their God?"[3]

There seems no point—and it would not serve us well—to rehearse the racial failures of America's churches at any great length here. What will serve us well is an honest recognition that what caused and sustained those failures on the ground were deep and far-reaching theological failures. In this chapter, I want to ask about the nature of the racist culture that seduced evangelical Christians in particular, about the kind of theology that allowed the seduction to occur with such apparent ease, and about the kind of theology that can empower Christians of every stripe to resist the racist seductions of our culture and pursue justice and equality for oppressed and marginalized people.

My own tradition, the Churches of Christ, offers a window into the way in which American evangelicals have all too often succumbed to the racist dimensions of American culture. A product of the American frontier in the early nineteenth century, Churches of Christ devoted themselves to restoring the primitive church of the apostolic age.[4] For that reason, they typically rejected evangelical churches as "man-made" traditions, born of the womb of human history instead of Scripture and the primitive church. Since the 1960s, however, Churches of Christ have increasingly embraced American evangelicalism.[5] But the racism Churches of Christ shared with the larger evangelical world predated the 1960s by many years.[6] Three vignettes from the history of Churches of Christ offer important clues into the nature of that tradition's theological failures with respect to race.

---

[3] Martin Luther King Jr., "Letter from Birmingham City Jail," in *A Testament of Hope: The Essential Writings and Speeches of Martin Luther King, Jr.*, ed. James Melvin Washington (San Francisco: Harper, 1986), 299.

[4] On Churches of Christ, see Gary Holloway and Douglas A. Foster, *Renewing God's People: A Concise History of Churches of Christ* (Abilene, TX: ACU Press, 2002).

[5] Richard T. Hughes, *Reviving the Ancient Faith: The Story of Churches of Christ in America* (Grand Rapids: Eerdmans, 1996), 373.

[6] On racism in Churches of Christ, see Douglas A. Foster, *A Life of Alexander Campbell* (Grand Rapids: Eerdmans, 2020), 273–88, 329; Foster, "Justice, Racism, and Churches of Christ," in Gary Holloway and John York, *Unfinished Reconciliation: Justice, Racism, and Churches of Christ*, rev. ed. (Abilene, TX: ACU Press, 2013), 115–33; and Wes Crawford, *Shattering the Illusion: How African American Churches of Christ Moved from Segregation to Independence* (Abilene, TX: ACU Press, 2013).

First, *Gospel Advocate*[7] editor James Allen reported in 1925 that "many of the preachers" of Churches of Christ belonged to the Ku Klux Klan.[8]

Second, famed Church of Christ preacher G. C. Brewer recalled that as a young man growing up in Tennessee in the early twentieth century, "None of us thought of inviting Negroes into our homes as guests or of sitting down to eat with them at the same table; we felt, as a matter of course, that they should have the same food that we ate, but that they should eat in the kitchen or in the servants' quarters." He continued, "This was the condition that prevailed and this we accepted as right and satisfactory," but concluded, "We were not prejudiced against the Negroes."[9]

Third, Anne Moody reported that in the aftermath of the murder of Medgar Evers in Jackson, Mississippi, in 1963, on the Sunday after Evers's funeral, young Black activists visited numerous churches in the city of Jackson. Moody recalled that "at each one, [the churches] had prepared for our visit with armed policemen, paddy wagons, and dogs." On the second Sunday, the group visited a Church of Christ where the ushers "offered to give us cab fare to the Negro extension of the church." When the young Blacks resisted that advice, the ushers "threatened to call the police if we didn't leave. We decided to go."[10]

These three reports should set off in our heads the alarm bells of a theology gone badly awry. What kind of theology would allow self-professed followers of Jesus to hold membership in the Klan? What kind of theology would allow a disciple of Jesus to practice racial discrimination and then claim, "We were not prejudiced against the Negroes"? And what kind of theology would allow Christians to refuse to worship with other believers, even to call the police if those "others" did not leave?

The answer to those questions is clear: a theology that offers believers no means of resistance against the bigotry of the popular culture. Before we explore the contours of such a weak and listless theology, we first must ask,

[7] The *Gospel Advocate* was a popular gospel paper serving the Churches of Christ.

[8] James Allen, "Scripture Studies," *Gospel Advocate* 67 (14 May 1925): 457.

[9] G. C. Brewer, "Saved by a Moonbeam," n.d. James David Bales Papers, Special Collections, Box 8, Folder 21 (MC 1256 II), The University of Arkansas Library.

[10] Anne Moody, *Coming of Age in Mississippi* (New York: Dell, 1968), 283–84.

what is it about American popular culture that pulls professed disciples of Jesus so easily into the sinkhole of racial bigotry and prejudice?

The Racialized Contours of Popular American Culture

The answer to that question is something most White Americans, including most White American Christians, neither recognize nor understand and something to which they typically give little or no thought, simply because it is hidden from their eyes, even though it pervades American culture. I am speaking of the myth of White supremacy.

When I use the word *myth*, I don't have in mind a story that is untrue, but rather a story that gives us meaning. John Westerhoff III helps us understand the meaning of myth when he writes, "We need a story to see in the dark" for "stories are the imaginative way of ordering our experience."[11] When I speak of *White supremacy*, I am not speaking of the Ku Klux Klan or other White nationalist groups that proclaim White supremacy from the rooftops. I am speaking, rather, of virtually all White Americans, including myself, for the myth of White supremacy is the very air we breathe, an ideology that is so deeply embedded in our common culture that we can escape the power it wields over our minds and emotions with great difficulty, if at all.

While many Whites might find this claim preposterous, even offensive, most Blacks, in my experience, acknowledge this claim as the central truth about the meaning of Black life in the United States. If we wish to know the truth, therefore, we must listen carefully to their assessment of ourselves.

White supremacy, obviously, is not a story shared in common by *all* Americans. Most Blacks understand that myth because they have suffered its bitter fruit and know no other way to explain that experience. Whites, on the other hand, embrace the myth but, for the most part, do so unconsciously. Nothing in their experience has forced them to recognize this myth, much less to regard it as America's primal narrative.[12]

---

[11] John H. Westerhoff III, *A Pilgrim People: Learning through the Church Year* (Minneapolis: Seabury Press, 1984), 3–4.

[12] The central argument of my book *Myths America Lives By: White Supremacy and the Stories That Give Us Meaning* is not that White supremacy is one American myth among others, but rather that White supremacy is the primal American myth that informs and drives all the others.

While David Billings's experience might have been more blatant and direct than that of most American Whites, his story is, for the most part, typical. Reflecting on his childhood in Mississippi and Arkansas in the 1950s and 1960s, Billings recalls:

> As a white person, even in my youth, I was taught that everything
> of significance that had happened in the United States had been
> accomplished by white people. . . . I was brought up to think
> and see my white world as normal. Everybody else around me
> seemed to me to see the world in the same way. . . . My world-
> view, shaped by this internalized sense of racial superiority,
> meant that I saw history, morality, the will of God, and scien-
> tific truth as the special province of white people, usually white
> men. . . . More than [to] laws or customs, my very understand-
> ing of myself was bound to the idea of white supremacy.

Billings goes on to explain that in his world, "whites were not self-reflective about race."[13] But why should they have been? Some of them—perhaps many of them—had experienced hardship and persecution. But not a single negative dimension in their lives was due to the color of their skin. On the contrary, the color of their skin ensured that most of them would not face the same limitations that they, themselves, imposed on their African American neighbors. There was simply no incentive for them, therefore, to reflect on what it meant to be White, on the privileges to which White skin entitled them, or on the myth of White supremacy which they simply took for granted.

Blacks, on the other hand, have been forced to think deeply about the notion of White supremacy. They have been forced to discern it, to reflect upon it, and to understand it, for that myth alone could provide to their minds the rationale for the realities of slavery, for Jim Crow segregation, for beatings and lynchings and castrations, and for denial of equal opportunity in a nation that claims that "all men are created equal."

White supremacy has worked powerfully not only on the bodies but also on the minds of Blacks in the United States. A young woman—one

---

[13] David Billings, *Deep Denial: The Persistence of White Supremacy in United States History and Life* (Roselle, NJ: Crandall, Dostie & Douglass Books, 2016), 13–14.

of my students in recent years—told how a teacher once asked her a question that pierced to the marrow of her being: "Why do you always draw White girls?" the teacher queried. Later that evening, my student recalled, "The image of my teacher kneeling down to ask the impossible question stomped through my mind and raged through my ears like a violent storm. The weight of the question bent me, splitting my mind and my heart." And then she said this:

> When I was in high school, I would often do what many girls did. I would imagine myself years from now, getting ready for work early in the morning. The house was quiet, I would be tranquil but moving quickly to beat the traffic. I'd check the mirror in the foyer before leaving, straighten my perfectly pressed collar, twist the ring on my wedding finger so that the beautiful carved diamond would face the right way. I'd check my long and silky hair for any strands that had fallen out of the elaborate style I'd wrapped it in. I'd check my skin for imperfections.
>
> It was always the skin that grabbed me, that pulled me away. It was always then that I realized the beautiful, successful, loved woman in my dreams was White. I have never felt more gut wrenching shame than those times, when I was suddenly torn from my unreachable dream to face a reality that was impossible to ignore. I could not be White. I wasn't White. . . .
>
> It is harrowing to live with a stress you can never escape . . . the fear that you will never be fully accepted.[14]

In her novel *The Bluest Eye*, Toni Morrison tells a similar story about a young girl named Pecola to whom "it had occurred . . . some time ago that if her eyes . . . were different, that is to say, beautiful, she herself would be different. . . . Each night, without fail, she prayed for blue eyes. Fervently, for a year she had prayed. Although somewhat discouraged, she was not without hope. To have something as wonderful as that happen would take

---

[14] Lesley Walker, "Words," essay in "Learning to Tell Our Stories," an honors first-year seminar at Lipscomb University, Fall 2016.

a long, long time."[15] In one way or another, Pecola's experience reflected reality for millions of American Blacks.

Over twenty-three years after writing that novel, Morrison reflected on its meaning:

> *The Bluest Eye* was my effort to say something about . . . why she [Pecola] had not, or possibly ever would have, the experience of what she possessed and also why she prayed for so radical an alteration. Implicit in her desire was racial self-loathing. And twenty years later I was still wondering about how one learns that. Who told her? Who . . . had looked at her and found her so wanting, so small a weight on the beauty scale?[16]

These kinds of experiences, so common to Blacks in the United States, help us understand why the Black appraisal of the American nation is so different from that of most Whites. The poet James M. Whitfield (1822–71), born in New Hampshire to free parents, spoke for millions of American Blacks when he described Black life in this country in the starkest of terms.

> America, it is to thee,
> Thou boasted land of liberty,—
> It is to thee that I raise my song,
> Thou land of blood, and crime, and wrong.
> It is to thee my native land,
> From which has issued many a band
> To tear the black man from his soil
> And force him here to delve and toil
> Chained on your blood-bemoistened sod,
> Cringing beneath a tyrant's rod.[17]

If one is tempted to think Whitfield's judgment extreme, that White supremacy has never been as pervasive as he suggests, consider the role White supremacy played in the thinking of America's founders and many

[15] Toni Morrison, *The Bluest Eye* (1970; repr., New York: Plume, 1994), 46.

[16] Morrison, *The Bluest Eye*, 209–10.

[17] James M. Whitfield, "America," http://www.historyisaweapon.com/defcon1/whitamer.html, accessed October 30, 2017.

other leaders of this Republic. It is common knowledge that when the founders affirmed that "all men are created equal," they limited the meaning of *all men* to White men (not women) who held property. Further, the man who actually wrote the words "all men are created equal"—Thomas Jefferson—offered something very different in his *Notes on the State of Virginia*. There he affirmed "that the blacks, whether originally a distinct race, or made distinct by time and circumstances, are inferior to the whites in the endowments both of body and mind." Like the promise of "Life, Liberty, and the pursuit of Happiness," Jefferson regarded the inferiority of Black people as a self-evident truth, also grounded in nature. "It is not their condition, then, but nature, which has produced the distinction."[18]

Likewise, Abraham Lincoln, in a debate with Stephen A. Douglas five years before he would sign the Emancipation Proclamation, affirmed this regarding Blacks:

> I am not, nor ever have been, in favor of bringing about in any way the social and political equality of the white and black races; that I am not, nor ever have been, in favor of making voters or jurors of negroes, nor of qualifying them to hold office, nor to intermarry with white people; . . . There is a physical difference between the white and black races which I believe will forever forbid the two races living together on terms of social and political equality. And inasmuch as they cannot so live, while they do remain together there must be the position of superior and inferior, and I as much as any other man am in favor of having the superior position assigned to the white race.[19]

And Andrew Johnson, Lincoln's vice president and the man who succeeded him in office, wrote to Missouri Governor Thomas C. Fletcher that "this is a country for white men, and by God, as long as I am President, it shall be a government for white men."[20]

---

[18] Thomas Jefferson, *Notes on the State of Virginia*, ed. William Peden (Chapel Hill: University of North Carolina Press, 1955), 138–43.

[19] Abraham Lincoln, "Fourth Debate with Stephen A. Douglas," Charleston, IL, September 18, 1858, https://www.nps.gov/liho/learn/historyculture/debate4.htm, accessed August 9, 2017.

[20] Reported in the *Cincinnati Inquirer* and cited in Hans Louis Trefousse, *Andrew Johnson* (New York: W. W. Norton and Company, 1997), 236.

Decades later, President Woodrow Wilson resegregated the federal civil service that had been integrated for years following Reconstruction and held in the White House a private screening of the film *Birth of a Nation,* which praised the rise of the Klan as symbolic of the White South's resurgence after Reconstruction.[21]

Then, in 2016, 81 percent of America's White evangelical Christians voted to place in the seat of the presidency of the United States a man who had built his political career on the utterly false and disproven claim that the nation's first Black president had been born in Kenya and therefore occupied the White House illegally, and a man whose racist comments and actions have been publicized so widely that, while some might ignore then, no American can deny them.

If we are beginning to grasp the depth and breadth and power of the myth of White supremacy in American life, and if we are willing to acknowledge the failures of the church in this regard, then we now must ask, What is it about the theology that many American Christians have embraced that has permitted—and even sanctioned—such complicity in the bigotry and racial oppression that is so much a part of America's popular culture?

Reading the Biblical Text through the Lens of the Dominant Culture

In his important book *The End of White Christian America,* Robert Jones wrote that "no segment of White Christian America has been more complicit in the nation's fraught racial history than white evangelical Protestants."[22] Two gross misreadings of Christian theology have allowed evangelicals, including members of Churches of Christ, to buy into the myth of White supremacy and to participate in the racist behavior that myth inevitably spawns.

The first is this—that many American Christians have read the biblical text through the lens of American popular culture while they should

---

[21] William Keylor, "The Long-Forgotten Racial Attitudes and Policies of Woodrow Wilson," *Professor Voices: Commentary, Insight, & Analysis,* Boston University, March 4, 2013, at http://www.bu.edu/professorvoices /2013/03/04/the-long-forgotten-racial-attitudes-and-policies-of-woodrow-wilson/, accessed August 13, 2017.

[22] Robert Jones, *The End of White Christian America* (New York: Simon and Schuster, 2016), 167.

read the culture through the lens of the biblical text. And through that misreading, they allow the American nation, its values, and its dominant culture to take the place of the only reality to which, as Christians, they should pledge their allegiance: the biblical vision of the kingdom of God.

The statement by G. C. Brewer, cited earlier in this essay, typifies that reversal of priorities. Recalling how he and others routinely humiliated Blacks when he was growing up in the early twentieth century, Brewer concluded, "This was the condition that prevailed, and this we accepted as right and satisfactory."

Brewer was a Christian minister who preached the gospel with extraordinary power. Yet on the question of race, he read the gospel through the lens of the racial biases that had defined his culture. Accordingly, "the condition that prevailed" apparently transformed the humiliation of Blacks into "right and satisfactory" behavior, regardless of anything Jesus or any writer of the biblical text might have said to the contrary. Christians like the young man Brewer—and there were many just like him—apparently found "the condition that prevailed" in the popular culture so overwhelming, so irresistible in the shaping of their hearts and minds, that they could somehow view racist behavior as thoroughly compatible with the Christian faith.

Or consider Landon Garland, the first chancellor of Vanderbilt University, an institution related at that time to the Methodist Episcopal Church, South, who expressed in 1869 his hope that this new Christian college would always exhibit "a proper conformity to the conventionalities of society."[23] The "conventionalities of society" in the American South at the time Garland wrote were rooted in the principle of White supremacy.

One of the factors that allowed so many evangelical Christians to transform the Christian faith into a handmaiden for the popular culture was the conviction common among Christian people that the United States was a Christian nation.[24] And if the nation was Christian, it would be dif-

[23] Landon Garland, *Nashville Christian Advocate* 29 (Feb. 27, 1869): 2. I am grateful to my colleague at Lipscomb University, Professor Richard Goode, for calling this story to my attention.

[24] On the United States as a Christian nation, see Martin E. Marty, *Righteous Empire: The Protestant Experience in America* (New York: Dial Press, 1970); Robert T. Handy, *A Christian America: Protestant Hopes and Historical Realities*, 2nd ed. (New York: Oxford University Press, 1984); John Fea, *Was America Founded as a Christian Nation? A Historical Introduction* (Philadelphia: Westminster John Knox Press, 2011); Steven K. Green, *Inventing a Christian America: The Myth of the Religious Founding* (Oxford: Oxford University Press, 2015); Kevin M. Kruse,

ficult to admit to the racial oppression, even the racial crimes, that the majority of America's citizens sanctioned.

How else can we explain the fact that professed Christians—thousands and thousands of them—took part in the lynching, the burning, the castration, and the brutalizing of Blacks throughout the United States between 1880 and 1940?[25] How do we know that many of these people identified themselves as Christians? Because lynch mobs almost always drew from a cross section of the community in which the lynching occurred, and because most lynchings occurred in America's "Bible Belt." As Leon F. Litwack wrote,

> The bulk of the lynchers tended to be ordinary and respectable people . . . , not so different from ourselves—merchants, farmers, laborers, machine operators, teachers, lawyers, doctors, policemen, students; they were good family men and women, good, decent churchgoing folk who came to believe that keeping black people in their place was nothing less than pest control, a way of combatting an epidemic or virus that if not checked would be detrimental to the health and security of the community.[26]

Indeed, "the mobs who meted out, '*summary justice*' were pronounced by one Georgian as 'composed of our best citizens, who are foremost in all works of public and private good.'"[27]

These racial zealots typically turned out by the thousands, as if lynching were some sort of spectator sport, and then gathered up souvenirs—fingers, toes, even genitals—to take back to their homes. Reflecting on the fact that Christians participated in these atrocities, James Cone, in his powerful book *The Cross and the Lynching Tree*, leaves us to ponder this massive contradiction—that Christians who believed in an innocent Jesus, lynched

---

One Nation Under God: How Corporate America Invented Christian America (New York: Basic Books, 2015); and Richard T. Hughes, *Christian America and the Kingdom of God* (Urbana: University of Illinois Press, 2009).

[25] The Equal Justice Initiative has documented approximately five thousand lynchings nationwide between 1877 and 1950. *Lynching in America: Confronting the Legacy of Racial Terror*, 3rd ed. (Montgomery: Equal Justice Initiative, 2017), 4.

[26] Leon F. Litwack, "Hellhounds," in *Without Sanctuary: Lynching Photography in America*, ed. James Allen (Santa Fe: Twin Palms Publishers, 2004), 19, 34.

[27] *Savannah Morning News*, as cited in Litwack, "Hellhounds," 19–20.

for their sins, lynched thousands of innocent Blacks on a comparable tree while never discerning the obvious similarity that connected both crimes or the obvious contradiction between their faith and their deeds.[28]

Half a century later, their conviction that the United States was a Christian nation led many evangelicals, including members of Churches of Christ, to regard the Freedom Movement, led by Martin Luther King Jr., as an unjustified complaint. How could this Christian nation have possibly denied equal rights and equal opportunity to any of its people? Martin Luther King and those for whom he spoke, therefore, were nothing more than agitators, inspired more by Communism than by anything resembling the Christian faith to which King so often appealed.

In 1968, Reuel Lemmons, editor of *The Firm Foundation*, a Texas gospel paper serving Churches of Christ, penned a letter to Jennings Davis, dean of students at George Pepperdine College in Los Angeles. There he made this point unmistakably clear. Lemmons wrote,

> A lot of people wanted to compare Martin Luther King to Jesus Christ, while in reality, King was a modernist, and denied faith in Jesus Christ as taught in the Bible. . . . If he was not an outright Communist, he certainly advocated Communist causes. His absolute disregard for law and order except those laws and orders which he wanted to obey leaves me cold. . . . J. Edgar Hoover branded King as a notorious liar and Harry Truman said he was a troublemaker. This kind of man, black or white, I cannot conscientiously praise.[29]

Significantly, when Lemmons sought to appraise King's character, the standard he erected was not one provided by Christian theology, but a standard provided by the director of the Federal Bureau of Investigation and a former president of the United States.

Those Christians who took their cues from this "Christian nation"— whether those who hung Blacks on the lynching tree or those who opposed the profoundly Christian work of the Freedom Movement—had

---

[28] James M. Cone, *The Cross and the Lynching Tree* (Maryknoll: Orbis Books, 2012).

[29] Reuel Lemmons (personal letter), May 23, 1968, "From Ruel Lemmons to Jennings Davis," John Allen Chalk files, Harding School of Theology, Brackett Library.

substituted the nation for the only reality to which Christians are called to pledge their allegiance: the kingdom of God. And the people who waged the struggle for equal rights, for equal housing, for equal access to food, education, and clothing were some of the people Jesus envisioned when he said, "He has anointed me to bring good news to the poor . . . and . . . let the oppressed go free" (Luke 4:18). But many evangelicals, including many in Churches of Christ, simply failed to make that connection.

There is a second misreading of Christian theology that has allowed evangelicals to buy into the myth of White supremacy. For the past 125 years at least, evangelicals have more often than not envisioned the gospel as a strictly private affair, involving just "Jesus and me," and a religion that has little to do with the affairs of this world but everything to do with otherworldly visions of an afterlife to come.[30] The theological problems with such a vision are immense. A privatized gospel completely severs the social or communal implications of the Christian message, and a gospel that is defined in purely otherworldly terms makes no room for social justice in the here and now. In cutting Christians off from the social implications of the gospel, these perspectives, even though they are embraced by millions of American Christians, essentially reject the heart of Jesus's teachings.

If one imagines that the Christian life is nothing more than a private, daily walk with Jesus, there can be no compelling theological motive for judging White supremacy and racist behavior to be fundamentally at odds with the core principles of the Christian faith. And if the goal of the Christian life is nothing more than securing an abode in the world to come and avoiding the fires of hell, then the Christian faith provides no compelling reason to come to terms with the pervasive power of White supremacy or to work to undermine racism in the larger society.

The Root of the Problem in Churches of Christ

While Churches of Christ, like the larger evangelical world, have often read the biblical text through the lens of American popular culture, have often worshipped a private Jesus, and have often defined the Christian faith

---

[30] James Davison Hunter explains why this has been true in *Evangelicalism: The Coming Generation* (Chicago: University of Chicago Press, 1987), 40–41.

chiefly as a journey to an otherworldly abode, there were other, additional factors that blinded them to the realities of White supremacy.

It was surely not the case that Churches of Christ were unfamiliar with the Bible, for the Bible has been the singular focus of Churches of Christ from the time of their inception in the early nineteenth century. But it is the case that Churches of Christ forced questions and concerns onto the biblical text that, at best, were marginal to the biblical witness. And it is also the case that Churches of Christ read the Bible in ways that simply obscured its central message.

Alexander Campbell set the agenda for Churches of Christ when he vigorously promoted the restoration of primitive Christianity. The problem was not the idea of restoration in its own right since the notion of restoration is an inherently useful vision. The problem lay in the fact that Campbell, indebted as he was to the principles of the Age of Reason, defined restoration in strictly rational terms. And the rational quality of Campbell's thought led him to view the New Testament not as a theological and ethical treatise that offers a vision of the kingdom of God, but as a scientific manual upon which rational and unbiased people might reconstruct in scientifically precise and accurate ways the forms and structures of the primitive church.

The notion of forms and structures is crucial to this conversation, for Campbell seldom asked what the Bible said about the poor. Instead, he asked about the biblical pattern for worship. He seldom asked what the Bible said about marginalized people. Instead, he asked about a rationally constructed plan of salvation. He seldom asked what the Bible said about people oppressed by imperial powers. Instead, he asked about the biblical model for the proper organization of the local church. In all these ways, Campbell diverted the eyes of Churches of Christ from the driving themes of the Christian gospel.

But there is more, for in his zeal to restore the forms and structures of the primitive church, Campbell argued that the Christian age began not with the birth of Jesus but with the birth of the church, an event recorded in Acts chapter two. Everything prior to Acts 2, he argued, rightly belonged to what he called the "Mosaic dispensation," which had no relevance for the grand task of restoring the primitive church. In effect, then, Campbell minimized the importance not only of the Hebrew Bible but also of the Gospels. Over time, that action would essentially sever Churches of Christ from the prophetic vision one finds especially in Jesus and the Hebrew prophets.

It is hardly surprising, then, that even in Campbell's lifetime, some in Churches of Christ had transformed Campbell's goal of restoring the primitive church into a fixed and settled conviction that they had, in fact, restored the one true church and that outside of that church, there could be no salvation. By the 1950s and 1960s, the notion that one's salvation depended on one's belonging to the one true church had become for many members and congregations in this tradition the most important consideration of all.

Having obscured the central themes of the biblical message, the White Churches of Christ, at the time of the Freedom Movement, were wholly unprepared to embrace their brothers and sisters of color who asked for nothing more than to be treated with respect as human beings. Indeed, they were wholly unprepared to discern in the Freedom Movement the faces of the kingdom of God.

Theological Resources

I know of no way to resist the shaping and defining power of the dominant culture apart from two theological assets. First, we must occupy a vantage point that allows us to look into our culture, as it were, from outside the culture itself. And second, that vantage point must provide us with a set of values that are foreign to the culture, that stand in judgment on the culture, and that challenge the culture's values in radical ways.

The Gospel of Grace

The fact is that every Christian has access to precisely that sort of vantage point. The New Testament describes that vantage point with the simple word *gospel*—the good news that God loves us infinitely more than we can fathom, has accepted us, and has said "yes" to us in spite of our inevitable failures, our brokenness, and our sin.

That is the gospel message, the heart of biblical faith. But there is a corollary to this central message—a corollary to which the New Testament writers return time and again. No one puts it better than John.

We know love by this, that he laid down his life for us—and we ought to lay down our lives for one another. How does God's love abide in anyone who has the world's goods and sees a brother or sister in need and yet refuses help? Little children, let us love, not in word or speech, but in truth and action. (1 John 3:16–18)

The gospel message, then, has two components. First, God extends his radical, self-giving love and grace to each of us, has accepted us, and has said "yes" to us in spite of our inevitable failures, our brokenness, and our sins. And second, God's love requires that we extend love and grace to others and say "yes" to them in spite of their inevitable failures, brokenness, and sin. The first component—God's own love and grace—is the driving, enabling power behind the second component, the grace we must extend to our neighbors.

But what happens when a Christian tradition seldom preaches the gospel of God's free and unmerited grace? What happens when a Christian tradition identifies God's grace with God's commands? What happens when a Christian tradition defines the "plan of salvation" not in terms of what God has done for us but rather in terms of the human response to divine commands?

What happens is this—the Christian tradition that fails to proclaim God's unmerited grace has severed the driving force behind the love and grace that, according to the gospel message, we must extend to others. And that is precisely what happened in Churches of Christ for a period of a hundred and fifty years—from the 1820s when Churches of Christ first began to identify God's grace with God's commands to the 1970s when Churches of Christ finally discovered and began to preach widely the gospel of unmerited grace.

When the Freedom Movement emerged in the mid-1950s, Churches of Christ almost entirely lacked the vantage point that might have allowed them to bring to that moment the insights of John: "How does God's love abide in anyone who has the world's goods and sees a brother or sister in need and yet refuses help?" Indeed, they almost entirely lacked the vantage point that might have prompted them to extend unmerited grace to their neighbors just as God had extended his unmerited grace to them.

The Gospel of the Kingdom

In addition to the gospel of grace, the New Testament offers Christians another vantage point from which we can resist the sirens of the dominant culture. Matthew describes that vantage point as "the gospel of the kingdom": "Jesus went throughout Galilee, teaching in their synagogues and proclaiming the good news [i.e., *the gospel*] of the kingdom and curing every disease and every sickness among the people" (4:23).

Matthew's phrase, "the gospel of the kingdom," offers an early introduction to a theme that resonates throughout the Gospels, namely, "the kingdom of God." While New Testament scholars differ over the meaning of that phrase, one of its meanings seems clear. In most of the instances where the phrase "kingdom of God" appears in the New Testament, the context links that phrase to concern for the poor, the dispossessed, those in prison, the maimed, the lame, the blind, and all those who suffer at the hands of the world's elites. In other words, the kingdom of God is where the powerless are empowered, where the hungry are fed, where the sick are healed, where the poor are sustained, and where those who find themselves marginalized by the rulers of this world are finally offered equality and justice.

Put another way, the "gospel of the kingdom of God" is the corollary to the "gospel of grace." It tells us that just as God has said "yes" to us in spite of our failures, so we must say "yes" to others in spite of their failures. Or, in the words of John, "We know love by this, that he laid down his life for us—and we ought to lay down our lives for one another" (1 John 3:16).

In this limited space, we cannot explore the biblical vision of the kingdom of God in great detail, but a handful of New Testament passages will help us grasp the point.

In the second chapter of Luke, an angel appears to shepherds in the field by night and proclaims "good news of great joy for all the people: [for] to you is born this day in the city of David a Savior, who is the Messiah, the Lord."

In the context of imperial Rome, the angel's proclamation was both revolutionary and seditious, for its two key words—Savior and Lord—were titles routinely applied to the emperor Caesar Augustus. Indeed, Caesar's titles included "Divine," "Son of God," "God," "God from God," "Redeemer," "Liberator," "Lord," and "Savior of the World."

It is one thing to proclaim that Jesus is Savior and Lord, but it is something else to ask what that Savior and Lord requires, and that is the question Luke answers with incredible clarity in Luke chapter three—a passage that contrasts the humble kingdom of God with the all-pervasive power and splendor of the Roman Empire. Luke sets up the contrast beautifully, referring first to the ruling elites of his day:

> In the fifteenth year of the reign of Emperor Tiberius, when
> Pontius Pilate was governor of Judea, and Herod was ruler of
> Galilee, and his brother Philip ruler of the region of Ituraea and
> Trachonitis, and Lysanias ruler of Abilene, during the high priest-
> hood of Annas and Caiaphas, the word of God came . . . . (3:1–2)

Came to whom? It came, Luke tells us, "to John son of Zechariah in the wilderness." Here Luke subtly contrasts the wilderness where John resided with the imperial courts of Tiberius Caesar, Herod, Philip, and Lysanias. Later in his Gospel, Luke was not so subtle, since he reports that Jesus himself contrasted John's poverty with the luxury of imperial power. "What then did you go out to see?" Jesus asked the people. "Someone dressed in soft robes? Look, those who put on fine clothing and live in luxury are in royal palaces. What then did you go out to see? A prophet? Yes, I tell you, and more than a prophet" (7:25–26).

Finally, what message did John proclaim? Did he preach the American gospel that "God helps those who help themselves"? Hardly. According to Luke, John preached a message of radical compassion for those in need. And when the crowds asked him, "What then should we do?" John replied, "Whoever has two coats must share with anyone who has none; and whoever has food must do likewise" (3:10–11).

The point is this—John the Baptist, both through the life he lived and the message he preached, offered those around him a vantage point that allowed them to look into their culture, as it were, from outside the culture and to claim a set of values that would challenge the culture in radical ways.

Jesus did the very same thing when he came to Nazareth and there, in the synagogue, announced his mission and his vocation. According to Luke,

When he came to Nazareth, where he had been brought up, he went to the synagogue on the Sabbath day, as was his custom. He stood up to read, and the scroll of the prophet Isaiah was given to him. He unrolled the scroll and found the place where it was written:
> "The Spirit of the Lord is upon me,
>> because he has anointed me
>>> to bring good news to the poor.
> He has sent me to proclaim release to the captives
>> and recovery of sight to the blind,
>>> to let the oppressed go free,
> to proclaim the year of the Lord's favor."

And he rolled up the scroll, gave it back to the attendant, and sat down. The eyes of all in the synagogue were fixed on him. Then he began to say to them, "Today this scripture has been fulfilled in your hearing." (4:16–21)

The Gospels record only one other instance when Jesus defined the concerns that would characterize his mission and vocation. Matthew reports that John the Baptist, languishing in prison, heard of the work Jesus was doing and "sent word by his disciples and said to him, 'Are you the one who is to come, or are we to wait for another?' Jesus answered them, 'Go and tell John what you hear and see: the blind receive their sight, the lame walk, the lepers are cleansed, the deaf hear, the dead are raised, and the poor have good news brought to them'" (Matt. 11:2–5).

By framing his mission and vocation in these terms, Jesus lined out the contours of what he often called "the kingdom of God." That kingdom provided then—and still provides—a transcendent point of reference that allows Jesus's followers in every time and place to look into their culture, as it were, from outside the culture and to claim a transcendent set of values that can challenge the culture in radical ways.

Numerous other passages flesh out this vision of the kingdom of God. In Luke, for example, those who are first (the rich and the powerful) will be last, while those who are last (the poor and oppressed) will be first

(13:29–30). Only those who are humble like little children can enter the kingdom of God (18:16–17). And Luke reports Jesus's comment: "How hard it is for those who have wealth to enter the kingdom of God" (18:24).

Conclusion

The myth of White supremacy is alive and well in the United States. The pressing question for Christians, then, must be this: "How can we resist?"

Our resistance will be stillborn unless we recognize that the problem we face is both real and pervasive. That will be difficult to do, simply because in the lives of most White Americans, there is nothing to compel them to reflect on the meaning of race, the meaning of White privilege, or the meaning of White supremacy. And without cause for reflection, it is easy enough to imagine that White supremacy thrives only in White nationalist organizations forthrightly committed to White control and dominance.

The sobering truth, however, is that White supremacy thrives in every nook and corner of the United States, including the nation's churches. Indeed, if we are honest, we will confess that it thrives even within our very own minds and hearts. Only when we come to terms with that reality can we effectively resist.

Once we admit that White supremacy is both real and pervasive in American culture, even in our churches, and even in our very own lives, we are then in a position to discover in the Christian gospel the great resources it offers for resistance: the gospel of grace and the gospel of the kingdom. Those truths assure us that God is love, that God has freely given his love and grace to each of us, and that God requires, in turn, that we extend that same love and grace to all human beings—those who live next door and those who live on the other side of the world. Indeed, the gospel requires that we love even our enemies.

If we internalize those great truths, they will drive the myth of White supremacy out of our hearts, out of our minds, and out of our churches. Indeed, the notion of White supremacy will cease to serve as a myth, will cease to function as a story that gives us meaning. For we will have built our lives on a story with infinite meaning—the gospel story of God's magnificent grace.

CHRISTIAN NATIONALISM AND RACIAL INJUSTICE
Where Do People of Faith Go from Here?

I have spent the better part of a fifty-year career trying to grasp what stands at the center of the American psyche, what defines the heart of the American experiment.

One of my teachers in graduate school argued with great force—and abundant evidence, I might add—that the principles of the eighteenth-century Enlightenment defined the meaning of the American nation. The Enlightenment, he said, gave birth to something crucial to the soul of the nation—the separation of church and state, enshrined in the First Amendment.

More than that, my teacher said, the Enlightenment inspired the American Creed—the affirmation that "all men are created equal and endowed by their Creator with certain unalienable rights, among which are Life, Liberty, and the pursuit of Happiness." Because the Creed legitimated diversity of all kinds—cultural diversity, ethnic diversity, and religious diversity—the Creed, my teacher said, was the heart of the American nation.

That teacher was Sidney E. Mead, widely acknowledged then as the dean of the field of American religious history.

Mead's argument would have made sense to Martin Luther King Jr., who appealed to the Creed time and again as he sought to gain equality for Black people in the United States. "I have a dream," King said. "It is a dream deeply rooted in the American dream that one day this nation will rise up and live out the true meaning of its creed—we hold these truths to be self-evident, that all men are created equal."[1] And it was the Creed that fueled the revolution of the 1960s across the board—the revolution that claimed equality for Blacks and Browns; for Asians and Native Americans; for women and LGBTQ people; for Hindus, Buddhists, Muslims, and Sikhs; along with Christians and Jews.

During that time there were many Christians—both mainline and evangelical—who actively fought for equal rights for all Americans and grounded their fight in the biblical vision of the kingdom of God. But other Americans—millions of them, in fact—rejected the radical diversity that increasingly defined the nation. In the Christian world, evangelical and Fundamentalist Christians fueled the protest against greater American diversity. They understood full well that equality for Blacks and Browns and women and LGBTQ people would become the norm so long as the Creed stood at the center of the American experiment. And so they took steps to replace the Creed with something far more constricting, far more limiting, and far more exclusive. They sought to replace the Creed with their vision of a Christian nation. Jerry Falwell's Moral Majority, organized in 1979, sought to impose evangelical control over American politics and, through the political process, over every level of government.

Only ten years after Falwell launched his Moral Majority, a group of young evangelical historians began to argue that Sidney Mead was wrong, that the center of the American experiment was not the American Creed and not the Enlightenment from which the Creed had emerged. Instead, they claimed that the heart of the American experiment had always been the evangelical Christian tradition. For proof they pointed to the Second

---

[1] Martin Luther King Jr., "I Have a Dream," in *I Have a Dream: Writings and Speeches That Changed the World*, ed. James M. Washington (San Francisco: Harper, 1986), 104.

Great Awakening that had, in fact, transformed the new Republic into a Protestant nation by 1830.

George Marsden, for example, found it remarkable that the "secular [Enlightenment] ideologies" that had inspired the American Creed had failed to capture the soul of America. Instead, he argued, the nation "had been guided, even driven, by resourceful evangelical leaders who effectively channeled the powers of revivals and voluntary religious organizations to counter the forces of purely secular change."[2]

Both Marsden and Falwell gave voice to one of the Great American Myths—the notion that the United States is a Christian nation—and there is a sense in which they were right. From the nation's founding, the Creed and the Christian nation myth have competed with each other for cultural dominance. They have danced in tandem, if you will. Sometimes the Creed has led the myth, and sometimes the myth has led the Creed. But the two are radically different and, in many respects, irreconcilable. If the Creed's intent is universal, affirming that "all men are created equal," the Christian nation myth is highly particular, even exclusive, by granting priority to people who pledge allegiance to a single religious tradition.

A myth, I should note, is not always false. Rather, a myth is a story that gives us meaning, that lights our path and helps us find our way.

Four other myths have also danced with the American Creed, transforming the Creed into something it is not, and each draws its strength and vigor from the conviction that the United States is, at heart, a Christian nation.

In one way or another, all of us—or at least those of us who are White—learned these myths when we were young. No one set us down and taught us these myths. Rather, we absorbed them, as it were, by osmosis. They were part of our culture, embedded in the very air we breathed.

We learned, for example, that the United States is a *Chosen Nation*, singled out by God for a special mission in the world.

We learned that the United States is *Nature's Nation*, rooted in the natural order of things. While other nations conformed to human wit and contrivance, our nation conformed to God's own design.

---

[2] George Marsden, *Understanding Fundamentalism and Evangelicalism* (Grand Rapids: Eerdmans, 1991), 11–12.

We learned that the United States is a *Millennial Nation*, destined to bless the earth with democracy, freedom, and true religion, and to create thereby a golden age for all humankind.

And we learned that the nation's Christian character, coupled with the nobility of our cause—to extend freedom around the globe—rendered the United States a perpetually *Innocent Nation*.

All of this I wrote about in the first edition of *Myths America Lives By*, published in 2003.

And then, in 2012, a Black scholar named James Noel turned my world upside-down and completely reframed my grasp of the American nation. After hearing me speak about the Great American Myths, he told me bluntly that I had left out the single most important myth, the one that had done the most to define the American nation. "And what might that be?" I asked. "The myth of White supremacy," Noel replied.

As I pondered Noel's words over the next few years, I began to see how right he was. I began to see that all the myths—the myths of the chosen nation, nature's nation, Christian nation, millennial nation, and innocent nation—that all these myths, from the nation's birth, have been placed in the service of Whiteness, in the service of the power, privilege, and supremacy of people who look like me.

I could not have heard and responded to James Noel as I did had it not been for Reverend Wayne Baxter who, when I taught at Messiah College in Grantham, Pennsylvania, befriended me, taught me, and mentored me for the better part of six years before I encountered James Noel.

And then, just weeks ago, I encountered another African American scholar who, like James Noel in 2012, completely reframed my grasp of the American nation. Her name is Isabel Wilkerson. Her book is *Caste: The Origins of Our Discontents*. Her argument is simple—that three nations have built themselves on systems of caste: India, Nazi Germany, and the United States of America.

If you find it disconcerting to apply the language of caste to the United States of America, consider, for example, the purity laws that governed the caste system in both the United States and India. Consider the requirement, widely practiced in this country, that Blacks could enter a White space only through the back door, if at all. Consider that Blacks were not permitted to shake a White hand. Consider the sundown laws that, in many American communities, required Black people to leave town before the sun had set. Or consider the consensus that prevailed across this nation that Blacks could not swim in the same pool with Whites, could not even touch the water lest it be defiled, and if that were to happen, the pool would be quickly drained and filled again with water that was pure.

Caste, Wilkerson says, is like the hidden framework—the joists, the studs, and the beams—that support a house. We cannot see this framework since it hides behind walls, and "the very invisibility [of caste] is what gives it power and longevity" as it "goes about its work in silence . . . , [moving] in the guise of normalcy, injustice looking just, atrocities looking unavoidable to keep the machinery humming."[3]

The language of caste deepens immeasurably the language of both Creed and myth, for it suggests neither goal nor ideal nor a vision for the future, but something grounded in the immutable past, something permanent, something intractable, something immovable. And when we reflect on the meaning of caste—that one group of people, along with their heirs, are assigned the lowest possible rung in a given culture from which they cannot escape—and when we reflect on the terrors that inevitably haunt those assigned to that caste, we realize the language of caste takes us far beyond the language of both myth and Creed.

Just how permanent and intractable caste has been in America comes into focus when Wilkerson reminds us that slavery defined this country for a full quarter of a millennium. Indeed, she writes,

> The institution of slavery was, for a quarter millennium, the conversion of human beings into currency, into machines who existed solely for the profit of their owners, to be worked as long as the owners desired, who had no rights over their bodies or loved ones, who could be mortgaged, bred, won in a bet, given as wedding presents, bequeathed to heirs, sold away from spouses or children to cover an owner's debt or to spite a rival or to settle an estate. They were regularly whipped, raped, and branded, subjected to any whim or distemper of the people who

---

[3] Isabel Wilkerson, *Caste: The Origins of Our Discontents* (New York: Random House, 2020), 17, 23.

owned them. Some were castrated or endured other tortures too grisly for these pages, tortures that the Geneva Convention would have banned as war crimes had the conventions applied to people of African descent on this soil.[4]

Yes, slavery did indeed define the United States for a full quarter of a millennium! And consider this. That mind-boggling span of years does not include the Jim Crow years that followed Reconstruction when White people imposed their self-proclaimed supremacy by lynching Black people, burning them at the stake, raping them, castrating them, bombing and burning their towns and settlements, keeping them subservient through the sharecropping system, and leasing them to private corporations to work the mines and the mills until they died—a reality Douglas Blackmon calls "slavery by another name." Nor does that mind-boggling span of time include those years when the American legal system at every level (municipal, county, state, and federal) conspired to ban Blacks from sharing America's wealth or owning homes in predominantly White neighborhoods—a fact that Richard Rothstein demonstrates in his marvelous book *The Color of Law*. Nor does that quarter of a millennium include our own time when Blacks, especially Black males, are subject to routine police harassment, brutality, and murder. Yes, caste is not too strong a word.

Isabel Wilkerson has helped me grasp more fully what James Noel meant when he told me that White supremacy is the dominant American myth, for it is the myth that sustains the system of caste.

It now seems clear to me that what stands at the heart of the American experiment is not one single theme, but rather three realities—the American Creed, the Great American Myths, and the American system of Caste.[5] Over the years, these partners, unwilling though they might be, have still danced with each other in various combinations and configurations. But in every case, the American system of Caste has been the dominant partner to which the Creed and the Myths have been forced to relate.

---

[4] Wilkerson, *Caste*, 45.

[5] From this point on, I capitalize the word "Caste" in order to acknowledge its status as an equal—or better than equal—player in the American saga, along with Creed and Myth.

Clearly, the very idea of Caste flies in the face of the American Creed. And while the Creed, with some success, has summoned the nation to abandon Caste, the myth of Christian America has come to the aid of Caste time and time again.

Indeed, the Christian religion in the United States, far from opposing the Caste system, has abetted that system, has sanctified and sustained it through a theology designed for that very purpose. That theology arose among Southern evangelicals, concerned with escaping the guilt the sin of slavery would otherwise bring. It rested on two crucial pillars: that the Christian religion is finally a private affair that involves just Jesus and me, and that the heart of the Christian religion is salvation in the world to come, with few implications for the here and now. Since they had accepted Jesus as their personal savior, Christians who held slaves or otherwise embraced the myth of White supremacy could do so with utter impunity. In due time, that theology would come to characterize large swaths of American Christianity, including many who belonged to mainline denominations.

We discover the fruit of that theology in Frederick Douglass's testimony, offered in his autobiography, that "of all slaveholders with whom I have ever met, religious slaveholders are the worst. I have ever found them the meanest and basest, the most cruel and cowardly, of all others."[6] He continued: "The man who wields the blood-clotted cowskin during the week fills the pulpit on Sunday and . . . the man who robs me of my earnings at the end of each week meets me as a class-leader on Sunday morning, to show me the way of life, the path of salvation." He concluded by affirming, "I can see no reason, but the most deceitful one, for calling the religion of this land Christianity."[7]

Fifty-four years later, in 1899, a Black man named Sam Hose was burned at the stake and his body lynched on a Sunday in the small town of Newman, Georgia, not far from Atlanta. Christians in Newman flocked to witness the murder, and "when Atlanta's white churches emptied from morning

---

[6] Frederick Douglass, *Narrative of the Life of Frederick Douglass, An American Slave, Written by Himself* (1845; repr., New York: Signet Books, 1968), 87.

[7] Douglass, *Narrative of the Life of Frederick Douglass*, 120–21.

services, [some 2,000] worshippers" boarded trains that took them to Newman where they gathered bits of bone and flesh to keep as souvenirs.[8]

Robert Jones, who relates this story, has done yeoman's work in helping us grasp truths about the Christian religion in the United States that we would rather not hear. He summarizes those truths in this poignant line: "White Christian churches composed the cultural score that made white supremacy sing."[9]

And so they did. In the 1950s and 1960s, for example, White-power organizations like the Citizens Council were filled with "pastors, deacons, Sunday school teachers, and other upstanding members of prominent white churches."[10] In our own time, through carefully controlled surveys and statistical work, Jones has found that

> in the United States . . . , the more racist attitudes a person holds, the more likely he or she is to identify as a white Christian. And when we control for a range of other attributes, this relation- ship exists not just among white evangelical Protestants but also equally strongly among white mainline Protestants and white Catholics. And there is a telling corollary: this relationship with racist attitudes has little hold among white religiously unaffili- ated Americans. If anything, the relationship is negative.[11]

Jones concludes that "white Christian churches have not just been complacent . . . ; rather, as the dominant cultural power in America, they have been responsible for constructing and sustaining a project to protect white supremacy and resist black equality. This project has framed the entire American story."[12]

And so it has.

The sum of the matter is this—Christian America is a White America, always and ever defined by Caste. That simple fact explains the depth and breadth of White Christian resistance to Dr. Martin Luther King Jr. and

---

[8] Robert P. Jones, *White Too Long: The Legacy of White Supremacy in American Christianity* (New York: Simon and Schuster, 2020), 28–32.

[9] Jones, *White Too Long*, 35

[10] Jones, *White Too Long*, 5.

[11] Jones, *White Too Long*, 175–76.

[12] Jones, *White Too Long*, 6.

the Freedom Movement that empowered people of color in the 1960s. It explains the depth and breadth of White Christian resistance to the nation's first Black president. It explains the depth and breadth of White Christian support for his successor who launched his political career by seeking to discredit the legitimacy of that Black president.[13] It explains the depth and breadth of White Christian support for that very same man after he spent four years seeking to destroy the Black president's legacy, banning Muslims, caging Latino children at the nation's southern border, and expressing his preference for immigrants from Norway, not from what he called "s-hole countries," composed of people of color.[14]

Perhaps no single act more fully captures that president's commitment to a White America than his Executive Order, issued on September 22, 2020, that bans racial sensitivity training from every federal agency and every private firm that contracts with the federal government, describing such training as "offensive and anti-American."[15] The net effect of that Order was to portray the nation as White and to make it clear that any effort to question the norms of Whiteness is an "anti-American" act.

For their part, large segments of the evangelical wing of White Christian America have honored that president by claiming he was chosen by God as a latter-day King Cyrus.[16] In return, that president has vowed to support, defend, and return the evangelical wing of White Christian America to its former position of cultural dominance and power.

In the face of the power the myth of Christian America has exerted over the nation for so many years, how do people of faith move forward?

---

[13] A total of 81 percent of White evangelicals, 64 percent of White Catholics, and 57 percent of White mainline Protestants voted for Donald Trump in the 2016 election.

[14] In the 2020 election, a majority of *all* White Christians, including 78 percent of evangelicals, voted for Donald Trump.

[15] Executive Order 13950, revoked by: EO 13985, January 1, 2021.

[16] What sustains this persistent pattern is a potent mix of the Great American Myths. Not only do many White Christians think of the United States as God's chosen nation; many also view President Trump as God's anointed. Some proclaimed him "a King Cyrus for our time." Recently elected US Senator from Alabama Tommy Tuberville proclaimed in a campaign ad that "God sent us Donald Trump." And Franklin Graham told the *Washington Post* that in the election of 2016, "God showed up." By August of 2019, the president himself embraced that mantle when he declared himself "the chosen one." Katherine Stewart, "Why Trump Reigns as King Cyrus," *New York Times*, December 31, 2018; Mike Cason, "Tuberville Says 'God Sent Us Donald Trump' in New Radio Ad," AL.com, January 27, 2020; Harriet Sherwood, "The Chosen One?" *The Guardian*, October 3, 2018; Chris Cillizza, "Yes, Donald Trump Really Believes He Is 'the Chosen One,'" *CNN Politics*, August 24, 2019.

Jesus tells us that in the kingdom of God, the last shall be first and the first shall be last, and precisely there, in that upside-down kingdom, we will find our way. Indeed, we will find our way when we are willing to learn from those Christians consigned to America's lowest Caste. For while many White Christians commit themselves to Christian America, many Black Christians commit themselves to the kingdom of God.

And the difference between the two is stark. If Christian America seeks power, the kingdom of God seeks justice. If Christian America seeks wealth, the kingdom of God exalts the poor. If Christian America seeks privilege, the kingdom of God turns its back on privilege for the sake of the neighbor.[17]

There is only one passage in the entire biblical text that paints a panoramic view of both the final judgment and the meaning of the kingdom of God. There, the King of the Universe gathers together the people of earth and divides the sheep from the goats. The King's concerns have nothing to do with the concerns of Christian America. Instead, the King is concerned about only one thing—how we treat our neighbors. "I was hungry," the King says, "and you gave me food, I was thirsty and you gave me something to drink, I was a stranger and you welcomed me, I was naked and you gave me clothing, I was sick and you took care of me, I was in prison and you visited me." And because of their selfless actions, the King welcomes the faithful into the kingdom of God.

There, in that kingdom, we will find our way.

[17] Richard T. Hughes, *Christian America and the Kingdom of God* (Urbana: University of Illinois Press, 2009).

HOW CAN WE RETHINK
THE RESTORATION VISION?

A t the meeting of the John Whitmer Historical Society in 2002, Robert Flanders delivered the Sterling McMurrin Lecture on the topic "Nauvoo on My Mind." During the course of that lecture, Flanders made several stunning remarks regarding the relationship the Reorganized Church of Jesus Christ of Latter-day Saints (RLDS)—known today as the Community of Christ—has sustained to its own particular history. Those remarks bear directly on the topic of this presentation—"How Can We Rethink the Restoration Vision?"—and therefore form the backdrop for what I wish to say today.

Flanders affirmed, "A fundamental epistemological problem for me as a young man was that the RLDS would not face its own past. Indeed, the Church fictionalized that past." In another passage, Flanders said, "Since the 1860s the Church had been systematically painting itself into a corner where its history was concerned." When he finally learned the truth regarding the origins of polygamy, he said, "I was disturbed. What else of what I had always believed was equally untrue? The RLDS, I began to fear, had suffered a long night of self-deception."[1]

[1] Robert Bruce Flanders, "Nauvoo on My Mind," the Sterling McMurrin Lecture delivered to the John Whitmer Historical Association, 2002 (typescript in possession of author), 1, 5–6.

When I read these words just a few weeks ago, a mystery that had baffled me since 1977—indeed, for almost thirty years—began to unravel. In the winter of that year, I began teaching at Southwest Missouri State University where Bob Flanders was my colleague and became my good friend.

I valued Bob for many reasons. He was—and remains—a good man. That was clear. Plus, I found him to be intellectually stimulating and enormously creative. But aside from all that, I valued Bob for his vast knowledge of Mormon history. I, too, was interested in the history of the Latter-day Saints. After all, the Latter-day Saints shared much in common with my own religious tradition, the Churches of Christ. Both these traditions emerged on the American frontier in the early nineteenth century, and both placed at the center of their work the restoration of original, authentic Christianity, after a long, dark night in which, they claimed, the true and ancient church had disappeared from the earth.

For all these reasons, I longed to talk with Bob about Mormon history and identity. How fortunate I was, I thought, to have as my friend and colleague the man who had written the book *Nauvoo: Kingdom on the Mississippi*, and who clearly was one of the most learned interpreters of Mormon history anywhere in the world.

But I quickly learned that Bob would not talk about Mormon history. I remember more than one occasion when I took Bob out for lunch, hoping to pick his brain about the history of the Latter-day Saints. I enjoyed those times with Bob enormously, and Bob became my very good friend. But I never learned from Bob much at all about Mormon history, for Bob just wouldn't talk about that subject. He couldn't even bring himself to explain why.

Now, from his Sterling McMurrin Lecture of 2002, I have learned why Bob Flanders could never speak to me about the history of the Latter-day Saints. It all had to do with his conviction that his own tradition had denied the plain and obvious facts of its own particular history.

My Theme and My Task

What is pertinent to this lecture today—and the reason I have told this story about Robert Flanders—is that those who embrace the restoration vision often deny not only their very own history, but they also deny—or at least ignore—the larger history of the Christian church. If they could only stand with Jesus and the Apostles in the first Christian age—or so they imagine—they could cloak themselves with the innocence of pure beginnings. But a preoccupation with one's innocence is finally a preoccupation with self, not a preoccupation with others, and for that reason, illusions of innocence make it very difficult to sustain a commitment to peace and justice.

How, then, can the Community of Christ embrace a commitment to peace and justice not *in spite of* your restorationist heritage, but precisely *because of* that heritage?

This question is pertinent since, on the one hand, you have always defined yourself as a restoration tradition, and since, on the other, you now have stated clearly and unambiguously that "because of our commitment to Christ and belief in the worth of all people and the value of community building, we dedicate our lives to the pursuit of peace and justice for all people."[2]

The truth is, restorationists in the United States have typically not committed themselves to others, for others often become "the other"—defiled, corrupted, and evil.

This is precisely the point Flanders made when he told the John Whitmer Historical Association in 2002 that he "grew up much like other middle class kids in a Midwestern town. *Except*—I was never allowed to forget that I was *not* one of those kids. I was special. We were in the world but not of it. We were the True Saints of the Latter Day. All other religions were basically false. We alone were legitimate and had a direct line to heaven."[3]

Bob Flanders closed his 2002 address to this organization with these poignant lines: "History is a civilizing and humanizing enterprise. . . . With *Nauvoo*, I began the long, often painful, always exciting historical journey in my quest to one day, indeed, join the human race."[4]

---

[2] Community of Christ, "Basic Beliefs," Community of Christ, accessed January 24, 2022, https://www.cofchrist.org/basic-beliefs.

[3] Flanders, "Nauvoo on My Mind," 5.

[4] Flanders, "Nauvoo on My Mind," 5–6.

When Flanders made the point that "history is a . . . humanizing enter-prise," he said in effect that the study of history undermines all pretensions to innocence, for it forces one to locate oneself not in the golden age of the past but in the stream of human history, with all its warts and imperfec-tions. This is precisely why the book he wrote—and the process of writing that book—turned out to be so terrifying. For through that book, Flanders slowly came to see that both he and his church were grounded squarely in the ambiguities of human history, in spite of the claims both he and his church had made to the contrary.

And when Flanders wrote, "With *Nauvoo*, I began the long, often pain-ful, always exciting historical journey in my quest to one day, indeed, join the human race," he said more than meets the eye. He said, in effect, that he longed to be part of a world that embraced the truth about the human condition—the truth that human beings, their cultures, and even their religions are inevitably finite and flawed, and they are finite and flawed because they inevitably are bound by time, place, and circumstance.

For the most part, however, the world Flanders longed to join is a world both alien and foreign to those who have embraced the cause of restoration in the United States. Where, then, might you look for a mean-ingful model for the sort of church you hope to become?

Rethinking the Restoration Vision

In the history of Protestantism, I know of only one version of the res-toration vision that has sustained a serious commitment to peace and justice over the course of many hundreds of years. We find that vision in the history—and in the living communities—of the radical reformers of sixteenth-century Switzerland, a people unkindly labeled by their oppo-nents as "Anabaptists" or "re-baptizers."

Before I explore this tradition, I want to make two preliminary com-ments. First, sixteenth-century Anabaptism was an incredibly complex phenomenon, ranging from violent revolutionaries to advocates of com-munitarianism to spiritualists and finally to evangelical pacifists. For the most part, I will restrict my comments to the latter—the evangelical pacifists. Second, I am happy to see that several historians both in the

Community of Christ and in the LDS are exploring the resources available to you from within that tradition.[5]

There are three crucial differences between the Anabaptist version of the restoration vision, on the one hand, and the typical American version of that vision, on the other. First, the Anabaptists were never interested in restoring an institution (i.e., the primitive church) or a state of nature (i.e., "Nature and Nature's God") or a body of pure and undefiled doctrine that may have existed in a golden age of the past. Instead, they hoped to restore the meaning of Christian discipleship. Put another way, if the American version of the restoration vision has typically focused on doctrines, institutions, or a state of nature, the Anabaptist version of the restoration vision focused on a person—Jesus the Christ—and what it might mean to be faithful to the way he taught his disciples to live.

Second, there is a sense in which the restoration vision of the Anabaptists had more to do with the future than the past. For what they sought to recover was not so much the forms and doctrines of an ancient church as a vision of an upside-down kingdom, a vision sketched out in the life and teachings of Jesus, but a vision they knew would never be realized until the kingdom of God triumphed over all the earth.

In a technical sense, this vision was neither post- nor premillennial, but it was profoundly ethical. The Anabaptists—at least the evangelical strain of this tradition that I am exploring today—did not concern themselves with when or how Jesus might usher in a final golden age. And they certainly took no thought for how they, themselves, might build a kingdom of perfection. Rather, their concern was to live in a way that was faithful to the principles of that kingdom, a kingdom whose outlines they had learned in the biblical text, but a kingdom that would remain inevitably in the future and whose realization was finally dependent on God himself. In the meantime, their task was to live their lives *as if* that kingdom

[5]Michael Quinn, "Socioreligious Radicalism of the Mormon Church: A Parallel to the Anabaptist," in *New Views of Mormon History: A Collection of Essays in Honor of Leonard J. Arrington*, ed. Davis Bitton and Maureen Ursenbach Beecher (Salt Lake City: University of Utah Press, 1987), 363–86; John L. Brooke, *The Refiner's Fire: The Making of Mormon Cosmology, 1644–1844* (Cambridge, UK: Cambridge University Press, 1994); Clyde R. Forsberg Jr., "Are Mormons Anabaptists? The Case of the Mormons and Heirs of the Anabaptist Tradition in the American Frontier, c. 1840," in *Radical Reformation Studies: Essays Presented to James M. Stayer*, ed., Werner O. Packull and Geoffrey L. Dipple (Brookfield, VT: Ashgate, 1999); and Andrew Bolton, "Anabaptism, the Book of Mormon, and the Peace Church Option," *Dialogue: A Journal of Mormon Thought* 37 (Spring 2004): 75–94.

were a reality in their own time and place, even though they knew it was not. Put another way, the Anabaptists lived in the shadow of the second coming, even as they lived in the shadow of Jesus and his disciples. And from the convergence of those shadows, they found a vision of the coming kingdom of God.

Third, even though these people sought to live out the principles of an upside-down kingdom that had its roots both in the ancient church and in the final reign of God, they never rejected the reality and meaning of history, especially their own particular history. In this way, they avoided illusions of innocence based on the naïve assumption that their church was identical in every respect with the primitive church of the apostolic period. And in this way, they were freed from preoccupation with self to serve the neighbor.

Obviously, the Anabaptists have always been susceptible to illusions of innocence based on the purity of life they sought to cultivate. But this was hardly a claim of innocence based on a rejection of history.

The clearest manifestation of the way Anabaptists have embraced their history is the fact that Anabaptist communities have always been story-formed communities. When I use the phrase "story-formed communities" I refer to stories that are rooted in the very concrete reality of human history. The stories that shape this tradition are stories of people who chose, over many centuries of Christian history, to serve as ambassadors of peace and justice even if that commitment meant suffering, persecution, and even death.

One of the most important stories that shapes Anabaptists today is the story of Dirk Willems, one of the hundreds of stories contained in *The Martyrs' Mirror*, a seventeenth-century Anabaptist martyrology. Dirk Willems was a Dutch Anabaptist of the sixteenth century who had been captured by the authorities, locked in prison, and sentenced to die. Willems managed to escape his prison cell, but now faced one more hurdle. To reach freedom, he also had to cross a rather wide river. Fortunately, it was the dead of winter and the river was covered with a sheet of ice. Willems was a small man, and he scampered across the river with ease.

But once he reached the river's far side, he heard the voice of a deputy in hot pursuit. Unlike Willems, the deputy was a large man, too heavy, really, to cross the river safely. Suddenly, Willems heard the sickening sound of the deputy crashing through the ice and plunging into the cold and icy water. Most of us, no doubt, would have viewed the deputy's misfortune as our ticket to freedom. But Dirk Willems turned back, retraced his steps, and pulled the deputy to safety, knowing that any attempt to rescue the deputy would likely lead to his execution. Indeed, just a few days later, the authorities burned Dirk Willems at the stake.[6]

But the most important sixteenth-century story that helps shape Anabaptists of the twenty-first century is the story of the birth of their own tradition and their earliest years. That tradition began in 1525 in Zurich, Switzerland, shortly after a small group of young people began seriously to read the Gospel accounts of Jesus and his call for discipleship. At that time, most of these people were in Huldreich Zwingli's circle of students, and most were trained as Christian humanists, that is, people who had been taught that genuine learning required reliance on original sources, not secondary ones. Put another way, they had been trained as good historians. This is precisely why they had so completely immersed themselves in the Gospel accounts of the life and teachings of Jesus.

But the more they read, the more they found those accounts deeply disturbing, for there they found a whole new meaning of the Christian life, a meaning they had never heard before. The Gospels seemed to suggest that the Christian life was, in fact, the way of the cross and a summons to radical discipleship. Here was a vision of an upside-down kingdom in which the last becomes first, one dies in order to live, and one serves in order to lead. And central to this vision was the commitment to peacemaking and justice for all humankind.

They found these accounts disturbing mainly in contrast to the established church, for in the medieval world, everyone in society was *ipso facto* a Christian and a member of the church, simply by virtue of one's baptism as an infant. It made no difference that one might grow up to become a thief, a liar, a cheat, or a rapist; one was still a Christian and a member of the church.

---

[6] Thieleman J. van Braght, comp., *The Bloody Theater or Martyrs Mirror of the Defenseless Christians Who Baptized Only Upon Confession of Faith, and Who Suffered and Died for the Testimony of Jesus, Their Saviour, From the Time of Christ to the Year A. D. 1660* (1660; repr., Scottdale, PA: Herald Press, 1950), 741–42.

Based on the radical teachings they found in the Gospels, these young people called for the baptism of adults as a visible sign of one's commitment to live as serious disciples of Jesus. But when the Zurich city council rejected that proposal, Zwingli rejected it as well and threatened these students with serious punishment should they actually engage in the baptism of adults.

In January of 1525, these young adults, determined to follow God rather than human decrees, met in the home of Felix Manz and proceeded to rebaptize one another as committed believers. The authorities, both Catholic and Protestant, viewed their actions as not only theologically wrong-headed but as fundamentally seditious as well, and launched an extended campaign to exterminate all who participated in this movement. For the next several years, they slaughtered Anabaptists all over central Europe. We have no idea how many died, but we can be certain that the number of deaths were in the thousands. Dirk Willems was counted in that number.

What is important for our purposes is the understanding of Christian history that these people embraced. Every restorationist movement obviously has some theory of the fall of the church. Otherwise, what is there to restore? Most American restorationist traditions have followed the lead of the Puritans in dating the fall of the church with the rise of Roman Catholic ecclesiastical and institutional practices they thought foreign to the biblical text.

The Anabaptists, however, consistently dated the fall of the church with the Emperor Constantine who, for the first time in Christian history, legalized the Christian faith, and with the Emperor Theodosius who in the late fourth century made Christianity the only legal religion in the Roman Empire. Before Constantine, these people argued, it cost to be a Christian. After Constantine, it paid. Before Constantine, Christians typically committed themselves to peace and justice. After Constantine, they fought the Empire's wars and served the Empire, even as the Empire perpetrated gross injustices. Before Constantine, Christians gave their allegiance to the upside-down kingdom, but after Constantine, the church served the empire even as the empire protected the church, and the notion of radical discipleship—with precious few exceptions—was lost.

The Anabaptists proposed to reverse those priorities by giving their allegiance to Jesus and the coming kingdom of God, not to the state. They therefore refused to fight in wars or engage in violence of any kind, sought the welfare of others even at their own expense, emptied themselves for those in need, and routinely offered up their lives on behalf of this vision of peace and justice for all human beings.

By grounding their vision in the concrete realities of human history, joined to a vision of the coming kingdom of God, contemporary Anabaptists are able to live out of an extraordinarily powerful narrative that stands in marked contrast with the dominant narratives of our time, be they secular or religious. Professor Lee Camp, a theologian at Lipscomb University in Nashville, Tennessee, and one of the last students John Howard Yoder taught before he died, explores the difference in these two narratives in his book called *Mere Discipleship*—a book profoundly informed by the Anabaptist vision and by his Mennonite teacher, John Howard Yoder.

Camp argues that while the Constantinian settlement may be ancient history, many American Christians nonetheless view the world through a "Constantinian cataract."[7] Many, for example, view themselves as *American* Christians whose first allegiance is to the United States, rather than as Christians who happen to live in the United States and whose first allegiance is not to America but to the kingdom of God.

For such Christians, "empire" defines reality, Jesus and his teachings become impractical and irrelevant to the "real world," and serious discipleship essentially disappears. Christians who define their identity in terms of empire, Camp argues, inevitably serve the goal of self-preservation. They therefore trust in the power of the state, the power of the market, and the power of the sword, rather than in the power of the cross that requires disciples to abandon themselves for the sake of the neighbor, even if the neighbor proves to be an enemy.

On the other hand, radical discipleship means that Christians render to the kingdom of God their complete and unqualified allegiance, even if that allegiance entails suffering. For Christians who find the notion of

[7] Lee Camp, *Mere Discipleship: Radical Christianity in a Rebellious World* (Grand Rapids: Brazos Press, 2003), 21.

suffering unsettling, Camp points out time and again that the cross—not power and privilege—defines the kingdom of God.

From this perspective, Camp explores the biblical meaning of non-violence. "Christians refuse to fight wars," he explains, "not because they naively believe they will thus rid the world of war; instead, we do not fight wars because the kingdom of God has come, in which war is banished, in which it is possible to order our lives according to the justice and peace of God. Christian non-violence, then, is always rooted in the narrative of redemption."[8]

In that context, Camp explores what he calls "the political meaning of baptism." In baptism, Camp explains, "Christians become part of a community that transcends all racial, cultural, national, geographical, and natural boundaries." Conversely, "the god of 'God and country' does not baptize into the Spirit of Christ, but the spirit of homeland security; this god baptizes not in the blood of the Lamb, but the blood of soil and country."[9]

Conclusion

In conclusion, the question we must raise is this: How might it be possible for a restorationist tradition like the Community of Christ to embrace the sort of narrative Camp describes?

We take the initial step toward embracing that sort of narrative when we take seriously the entire history of the Christian church and especially the history of our own particular traditions with their triumphs and their failures. Robert Flanders spoke a great truth when he said at this meeting two years ago that "history is a civilizing and humanizing enterprise," and the embrace of one's history is the very first step on that "long, often painful, always exciting historical journey . . . to one day . . . join the human race."[10]

But as President Grant McMurray reminded you in his keynote address to this conference in May 2003, there are two ways to take history seriously. On the one hand, you can absolutize your history and make it wooden and

---

[8] Camp, *Mere Discipleship*, 127.

[9] Camp, *Mere Discipleship*, 145.

[10] Flanders, "Nauvoo on My Mind," 5–6.

brittle and restrictive. In this way, as President McMurray observed, one's history becomes one's theology.

On the other hand, we can embrace our history and say with the Psalmist, "I have a goodly heritage," but learn, at the very same time, to break through that history to the deeper truths it has to teach.

President McMurray offered as an illustration the account of Joseph Smith's First Vision. The question, he said,

> is whether the specific content of the experience is its primary value, or whether the real point is that a teenage boy put his knee to the ground in a search for truth and had some kind of spiritual encounter that changed his life and led to the formation of a major religious movement. Perhaps that is a far more important awareness than the number of personages remembered by Joseph two decades later, or the words spoken by them.[11]

President McMurray offered another example as well—the very concept of restoration. "If restoration is perceived as the restoring of a set of doctrines in their pure and undefiled form," he pointed out, "we have already lost the principle at the heart of the concept. That provides us doctrinal rigidity instead of the principle that the gospel is now understood in the culture and time in which it is expressed—central truths restored, if you will, in a new era of human history."[12]

We take the second step toward embracing a narrative of peace and justice when we realize that the narrative we seek is embodied—at least for Christians—not in doctrines or institutions but in the life and teachings of Jesus the Christ and in the upside-down kingdom over which he rules.

And we take the third step when we find colleagues and allies who have already discovered that narrative and who can help us on our journey. We may find those allies in the annals of Christian history, or we may find them even today in communities of faith that have committed themselves to a rigorous pursuit of peace and justice for all humankind. The Anabaptists who descend from the sixteenth century are only the

---

[11] W. Grant McMurray, "A 'Goodly Heritage' in a Time of Transformation: History and Identity in the Community of Christ," *Journal of Mormon History* 30 (Spring 2004): 72-73.

[12] McMurray, "A 'Goodly Heritage,'" 72.

most obvious example of the sorts of allies we need. You cannot become Anabaptists for their history is not your history. But they can be friends who offer strength for this terribly important journey on which you have now embarked.

THE PEOPLE WHO ISSUED THE MANY CALLS THAT SHAPED MY VOCATION

THE PEOPLE WHO SHAPED MY VOCATION

Over the years, countless people have shaped my sense of vocation. Standing at the head of that line of saints were my parents who told me time and time again that I should never consider money when choosing a career. Rather, they said, ask how you might serve and what sort of work will bring you joy and fulfillment.

And while they were faithful members of the Church of Christ, they encouraged me to question, to wonder, and to critique my own tradition. In a word, they embodied the best of Churches of Christ—that part of our heritage that prized the search for truth.

Beyond my parents, no one has shaped my sense of vocation more than my wife, Jan, for she and I have been on a common journey that has lasted now for almost sixty years. From the beginning, we have wondered together, explored together, and questioned together. There has not been a single issue of substance that we have not shared, and in that way, her vocation became my vocation and my vocation became hers.

Beyond my parents and my spouse, scores of other people have helped shape my sense of self, my sense of meaning, and my sense of vocation. Often they were unaware of the way they were shaping my sense of calling, but shape it they did. Those people ranged from my teachers in Stonewall Jackson Elementary School in Dallas to my teachers in Davy Crockett Elementary School, Robert E. Lee Junior High School, and Central High School in San Angelo, Texas; from my teachers at Harding College and Abilene Christian College and finally to my teachers at the University of Iowa.

Beyond those people who taught me in formal settings, hundreds—perhaps thousands—of people have taught me, instructed me, molded me, and helped shape me into the person I have finally become. Chief among those "others" was a Black pastor in Harrisburg, Pennsylvania, who took me under his wing, mentored me, and made me a better person.

In the essays that follow, I seek to pay tribute to some of those people who have shaped my life and my sense of calling.

FINDING SOMEONE TO LOVE

The journey of life, writes Frederick Buechner in his book *The Sacred Journey*, is "a journey *in search*," and there are three things, at least, that each of us seeks to find. "We search," Buechner tells us, "for a self to be. We search for other selves to love. We search for work to do." This is the story of my finding someone to love and how that love has called me into work I never dreamed I would do.

I grew up in West Texas where, for the most part, the tallest trees were what people back east would call large shrubs. So when I first saw Harding College in Searcy, Arkansas, it was love at first sight. The campus was full of magnificent trees—huge oaks and maples and other trees that reached to the sky. Large, white porch swings, suspended from sturdy white frames, dotted the Harding landscape.

I thought the Harding campus was the most beautiful place I had ever seen. It swept me off my feet and won my heart. And I choose the word "heart" quite deliberately since my decision to attend Harding was far more a decision of the heart than of the head.

If my head had played a role in that decision, I might have decided to go elsewhere after I visited there in the spring of my senior year in high school and heard the president—Dr. George S. Benson—make a chapel announcement that I found extraordinarily odd.

Benson had a nasal quality to his voice and always spoke as if he was suffering from a vicious cold. That morning, in his pinched, nasal voice, his announcement went something like this: "Young people, this morning as I was walking from my house to my office, I saw a sight that almost scared me to death. I saw a young man and a young woman sitting in a swing, and then, when I looked more closely, I saw a snaaaaaake around that young woman's shoulder." He elongated the word, "snake" for effect, and then concluded, "Now, young people, let's not be snaaaakeeeey!"

Benson's announcement wasn't enough to offset the magic of the trees, however, and I enrolled at Harding the following fall.

During my first year there, I was homesick for West Texas much of the time and seriously considered transferring to a school closer to my home. But then a young woman came into my life. She did more than steal my heart, for once we met she dominated my dreams at night and my thoughts during the day. The truth is, I was madly in love.

Her name was Janice Wright. She was from Chicago, she was pretty and charming and smart, and our relationship was so spectacular that I soon abandoned any thought of leaving Harding for another college. In fact, we married when we were both only twenty years old.

How we met is a story of extraordinary grace.

Harding had rules upon rules that governed student behavior. Many I thought were ridiculous, but the rule about cafeteria decorum was one of those things to which you never give a second thought at the time but, looking back, you realize how it completely changed your life.

Harding required students to sit at the same table with the people with whom they had gone through the cafeteria line. That rule discouraged cliques and encouraged kids to get acquainted with a wide assortment of other students. The other rule was that no one could leave the table until everyone had finished eating.

One day I went through the line with Jan. I had never seen her before, but because of Harding's rule, we sat together at the table. On that particular day, I talked and talked and talked and forgot to eat my meal. The other kids grew impatient and eventually broke one of the cardinal rules when they all got up and left. All, that is, except Jan. She stayed. And that was the beginning of a romance that has now topped fifty years.

Jan and I both sang in the Harding College A Cappella Chorus, and in the spring, when she was a sophomore and I was a freshman, the chorus toured from Arkansas to New York City, singing for various Churches of Christ along the way. Jan and I sat together on the big tour bus, and each and every day, for the duration of the tour, we gazed into each other's eyes, each transfixed by the other.

But I almost blew my relationship with Jan early on. Jan was light-hearted and loved to laugh and joke and have fun. But I was deadly serious. Once she gave me a greeting card that said on the front, "Someone told me that you're obnoxious, but I stuck up for you." When I opened the card, the punch line said, "I told them you can't help it." Jan meant that card for a joke, but I was devastated.

I was so serious that on almost every date, I wanted to talk about the meaning of life. Jan put up with that for a while, but on one of those dates, when I brought up the meaning of life, she told me that if I couldn't lighten up, our relationship was over. I lightened up really fast.

Jan and I paid no attention to President Benson's warning to the students to "not be snaaaakeeeey" in the Harding swings. One night all the swings were occupied, so Jan and I decided to find another location for our courtship. We picked a dimly lit, recessed outdoor entry to the American Studies Building, and there we talked and hugged and kissed until, suddenly, the outside door swung open and the college vice-president, Dr. Clifton Ganus, emerged. He knew us both and had known Jan's parents for years.

"Jan and Richard," he said, "this is not a very good place for what you're doing. It's far too bright." And he suggested we sit in the shadow of an old stone wall that ran the width of the campus, dividing it from the street.

That old stone wall seemed perfect, and we found an ideal spot where we sat on the grass in the shadow of the wall. But all too soon we heard steps approaching. It was the wife of the dean of the college, Bessie Mae Pryor. She knew Jan well since she sponsored Regina, Jan's social club. (Harding had social clubs, not fraternities and sororities.)

"Jan and Richard," she said, "this is not a very good place for you. It's far too close to the street," and she pointed us to some bushes further down the wall. This was the third location we had tried, and as Goldilocks said of the third bowl of porridge, this one was "just right."

On a beautiful Sunday afternoon in September of 1963, at the beginning of her senior year and my junior year at Harding, Jan and I married in the College Church of Christ in Searcy, and after the wedding reception, we began our trek to Roaring River State Park in Missouri where we would honeymoon. We had just passed through the hamlet of Toad Suck Ferry when we noticed it was almost 6:00 p.m., the normal time for Sunday evening services in virtually every Church of Christ across the country.

In our twenty years on this earth, neither Jan nor I had missed a Sunday evening church service unless some emergency had dictated otherwise. So partly out of habit and partly out of duty, Jan and I located one of the Churches of Christ in Conway, Arkansas, and there, to launch both our honeymoon and our marriage, we attended church.

We hoped no one there would know we had just been married, so we parked the car—covered as it was with balloons and "Just Married" signs—behind the church where we thought it would not be noticed. But after church, Jan discovered that rice still nested in the curls of her hair.

Over the years, Jan has saved me from myself on countless occasions. When we first started dating, she saved me from my preoccupation with the meaning of life. On many occasions, she has saved me—and her—from serious car crashes when I have been too preoccupied with other matters to pay attention to the road. And once she saved me from myself in Iowa City, Iowa, where we moved in the fall of 1967 for my doctoral studies.

We had been in Iowa City for only two days when we had to tank up our car with gas. Those were the days of full-service gas stations, and when the attendant approached my window, he asked that simple question, "May I help you, sir?" I told him in my normal Texas drawl to "fill it with reglar" and "check the all." The attendant, who spoke like most Iowans—in good, standard radio speech—promptly replied, "I will, sir, but all the what?" Exasperated, I repeated, "Check the *all!*" "Yes sir!" replied the attendant once again. "But all the what?" I could hardly believe this guy could be so dense. "The *all!*" I was beginning now to raise my voice. "The *all!*" I said again. By now, he was showing his frustration, too. "Yes, sir, but all the *what*?" "Would you please check under the hood?" I finally muttered in defeat.

When I got home, I told Jan about my experience with Iowans who didn't know how to speak properly. She had a different assessment. She told me that I was the one with the problem. But she would work with me, she said, and she did. "Oil," she said. "All," I responded. Slowly, I improved. "Oil," she said. "Oiyal," I repeated.

I never got the word "oil" down quite right, but thanks to Jan, by the end of our four years in Iowa City, I had begun for the most part to sound like a native Iowan.

We learned a lot about Iowa during our sojourn there. Once we needed a simple doorstop and thought an old-fashioned flatiron might do the trick. We saw an ad in the *Iowa City Press-Citizen* about a farm auction where several flat irons would be auctioned off. How fortunate for us, we thought.

So on the appointed day, we headed into the Iowa countryside and located the farm in question. We had never attended an auction, much less a farm auction, so once the bidding began, we carefully observed to see how it was done. We noticed that people who wished to bid simply raised their index finger, silently and unobtrusively.

When the auctioneer announced that the bidding for the first flatiron would begin at fifty cents, I silently raised my finger. "I've got fifty cents," the auctioneer said. "Who will give me a dollar?" And someone bid a dollar. "Who'll give me a dollar, fifty?" he asked, and once again I raised my finger. "Who'll give me two?" he asked. And someone gave him two. "Who'll give me two-fifty," he asked, and again I raised my finger. The bidding went on and on. Someone continued to bid against me, and the price for the flatiron that began with fifty cents got up to ten dollars.

Someone else wants that flatiron badly, I thought to myself. And that's when the auctioneer stopped the bidding, looked right at Jan and me, and bellowed out the question that betrayed his sheer amazement that two city slickers could be so naïve. "Are you two together?" he asked.

We took that flatiron home, and to this day, some fifty years later, it adorns our laundry room floor.

Jan is so creative that artistry oozes out of her pores. Anyone who has been inside our home knows the truth of that statement. Give her a room and she will transform it into a space of exquisite beauty. Somehow, with no formal training, she knows how to work with color and balance and depth. She doesn't require much money to achieve her goals. In fact, she shuns the trappings of wealth. Simplicity and understatement define her work, and thanks to her, I have been privileged to live in spectacularly beautiful spaces for almost sixty years.

Moreover, Jan is a builder, a doer, and a fix-it person. She has painted walls, laid wood floors, hung wallpaper, fixed the plumbing, and so much more.

Once, in Springfield, Missouri, a plumber learned about Jan's abilities the hard way. It was a bitterly cold day when he came to our house. Snow covered the ground and the wind was howling. The outside temperature was twenty or twenty-five degrees, but it felt like minus twenty.

We had just moved to Springfield from Malibu, California, and the house was new. The plumber had come because the pipe that vented the hot water heater up through the roof was too short and the wind that swept over the roof blew the fumes back into the room.

It was mid-afternoon when the plumber arrived. I was at the university, though Jan knew I would be home within an hour or two.

"I'd like to speak with Mr. Hughes," the plumber told Jan when she opened the door.

"He's not here," she replied. "May I help you?"

"I'm here to fix that vent pipe," he said. "How long until Mr. Hughes gets here?"

"Maybe an hour, maybe more, maybe less. But I can help you with that," she told him.

"Nope," the plumber said, flatly rejecting her offer. "I want to speak with Mr. Hughes."

So Jan offered again. "I know all about that pipe," she said. "Please come in. I can help you."

"Nope," the plumber said, "I'll just wait on Mr. Hughes."

So he sat in his truck that was parked on our driveway and waited. Thirty minutes passed. Forty-five minutes. An hour. An hour and fifteen minutes. An hour and a half. For a full two hours, the plumber sat in his truck, running his motor, trying to stay warm.

Finally, I drove into the driveway and parked next to the plumber. He jumped out of his truck and introduced himself. "I'm the plumber," he said. "I'm here to fix that vent pipe."

"Oh, you'll have to see my wife about that," I said.

Jan told me later that she'd never loved me more.

Over the years, Jan has given me some extraordinary gifts, beginning with the gift of herself. She taught school for seven years so I could pursue my vocation. She was fully present, caring for me in every conceivable way when I succumbed to a heart attack that both of us thought would likely take my life. And for all these years of marriage—fifty-eight and counting—she has been my very best friend.

For as long as I can remember, Jan has loved stories—not just any stories, but sacramental stories, the kind of stories that help us see the grace of God at work in the ordinary and the mundane.

Years ago, she discovered these sorts of stories in writers like Madeleine L'Engle, Annie Dillard, Kathleen Norris, Anne Lamott, and Frederick Buechner, and she shared those stories with me. Always on the lookout for sacramental stories, she finds them on the web, in books, in newspapers, in magazines—everywhere, really. And while some purists wouldn't be caught dead with a television in their houses, Jan watches TV news and documentaries on a regular basis, always alert for those incredible stories that speak of the grace God extends to broken people through people who are equally broken, but just in different ways.

And then, in the mid-1980s, Jan began to write stories of her own. Those stories inevitably carried such power that when she presented them orally, some people began to quietly weep. She never set out to write tear-jerking stories that played on people's emotions. She just told stories that were true to life, that celebrate the ordinary in each of our lives, and that help us find meaning in events that we might otherwise regard as so tragic that meaning is hard to find.

Slowly and inevitably, she drew me into the web of her stories. And while I have devoted fifty years of my life to teaching and writing about Christian history—a discipline that all too often stands far removed from the storyteller's craft—I decided when we moved to Messiah College in 2006 to join Jan in the kind of work she did.

From that first year at Messiah College until now—for eight years at Messiah College and six years now at Lipscomb University—she and I have team-taught an honors first-year seminar on the theme "Learning to Tell Our Stories." We ask our students to read some powerful memoirs—books like Frederick Buechner's *The Sacred Journey*, James McBride's *The Color of Water*, Anne Lamott's *Traveling Mercies*, and Rick Bragg's *All Over but the Shoutin'*.

Then, following their reading of each of those books, our students write two-page papers. But they don't so much write about the books they read as about the stories their own lives were telling—personal stories triggered by a given memoir. And then, in the protective intimacy of the circle the class has formed, they share those stories out loud with one another. It seems like sacred space, like holy ground. And the stories the students tell, week after week, are nothing short of remarkable.

By any measure, this class has been the highlight of my career.

And by any measure, Jan—the woman who stayed with me when the other kids grew weary of my incessant chatter, who taught me how to speak the dialect of native Iowans, who has loved me through thick and thin, and who, in recent years, has drawn me into the web of her love for story—this spectacular woman, has been an extraordinary gift of grace.

"Next Time, Send Jan"

E ach year, Jan and I ask our students to evaluate our team-taught class, and one of the questions on the evaluation form always reads, "What did you like best about this course?" One year, the students were in lock-step agreement. "Jan," they chirped in unison.

Some fifty years earlier, Jan drew similar ratings from one of my professors at the University of Iowa. This was no ordinary professor, mind you. This was Sidney E. Mead, the widely acknowledged dean of historians of American religious history in the 1960s.

Mead's reputation was the reason I selected the University of Iowa for my doctoral work in the first place. But as it turned out, I focused my work on Reformation studies, not on American religion, and never took a single course for credit under Sidney Mead.

But while Mead was never my teacher at Iowa in a formal sense, he became my teacher for the next forty years. I have returned to Mead's books time and again and invariably find myself enriched, inspired, and instructed. In addition, until he died on June 9, 1999, he and I kept up a lively correspondence, exchanging four or five letters every year for the better part of three decades.

Our relationship began when James Spalding, my doctoral advisor, asked if I would team teach a course with Mead at the United School of the

Church, a summer study/retreat for mainline Christians—Presbyterians, United Methodists, and members of the United Church of Christ—during the summer after my graduation from Iowa.

My sectarian roots and Mead's Unitarian faith meant neither of us had all that much in common with mainline Protestants. So he and I spent hours that week getting acquainted.

How foolish I was to pass up the opportunity to study with this immensely learned and creative man became all too apparent during the course of my comprehensive exams. At Iowa in those days, the comps gave five different professors the opportunity to grill a doctoral student over the highly specialized subject area that each of those professors taught. If the student passed the comps, then he or she moved on to write the dissertation. But if even two of the five professors flunked the student, that student was out of the program.

I was comfortable with the first four examiners since all four represented my major field of Reformation studies, and for the most part, I breezed through their questions with ease. But then came Mead.

I had dreaded this encounter with Mead since I had done no formal work under his direction. And it didn't take Mead long to discover my deficiencies. To make matters worse, I grew increasingly nervous once his line of questioning began.

Mead asked questions designed to get me to talk about the shape of religious pluralism in the American republic—one of the subjects to which he had devoted his career. But to each of his questions, I froze and drew a complete blank.

Finally, frustrated with the incredible level of my stupidity, Mead said, "Now look here, Hughes. I'm going to ask you one more question, and I'm going to make this question as simple as I possibly can. If you were walking down the street in downtown Iowa City and someone came up to you and asked, 'Pardon me, sir, could you tell me, where is the church?' What would you say?" He emphasized the word *the* when he said "*the* church," as if to give me one last and very important clue. He hoped I would somehow latch onto the obvious point that the term "*the* church" makes no sense in America where there are many denominations and sects but not a single established church. The obvious answer to Mead's question—but the answer that somehow kept eluding me—was simply, "*Which* church?"

The room was deathly silent as I pondered Mead's weighty question for at least a full two minutes. Finally, I blurted out with what was really more of a question than a statement. "Well, Dr. Mead, I suppose I would say, 'On the corner'?"

"Aauuugggh," Mead said, as he hit his forehead with the palm of his hand. He pulled a book off the shelf beside him and began to read, as if to signal his complete disgust with my imbecility. He clearly had no more questions. In retrospect, I'm sure he must have failed me on that exam, but thankfully, a four-out-of-five vote was sufficient to advance me on to the dissertation stage.

As a child of Churches of Christ, I likely struggled with Mead's question because, deep inside, I still believed at some subliminal level that there truly was only one legitimate church—the fruit of the true church mythology with which I had been raised—and I simply resisted the implications of Mead's line of thought.

At any rate, that evening I told Jan about the exam. I told her that Mead had asked what I would say if someone asked me, "Where is the church?"

"*Which* church?" Jan asked.

During our week together at the United School of the Church, I told Mead of Jan's response to his question. From that day until the end of his life, he always contended—facetiously, I often thought, though now I'm not so sure—that Iowa had awarded the PhD to the wrong person. "We should have given the degree to Jan," he often quipped. And as time went on, he came to know Jan and liked her a very great deal.

In 1998, Jan and I were living in Malibu, California, where I served as a religion professor at Pepperdine University. In June of that year, in the midst of a marvelous vacation in Door County, Wisconsin, I suffered a debilitating heart attack and landed in Bellin Hospital in Green Bay, Wisconsin, for the better part of a week. Following my recovery, I wrote to Mead and told him the story of this extraordinary adventure.

I told him how the heart attack had occurred while Jan and I were watching *Sleepless in Seattle* in our hotel in the tiny village of Fish Creek, Wisconsin; how we called a doctor in another village, Sister Bay; how the ambulance arrived and took me to a small county hospital in Sturgeon Bay; and how another ambulance finally took me to Bellin Hospital in Green Bay for treatment. After telling this fairly lengthy story, I shared with Mead what I viewed as the spiritual dimensions of this crisis. My letter was dated September 1, 1998.

Exactly one month later, on October 1, 1998, Mead responded. He appreciated my story. Still and all, he said,

> By the time you got to Bellin [Hospital] I had almost forgotten you in wondering where Jan was and what she was doing—did she drive you on the first two laps, did she ride with you in the ambulance to Bellin or follow in your car? After you were settled in Bellin did she have to go back to Sister Bay to settle with the hotel & with the purveyors of *Sleepless in Seattle*—whatever, she must have been sleepless in Door County all night and much of the following five nights while your heart was deciding to go to work again! I am tempted to be more proud of her than you say you are proud of yourself.

Just prior to the heart attack—in fact, on the plane that flew us from Los Angeles to Door County—I read the marvelous book *Tuesdays with Morrie*. Mitch Albom, who wrote that book, had lost touch with his old Brandeis professor, Morrie Schwartz, and after a fifteen-year period of no communication, the two reconnected as Morrie lay dying with Lou Gehrig's disease. The title, *Tuesdays with Morrie*, reflects the fact that Mitch and Morrie met each and every Tuesday for the rest of Morrie's life to explore together the meaning of life in the face of Morrie's imminent death.

Even though Sidney Mead and I had stayed in touch by mail every year for almost thirty years, I had not actually seen him in perhaps a decade. *Tuesdays with Morrie* made me realize that my chances to see Mead face to face were growing increasingly limited as the days passed by.

So I called him and told him I wanted to fly over for a visit. He and his wife, Millie, were living in Tucson then, and he told me he would be happy to see me. He told me he had just celebrated his ninety-fourth birthday and, what was more, his driver's license had just been renewed. The next time he renewed his license, he said, he would be ninety-nine years old!

A few days after my call, he wrote in a letter of our "proposed visit sometime around the middle of this month—it would be, will be wonderful, a blessing to see you, to talk about anything from Tuesday's questions to recent gossip."

Sometime later, I made the short flight from Los Angeles to Tucson. We had what I thought was a wonderful visit that lasted perhaps three or four hours. He and Millie even gave me some diaries written by Millie's mother, a Pentecostal preacher in Minnesota in the early twentieth century. They wanted me to get those diaries to the Minnesota Historical Library. I told them that I would.

Four months later, Mead was dead. He apparently died of a broken heart, crushed by the changes that were overtaking his Millie, the love of his life and a victim of Alzheimer's disease.

I will always be grateful I made that trip to visit my old professor. And I will always remember the last words I heard from his lips.

When I checked my watch and realized my flight back to Los Angeles was coming up soon, I told him and Millie that I had better be on my way if I wanted to make my flight.

Mead got up from his chair and walked me to the door. He walked slowly at a pace befitting a ninety-four-year-old man. We stood on his porch, and I told him how much I had enjoyed my visit. We exchanged a few other pleasantries before I walked from his porch to my car.

And then, as if to cap off those thirty years of wonderful interaction and correspondence, Mead spoke the last words I ever heard him utter. He spoke loudly to make sure I could hear. He peered at me through eyes grown dim with age and then, without so much as a smile, spoke simply and directly.

"Next time," he said, "send Jan."

And I understood and still do understand, for Jan has graced so many lives—his and mine and those of our students who were unanimous in their praise of her wit, her wisdom, and the stories she shared with them and with me as she has helped us all learn to tell our stories.

THEY BELIEVED IN ME
The Grace of Good Teachers

I've been graced, mentored, nurtured, and taught by some of the best teachers you could ever find. And the beauty of it is that marvelous teachers have continued to enter my life, shape my thinking, and enhance my work over all these years. To say that I am grateful would be an understatement of the grossest kind.

As if it were only yesterday, I can still recall sitting in Mrs. Lewis's first-grade class at Stonewall Jackson Elementary School in Dallas as she taught us how to make our letters, round and even.

I remember Mrs. Derryberry who took our fourth-grade class on a Saturday cotton-picking expedition to help us at least begin to see the world through the eyes of migrant farmers.

And I remember Mrs. Satchel who taught us art. I was probably in the second grade when, one day, a student answered one of her questions so profoundly that she exclaimed, "My, you just said a mouthful!" Suspecting that I had not been listening, she then turned to me and asked me what that student had just said. "A mouthful," I replied, to the unbridled laughter of my classmates.

Mrs. Satchel would have been within her rights to punish me for insubordination, but somehow she knew that I had given as honest an answer as I knew to give.

After only five years in Dallas, General Telephone (now Verizon) transferred my dad to San Angelo, a charming West Texas town that grew up on the banks of the north, south, and middle forks of the Concho River. I was ten years old and there I entered fifth grade at Davy Crockett Elementary School.

One day a girl named Paula annoyed me so badly that, after picking my nose, I threw an especially large booger directly at her face. It stuck to her cheek, and when she removed it and saw what it was, she screamed bloody murder. For the rest of the year, my classmates referred to me as "booger boy."

In spite of my antics, my teachers took me seriously and I continued to grow and learn.

At Robert E. Lee Junior High School, Maureen Bullock taught Texas history. More than a teacher, Mrs. Bullock became a guide and a special friend. When the principal left Lee and transferred to another school, Mrs. Bullock called a special assembly and, out of all the students in that school, asked me to honor the principal with a tribute speech. Later, when she published a junior high school-level textbook on Texas history, she gave me an autographed copy. In so many ways, she embodied God's grace as she lavished me with love, respect, and acceptance.

At Central High School, I studied English literature under Mr. Windsor. I can see him even now with his bow tie and horn-rimmed glasses, looking for the world like a Brit who belonged in some romantic Cotswoldian village like Chipping Campden. He taught us Chaucer's *Canterbury Tales*, which I learned so well that now, after more than fifty years, I can still recite its opening lines.

I honestly thought San Angelo was the center of the universe. But the universe I knew was so provincial and small that in 1960 my friends and I practically worshipped Barry Goldwater, whose recently published book, *The Conscience of a Conservative*, had become our Bible.

So Kathryn Eillers, our government teacher at Central, decided to broaden us a bit. Senator Bobby Kennedy was scheduled to speak at San

Angelo College on behalf of the presidential bid of his brother Jack, and Mrs. Eillers strongly encouraged us to attend.

Informed as we were by Goldwater's *Conscience of a Conservative*, my friends and I had no use either for the Kennedy clan or for what we regarded as the ultra-liberal principles of the Democratic Party. So when Bobby Kennedy completed his speech in the college auditorium, one of my friends—Charles Haworth—did something that the Secret Service would never permit today. As Kennedy walked from the auditorium to his waiting car, Charles—with the rest of us gathered around him—planted himself in the middle of the sidewalk where he could force the Senator into a verbal confrontation. And there he tried to trap Kennedy with some smart-alec questions gleaned from Goldwater's book.

WHAT'S THIS? — When Robert F. Kennedy appeared at San Angelo College Tuesday, the photographer found he had a strange emblem smack in the middle of the picture. Wearing the Nixon booster is Barbara Ann Elliott of 2228 Waco. At right is Richard Hughes of 2656 W. Ave. N. (Staff Photo by Smith)

A photographer from the *San Angelo Standard Times*, our local newspaper, snapped a photo of Kennedy surrounded by Charles and his conservative friends. But the photo that appeared on the front page of the next morning's paper was not of Charles and Kennedy, as it should have been, but of Kennedy, me, and a young woman sporting a pin that read, "If I were 21, I'd vote for NIXON." It seemed to the world as if I were the one grilling Kennedy, and how I wished at the time that what that photo portrayed were actually true!

Of all my high school teachers, the man who did the most to shape my life and help me discover a vocation was a crusty old journalist named Ed Cole. A former newspaperman with the *San Angelo Standard-Times*, it was Mr. Cole who first taught me how to write. When I was a sophomore, he named me sports editor of the *Campus Corral*, the student newspaper, and then, during my junior year, I became editor-in-chief.

Thanks to Mr. Cole, the *Campus Corral* was no typical high school rag. Though smaller in size, it rivaled the *Standard-Times* for the quality of its page design and overall appearance.

On Friday nights, when the San Angelo Bobcats football team played at home, Mr. Cole and I sat together in the press box of that magnificent stadium, high above the playing field below, and there he called the plays—"number 12 hands off to number 25, 25 sweeps around right end, tackled by 17, down on the 45 yard line for a 7 yard gain"—and almost as quickly as he spoke, I typed the information he provided. The next day I wrote the story for the *Campus Corral*.

As a sophomore at Harding College, an extraordinary scholar and teacher named Raymond Muncy first inspired me to study history, especially Christian history. When I couldn't find a topic for my research paper in his European history class, he called me into his office, and there he gently led me to explore my own deepest interests and concerns. Once he discovered my passion to understand more about the Christian religion, he suggested that I write a paper on the sixteenth-century debate between Luther and Erasmus on whether human beings possess free will.

Thanks to Muncy, my eyes began to open onto a larger Christian world than I had ever known before. But myopia still blurred my intellectual vision, and since I could discern no connection between this larger Christian world and the one true church to which I belonged, I was able, finally, to dismiss the Luther-Erasmus debate as interesting—immensely so—but essentially irrelevant to anything that really mattered.

Three years later, as a first-year graduate student at the Harding Graduate School of Religion, a professor named Jack P. Lewis taught me a lesson about the value of books that I've never forgotten. Lewis had earned two PhDs—one in New Testament from Harvard and one in Hebrew Bible from Hebrew Union—and he spoke with the kind of authority that inspired awe on the part of the students.

Even though Jan taught school that year, her salary was low and we were strapped for cash. So I seriously entertained taking a position as a youth minister at a Memphis-area church. When I casually mentioned to Lewis that I might take that job, he took me to the porch of the main building of the Harding Graduate School and pointed to the library.

"Do you see that building?" Lewis asked with emotion in his voice. "Yes," I said. "What is that building?" he demanded. "The library," I responded. "Do you know how many books are in that building?" he inquired. "I have no idea," I replied. Lewis told me the astounding number of volumes that the library housed and then asked, "How long do you think it would take you to read all those books?" "A lifetime," I replied. "And you seriously think you have time to take that job?" I got his point. It was clear to me then that we could tighten our belts and live on less. I decided to forget the job at the church and focus on my studies.

That very same year I signed up for a class on the history of my own tradition taught by the man who had written a multivolume history of our church, Earl Irvin West. That class opened for me a world of discovery, since it had never occurred to me that the Church of Christ had a history other than Jesus and the apostles. What I learned was so engaging and compelling that, for the very first time, I found myself called to the study of Christian history.

Just a year later, at Abilene Christian University, Professor Everett Ferguson introduced me to the sixteenth-century Anabaptists—a simple act that changed my life in ways that I explained in Chapter Four.

Over the years, several scholars have taught me and shaped me and sometimes saved me from my ignorance, my biases, and even from myself. In the fall of 1982, contract in hand, I returned to Abilene Christian University to begin my research for a history of the Churches of Christ for Greenwood Press. I thought I knew a lot about that topic, but the Brown Library archivist R. L. Roberts called my bluff. "I bet you think the history of Churches of Christ is the history of Alexander Campbell writ large," he said. I had to admit that, indeed, I did. "Well, you're wrong," Roberts said, "and if you don't understand the massive contributions that Barton W. Stone made to this tradition, you'll miss the genius of the entire heritage."

Over the course of that year, Roberts became my mentor, guiding me into a wealth of literature by Barton Stone and the many people he inspired. And while I am ultimately responsible for the errors and omissions in *Reviving the Ancient Faith: The Story of Churches of Christ in America,*[1] I

---

[1] Richard T. Hughes, *Reviving the Ancient Faith: The Story of Churches of Christ in America* (Grand Rapids: Eerdmans, 1996).

owe to R. L. Roberts a debt I can never repay, for he opened to me a world of information and insight I might have learned in no other way.

In 1976 I studied with a leading public intellectual, Robert N. Bellah, in an NEH Summer Seminar at the University of California at Berkeley on the theme "Civil Religion in America." Roughly twenty-five years later, I asked Bellah to write a foreword for the first edition of my book *Myths America Lives By*,[2] but he declined. "The myths you identify," he wrote, "are the only myths this nation has, but you have annihilated them. I want you to show that each of these stories, while often abused and misused, has redemptive power and potential for good." Bellah's advice helped to inform that book in significant ways; and when all was said and done, he wrote the foreword.

In 2011, I completed my manuscript for another book that I called *Christian America and the Kingdom of God*.[3] Two of the external reviewers gave the manuscript a green light, but one reviewer flatly advised, "Don't publish it!" That reviewer was Martin E. Marty, widely regarded for almost half a century as the leading historian of religion in the United States. "But tell Hughes," Marty advised the prospective publisher, "that I'm the road-block and ask him to call me."

I had never studied with Marty in any formal setting, but I had known him for years. When we spoke by phone, he told me my treatment of the kingdom of God in the biblical text was far too skimpy and needed to be significantly expanded. Holding Marty in the highest possible esteem,

Samuel S. Hill Jr.

I did exactly what he advised. The next year, the University of Illinois Press published that book with a lovely endorsement from Marty.

Aside from my formal teachers, no one mentored me more faithfully or more graciously than Samuel S. Hill Jr., the kind and gentle scholar who taught first at the University of North Carolina and then at the University of Florida, and who was widely regarded as the dean of historians of

---

[2] Richard T. Hughes, *Myths America Lives By* (Urbana: University of Illinois Press, 2003).

[3] Richard T. Hughes, *Christian America and the Kingdom of God* (Urbana: University of Illinois Press, 2012).

religion in the South. His intimate knowledge of Southern religion enabled Sam to locate Churches of Christ squarely in their Southern context.

Although he became an Episcopalian later in life, Sam was Baptist to the bone, and his deep appreciation for the Baptist heritage enabled him to both understand and appreciate the Churches of Christ. With his intensely curious mind and his devotion to the virtue of wonder, Sam would often say to me, "Richard, have you thought about this?" or "Richard, have you thought about that?" He prodded and pushed me to think more deeply about my tradition, and he performed that task so well that I often thought that Sam understood both me and my tradition even better than I understood myself.

I explained both in Chapter Ten and Chapter Eighteen how pivotal Sidney Mead has been in shaping the way I understand the history of American religion. But it was James C. Spalding at  the University of Iowa to whom I owe the greatest debt of all, for it was Spalding who helped determine the kind of historian I would become. Early on in my doctoral studies, Spalding asked if I had given thought to a dissertation topic. I told Spalding I wanted to write about Alexander Campbell, one of the founders of my own tradition—the Church of Christ. When Spalding heard that, he grew apoplectic. "Not here," he said. "Not

James C. Spalding

at Iowa!" He was determined that my studies at Iowa take me far beyond the narrow confines of my own faith tradition. More than that, Spalding befriended me and nurtured me during my years at Iowa and even beyond. Many others felt exactly the same way, for virtually all the graduate students thought of Spalding as "the students' friend."

Spalding suffered from narcolepsy—an irresistible urge to sleep. I once sat in one of Spalding's graduate seminars that he team-taught with a professor from the history department. When Spalding finished his part, he went to sleep.

When I attended my first professional meeting, Spalding and I together attended a session on the English Reformation, the area of Christian history in which Spalding specialized. All the big names in that field were

The Grace of Troublesome Questions

there. I was awed and impressed. But shortly after the session began, Spalding went to sleep. He didn't just sleep. He slumped to the side of his chair, looking for the world as if he might fall on the floor at any minute. I was mortified. Here were all the big names in my field, people whose books I had read, people whose scholarship had shaped the discipline, people whose importance was beyond question. And here was my man, slumped over and sound asleep.

After the first scholar had read his paper, the person chairing the session suggested a change in the proceedings. Instead of postponing comments and questions until all three papers had been read, he would welcome questions and comments after each paper, and did anyone have anything to say about the paper that had just been presented?

At that, Spalding sprang to his feet, ruthlessly critiqued the paper, and then sat down, slumped over, and went back to sleep. I was so proud! He had been awake after all and emerged as the master of his field—something I had known him to be all along.

334

Five Words That
Made a Difference—And
the Man Who Spoke Them

I met him on a cold and snowy winter's evening in January of 2008. I had heard his name spoken on the Messiah College campus with something close to reverence. And now I both saw him and heard him for the very first time.

It was an evening to celebrate the music of Black people enslaved in the United States. Professor Luke Powery, a specialist in African American music at Princeton Seminary, had come to Messiah College to share his insights on that topic.

But the high point for both Jan and me was what we saw and heard as we entered the chapel that night. A Black pastor was playing the piano, and the music he made was extraordinary. But what compelled our attention as much as his music was his face—the sheer joy and delight his face expressed with every note he played.

As I watched and heard him play, I could not have guessed that I would soon regard this man as one of the most remarkable people I have known over the long course of my life.

His name, as far as I knew at the time, was simply Reverend Baxter. Later, I would learn his full name—Charles Wayne Baxter—and that he pastored a small Church of God in Christ on the east side of Harrisburg, Pennsylvania. He supplemented a meager income from the church by

serving as a receptionist and security guard at Sci-Tech High School in downtown Harrisburg, where he also directed the Sci-Tech Gospel Choir.

On this cold and snowy night when we gathered to celebrate the music of enslaved people, Baxter's gospel choir had been scheduled to perform. But the snow was so deep that only the pastor and a couple of his students had managed to make the twelve-mile trek south from Harrisburg to Messiah College.

Reverend Charles Wayne Baxter

When the program was over, I made my way to the chapel's foyer, and there I saw him, standing to the side by himself. I introduced myself and told him how much I had enjoyed his music, but that I had especially enjoyed watching the joy that radiated from his face as he played those great gospel songs.

And then, for some reason—I can't explain why—I asked, "Would you be willing to have breakfast with me one of these days?"

"Why, sure," he said. And he told me to meet him at the Downtown Deli, just steps away from Sci-Tech High School, at a certain date and time. And when we met for breakfast on the appointed day, a marvelous friendship was born.

He often claims that I have been his teacher. From my perspective, just the reverse is true. For every time we meet, he teaches me fresh and vibrant lessons about the meaning of the Christian faith, especially about forgiveness and compassion.

When I first met Reverend Baxter on that snowy night in 2008, I was serving as Senior Fellow in the Ernest L. Boyer Center at Messiah College and was hard at work planning an initiative we called "Community Conversations on Race, Education, and Faith." With that project, we hoped to address in some meaningful way the great racial divide in the Capital City region.

There are many towns in America where the dividing line between wealthy and middle-class Whites, on the one hand, and impoverished people of color, on the other, is a street, or a bridge, or a railroad track. In the Harrisburg, Pennsylvania, region, the dividing line is the Susquehanna River.

Predominantly composed of people of color living below the poverty line, Harrisburg sits on the east side of the river—what people often call "the East Shore." But if one travels across the River to the West Shore (what many people of color call "the white shore"), one discovers charming and affluent towns like LeMoyne, Camp Hill, and New Cumberland. There is poverty in those communities, to be sure, but the poverty there hardly compares to the poverty in Harrisburg.

Strikingly, almost all the residents in those West Shore communities are White. And the vast inequalities that divide the East and West Shores from each other play themselves out in the quality of education available to children on both sides of the river.

We knew there was already some level of collaboration between churches on the East and West Shores, but we hoped that the "Community Conversations on Race, Education, and Faith" might bring Blacks and Whites and churches and schools from both the East and West Shores into a larger and richer conversation, and we hoped that conversation might swell into a partnership for the sake of impoverished children in the Harrisburg schools.

We knew from the start that the success of this project would depend to a great degree on the support and involvement of the people of color who lived in the city. For that reason, among others, we invited Dr. Beverly Daniel Tatum, president of Spelman College in Atlanta, to launch the project with a keynote address.

Now, sitting across from Reverend Baxter as we broke bread together, I told him about this event and how much I hoped that many Blacks would come to Messiah to hear President Tatum speak.

And that's when he looked me in the eye and quietly asked, "Richard, may I speak candidly with you?"

"I hope you will," I responded.

"All right," he said. "Then get out a pen and a piece of paper and write what I tell you."

Once I was ready to write, he doled out a simple message, one word at a time.

"First," he said, "write the word 'it's.'" And I did.

"Now write the word 'all,'" he continued. And I wrote down that word, too.

"Now write the word 'about.'" And I scribbled "about" on my notepad.

"Now write the word 'relationships.'"

And once I had written that word, he made his point. "It's all about relationships!" he said. "And that's what you don't have."

He paused for a moment, as if reflecting on what he was about to say. And then he said those five magical words that launched our friendship: "But I will help you."

Embedded in those five words were all the reasons I found—and continue to find—this man to be such an extraordinary human being.

For why should he have helped me—a White man who was essentially a stranger both to him and to his world? After all, I am a White professor who has led a life of privilege for a very long time, while he—like virtually all Black Americans—has been on the receiving end of systemic racism all his life.

His father, Reverend Belgium Baxter, was an extraordinarily talented preacher and poet who, had he been White, would have enjoyed countless open doors to professional and monetary success. But he was Black, and most of those doors were closed. As a result, the Baxter family—like most Black families in the United States—waged a constant struggle with the debilitating power of poverty.

When Wayne was a young man, he inherited his father's church; and the poverty that haunted his father and his mother years ago has haunted him and his family as well.

Beyond that, Reverend Baxter has experienced firsthand the full brunt of racial hatred. Some years ago, when preaching in eastern Ohio, he came home from his church late one afternoon to rest. He sat on his living room couch to watch the evening news when suddenly he heard a loud thud. Something had hit his house.

In the time it took to get up from the couch and walk to the front door, the flames from the Molotov cocktail that someone had hurled at his home were raging out of control. He and his wife lost not only their house but every possession they owned. Only their garage still stood, but on the garage, someone had scrawled, "Nigger, go home!"

And yet, here he was, a Black man, saying to a White man he barely knew, "I will help you."

The truth about Reverend Baxter is this: in the face of brutal hatred and systemic racism, he has refused to hate in return.

Shortly after seeing Quentin Tarantino's *Django Unchained*, I asked Reverend Baxter what he thought about that film. Knowing the history of slavery as I do, I understood why Django had taken vengeance on Whites who had oppressed both him and his kin. But Baxter rejected the film and its premise out of hand.

"It's a feel-good film for Blacks," he said. "Hatred begets hatred, vengeance begets vengeance, and violence begets violence. Someone somewhere has got to reject the temptation to hate in return."

That perspective is remarkable enough, but I have found in Reverend Baxter yet another remarkable trait. As poor as he is, he has every right to focus on himself and his own very pressing needs. Instead, he carries the burden of what he calls "America's disposable children"—the children of the hood.

He reminds me of Jeremiah, "the lamenting prophet," or of Jesus who wept over Jerusalem. I could almost feel the tears when I read in one of his letters, "Richard, when I think of my people, I lament. I lament because [of] the lives that we deem worthy of discarding.

"Listen, Richard," he told me one day. "In this country we throw away everything. We throw away razor blades, clothes, cell phones, television sets, even cars. But the greatest tragedy is the way we throw away our kids.

"When most people see these kids," he said, "they only see hoodlums. But the truth is this—that many kids in the hood are as talented and smart as suburban kids, and they have the potential to achieve in remarkable ways.

"But most people never grasp," he said, "the way the cards are stacked against them." And he spoke of the poverty that haunts them. He told how they often sleep in cars, or in ramshackle houses with no heat, or even on the street. And he spoke of the debilitating hunger that makes it virtually impossible for these kids to learn. "The legacy of slavery," he said, "still plays itself out today.

"These kids may graduate," he said, "but because some teacher along the way decides that Johnny can't read, Johnny is placed in an alternative school. And, of course, in that school of low expectations, the chances that Johnny will learn to read and write and do basic math are slim to none. Johnny may well graduate, but with no marketable skills, so he turns to peddling crack, gets busted, and lands in prison."

Baxter has often lamented that America's prisons, run as they are by private industry, need a steady flow of bodies to turn a profit. Once he told me that "my brother Nathan was visiting a prison once when a guard asked him where he was from. When Nathan told him 'Harrisburg,' the guard replied, 'Oh, Harrisburg! We love Harrisburg! Just keep those boys coming. Just keep those boys coming.'

"And that," he said, "is how this country disposes of its unwanted children.

"That we could dispose in this way of even one child is troubling enough," he said, "but the pile of disposable children in this country is getting so high that it has already crippled the nation. In fact," he said, "many of the answers to the challenging issues of our time lie cold and still . . . in our graveyards and our prisons."

And then he looked at me with eyes that seemed to pierce to the bottom of my soul and said, "Richard, we've got to do what we can to change things for these kids."

And with those words—and with so many others that he spoke to me over the course of our long friendship—he enlarged the calling that I first heard in the book that spoke my name and pointed me toward Jesus, the book my professor placed in my hands so many years ago.

AFTERWORD

My prayer is that Richard Hughes's "troublesome questions" will incite robust and sustained conversations around matters of race, vocation, and the restoration of our kingdom commitments. When those dialogs occur, two groups in particular need a seat at the table.

First, these chapters should be required reading for students, faculty, and administrators at Christian colleges and universities inasmuch as Richard's decades-long work connecting faith, learning, and vocation offers a necessary corrective to our often misguided and tepid notions of Christian higher education.

Perhaps we have all had experiences of hearing self-ascribed Christian scholars present their research, only to discover that their findings are essentially indistinguishable from those produced by most any thoughtful, well-trained, inquisitive researcher from most any institution of higher learning. Stated otherwise, without a byline to identify an employer or alma mater, it is hard to discern whether these scholars are affiliated with Pepperdine University or Cal State, Messiah College or Penn State, Lipscomb University or the University of Tennessee. Lamentably, Christian colleges and universities all too often operate from the same canons and criteria as state institutions and succumb to the same methodological "agnosticism"[1] that defines research across the academy.

---

[1] D. G. Hart, "History in Search of Meaning: The Conference on Faith and History," in *History and the Christian Historian*, ed. Ronald Wells (Grand Rapids: Eerdmans, 1998), 85.

Consequently, higher education in the US tends to produce "an American society of achievers and consumers," Ivan Illich warns, with blind faith in free enterprise and "family-car affluence"—an ungodly and expensive myth from which students and our communities will unlikely profit.[2] The academy certifies its graduates "as belonging to a super race [*homo educandus*] that has the duty to govern," likewise condemning those who lack such exclusive credentials to a status of incompetence, inferiority, and disenfranchisement. The education process, often touted as a liberating force—as the "savior of the poor"—functions as a "soul-shredder that junks the majority and hardens an elite to govern it."[3] The academy, Illich concludes, is a "faith," a "religion" seeking to do "what God cannot, namely, manipulate others for their own salvation."[4]

Education is an exercise in community formation, a catechetical act that far too often instructs students in the "gospel" of the principalities and powers. When we operate according to that competing credo, our Christian colleges and universities produce graduates prepared to act like most everyone else pursuing the comfortable and contented American subculture. This, Richard announces, is the vocation of neither Christian higher education nor the Christian scholar.

Richard has been asking the all-important and disquieting questions. For which community are we forming allegiances? Does the kingdom of God—and its irrepressible resistance toward the ways and wants of the world—truly form our thinking, research, teaching, and living? What's the evidence? Whose norms define our values and outcomes? Are our alumni/ae called to live as committed pilgrims and empowered sojourners while in Babylon, or as loyal functionaries of the nation-state?

A few Christian historians have chided Richard for his scholarly crusading, lamenting that he is "preaching through history,"[5] or that his

[2] Ivan Illich, "To Hell with Good Intentions," The Conference on InterAmerican Student Projects, Cuernavaca, Mexico, April 20, 1968, https://www.uvm.edu/~jashman/CDAE195_ESCI375/To%20Hell%20with%20Good%20Intentions.pdf.

[3] Illich, "To Hell with Good Intentions," 2.

[4] Illich, *Deschooling Society* (London: Marion Boyars, 1971), 50.

[5] James Lagrand, "The Problems of Preaching Through History," in *Confessing History: Explorations in Christian Faith and the Historian's Vocation*, ed. John Fea, Jay Green, and Eric Miller (Notre Dame: University of Notre Dame Press, 2010), 188–89.

"sermons" represent a "value-ladened leftist Christian historiography."[6] But such an appraisal misses Richard's point that disciples operate from an epistemic prioritizing of the upside-down kingdom. Thus, in the tradition of the Radical Reformation, Christians must introduce some cognitive dissonance in the academy and in the public square. Graduates of Christian colleges and universities must operate from a kerygma that privileges society's scorned. Insofar as we ascend by descending, our icons of success are culture's disregarded, and we learn to grow by emptying ourselves. Here is Richard's prophetic vocation transforming the conversation and restoring the practice of Christian higher education.

This collection must generate vigorous and incisive dialog, not only in our Christian colleges and universities, but also in our comfortable and complacent churches—especially those of the Stone-Campbell tradition. Richard has always manifested an authentically ecumenical spirit of love, thereby contributing to the unity of the Spirit in the bond of peace among the larger Christian family. At the same time, he has invested his life and work in the Churches of Christ—the fellowship of his birth. He knows our Stone-Campbell story and why we exist.

As evidenced in the foregoing essays, Richard will chastise our tradition, telling stories of its sectarianism and exposing its provincialism, warts and all. Such disclosures, however, stem from his deep appreciation for the great potential of the Churches of Christ. He champions the tradition's noblest gifts and seeks to reinvigorate its highest ideals. Inspired to serve his faith community, he refuses to let the Churches of Christ off easy, for he is committed to holding the fellowship to a true and just fulfillment of its pledge that God's will shall be fully and unapologetically done on earth today as it is being lived in heaven—in all its countercultural beauty.

At the end of the day, he asks of his tradition the same work of reconciliation, justice, and mercy that he has demanded of himself. Consequently, one finds in Richard's life and writing the commitment that Churches of Christ must operate from God's preferential option for the poor, marginalized, and scorned. The work of the Churches of Christ must liberate all our neighbors from pernicious oppression, including racial supremacy, ethnic

---

[6] Jay Green, *Christian Historiography: Five Rival Versions* (Waco: Baylor University Press, 2015), 77–78.

arrogance, national militarism, gender chauvinism, and socioeconomic exploitation. When it comes to his writing on, and engagement with, the Churches of Christ, Richard's thesis is that the fellowship will only restore its vocation and contribute to the healing of the world to the extent that it is an inbreaking of the upside-down kingdom of God into the world. Love of God and neighbor will abide nothing less.

If one misses this radical, insurgent, scandalous punch, one has missed the genius of Richard's work and the witness of his life.

Richard C. Goode
Professor of History, Lipscomb University

PERMISSIONS

Chapter One, "The Grace of Troublesome Questions," first appeared in *Vocation Matters*, the official blog of NetVUE (Network for Vocation in Undergraduate Education), May 12, 2020, and is published here with the permission of NetVUE.

Chapter Two, "The Apocalyptic Origins of Churches of Christ and the Triumph of Modernism," first appeared in *Religion and American Culture: A Journal of Interpretation* 2 (Summer 1992): 181–214, and is published here with the permission of *Religion and Culture: A Journal of Interpretation*.

Chapter Three, "Two Restoration Traditions: Mormons and Churches of Christ in the Nineteenth Century," originated as the Tanner Lecture for the Mormon Historical Association, 1992, and first appeared in the *Journal of Mormon History* 19 (Spring 1993): 34–51, and is published here with permission from the *Journal of Mormon History*.

Chapter Four, "Called by a Book," first appeared in *Vocation Matters*, the official blog of NetVUE, October 27, 2020, and is published here with the permission of NetVUE.

Chapter Five, "Restoring First Times in the Anglo-American Experience," first appeared in Richard T. Hughes and C. Leonard Allen, *Illusions of Innocence: Protestant Primitivism in America, 1630–1875* (Chicago:

University of Chicago Press, 1988; repr., Abilene: ACU Press, 2008), 1–24, and is published here with the permission of ACU Press.

Chapter Six, "Why Restorationists Don't Fit the Evangelical Mold," first appeared in Douglas Jacobsen and William Vance Trollinger Jr., eds., *Re-forming the Center: American Protestantism, 1900 to the Present* (Grand Rapids: Eerdmans, 1998), 194–214, and was republished in Richard T. Hughes, *Reclaiming a Heritage: Reflections on the Heart, Soul, and Future of Churches of Christ*, exp. ed. (Abilene: ACU Press, 2019). It is reprinted by permission of the original publisher.

Chapter Seven, "How a Teacher Heard the Call of Racial Justice," first appeared under the title, "Escaping the Web of White Supremacy: Our Most Urgent Task in the Work of Character Formation," *The Cresset: A Review of Literature, the Arts, and Public Affairs* 83 (Advent-Christmas 2019): 4–8, and is published here with the permission of *The Cresset*.

Chapter Eight, "The Summons from the Biblical Text," is from Richard T. Hughes, *Christian America and the Kingdom of God*. Copyright 2009 by the Board of Trustees of the University of Illinois. Used with permission of the University of Illinois Press.

Chapter Nine, "Why I Am Not an Evangelical Christian," first appeared under the title "Remembering Amos: Where White Evangelicals Lost Their Way," *Baptist News Global*, October 15, 2020, and is published here with the permission of *Baptist News Global*.

Chapter Eleven, "The Restoration Vision and the Myth of the Innocent Nation," is from Richard T. Hughes, *Myths America Lives By: White Supremacy and the Stories That Give Us Meaning*. Copyright 2018 by the Board of Trustees of the University of Illinois. Used with permission of the University of Illinois Press.

Chapter Twelve, "How Slavery Still Shapes the World of White Evangelical Christians," first appeared in *Baptist News Global*, March 2, 2021, and is published here with the permission of *Baptist News Global*.

Chapter Thirteen, "Resisting White Supremacy," first appeared in *Slavery's Long Shadow: Race and Reconciliation in American Christianity*, ed. James L. Gorman, Jeff W. Childers, and Mark W. Hamilton (Grand Rapids: Eerdmans, 2019), 213–30, and is reprinted by permission of the publisher.

Chapter Fourteen, "Christian Nationalism and Racial Injustice: Where Do People of Faith Go from Here?" was a lecture delivered to a class taught by Bishop Nathan Baxter, Lancaster Theological Seminary, Lancaster, Pennsylvania, December 3, 2020, and is published here with the permission of Bishop Baxter.

Chapter Fifteen, "How Can We Rethink the Restoration Vision?" originated as the Sterling McMurrin Lecture at the annual meeting of the John Whitmer Historical Association, Omaha, Nebraska, September 23, 2004, was published in the *Journal of the John Whitmer Historical Association* 25 (2005): 18–35, and a condensed version of that lecture is published here with the permission of the John Whitmer Historical Association.

Chapter Twenty, "Five Words That Made a Difference—And the Man Who Spoke Them," first appeared in the *Harrisburg Patriot News*, March 3, 2013, and is published here with the permission of the *Harrisburg Patriot News*.

"A veritable cornucopia of insights and challenges, this collection of essays distills a lifetime of theological reflection, historical insight, and earnest Christian discipleship, always anchored in the teachings of Jesus and the example of the Early Church. Richard Hughes never disappoints. His writing is provocative, confessional, courageous, and inspiring. You will see the world differently after reading this book!"

—**John Roth,** Editor, *Mennonite Quarterly Review,* Director, Mennonite Historical Library, Professor of History, Goshen College

"In this remarkable and comprehensive book, Richard Hughes lets his life speak through his work as a faithful interpreter of restorationist church history and the challenges posed by contemporary American culture, particularly the myth of Christian America. He allows us to hear the voices that have influenced his vocational journey, and he urges us to hear afresh the call to justice and mercy as reflected in the eighth-century prophets of Israel and the upside-down kingdom as revealed by Jesus in the Gospels."

—**D'Esta Love,** Chaplain Emerita, Pepperdine University

"Richard Hughes has long been one of my guides as I've thought through my faith heritage and the Way of Jesus. The challenges in this book are no exception. Once again, he's forcing me (and us) to live up to the ideas of kingdom and restoration, urging us to embrace the paths of peace and justice."

—**Mike Cope,** Director of Ministry Outreach, Pepperdine University

"Confronting the most urgent questions of a lifetime in the public square demands a rigorous ethic of truth telling and uncommon courage. In this memoir, Richard Hughes practices courageous truth telling with a rare sense of wonder, curiosity, and hopefulness. In doing so, Hughes wrestles deeply with the questions of vocation, race, and restoration—ones that have transformed his relentless search for truth and justice."

—**Tabatha L. Jones Jolivet,** PhD, Associate Professor of Higher Education, Azusa Pacific University, community organizer, coauthor of *White Jesus: The Architecture of Racism in Religion and Education*

"Richard Hughes is a church historian of note, and what he has written regarding restoration movements and the development of Churches of Christ is enormously informative. He has connected his scholarly work and the prophetic voice of Old and New Testaments to the culture in which he lives, as seen in his highly regarded writings on racism and White supremacy. In a day of persistent decline in the culture and the church, this book with Hughes's discussion of the upside-down Kingdom of God may shine light on a path forward."

—**Joel E. Anderson,** Chancellor Emeritus, University of Arkansas at Little Rock

"This is the fruit of years of teaching and research by one of the most respected historians of the American Restoration Movement. From the apocalyptic origins of the Churches of Christ and its understanding of restorationism to its differentiation from Evangelicalism, Hughes offers us an opportunity for deeper self-understanding. At the same time, he addresses pressing questions of Christian nationalism and White Supremacy in the context of his own journey to make sense of his inherited faith. His path illuminates our own histories, experiences, and challenges, and it invites us to see and hear more clearly the radical call of the gospel."

—**John Mark Hicks,** Professor of Theology, Lipscomb University, author of *Around the Bible in 80 Days*

"Richard Hughes's retrospective volume is an unusual combination of a lifetime of historical scholarship and some of the key episodes in his personal story that lie behind it. The focus is the enduring theme of 'restoration,' and he shows us in a deeply engaging way where it came from and why it matters so much. A rich and inspiring read!"

—**Leonard Allen,** author of *In the Great Stream: Imagining Churches of Christ in the Christian Tradition*, Dean of the College of Bible and Ministry, Lipscomb University

"Richard Hughes is a teacher, and like any good teacher, he has never stopped learning. This book is a testimony to a life of learning. But Richard Hughes is also a preacher, not in the literal sense of speaking from a pulpit but in the existential sense of pouring his soul into what he says and does. It is this merging of mind and soul, of critical analysis and heartfelt passion, that makes Richard special and makes this volume so simultaneously instructive and inspiring."

—**Douglas Jacobsen,** Distinguished Professor Emeritus of Christian History and Theology, Messiah University